MW00464238

THE CASE OF THE BONSAI MANAGER

THE CASE OF THE BONSAI MANAGER

Lessons from Nature on Growing

R. Gopalakrishnan

PENGUIN
PORTFOLIO

PORTFOLIO

Published by the Penguin Group

Penguin Books India Pvt. Ltd, 11 Community Centre, Panchsheel Park,
New Delhi 110 017, India

Penguin Group (USA) Inc., 375 Hudson Street, New York, New York 10014, USA

Penguin Group (Canada), 10 Alcorn Avenue, Toronto, Ontario, Canada M4V 3B2
(a division of Pearson Penguin Canada Inc.)

Penguin Books Ltd, 80 Strand, London WC2R 0RL, England

Penguin Ireland, 25 St Stephen's Green, Dublin 2, Ireland
(a division of Penguin Books Ltd)

Penguin Group (Australia), 250 Camberwell Road, Camberwell,
Victoria 3124, Australia (a division of Pearson Australia Group Pty Ltd)

Penguin Group (NZ), 67 Apollo Drive, Rosedale, North Shore 0632,
New Zealand (a division of Pearson New Zealand Ltd)

Penguin Group (South Africa) (Pty) Ltd, 24 Sturdee Avenue, Rosebank,
Johannesburg 2196, South Africa

Penguin Books Ltd, Registered Offices: 80 Strand, London WC2R 0RL, England

First published in Portfolio by Penguin Books India 2007

ISBN-10: 0-67008-131-0   ISBN-13: 978-0-67008-131-8

Typeset in Sabon Roman by SÜRYA, New Delhi
Printed at Chaman Offset Printers, New Delhi

CONTENTS

FOREWORD

This book is about effective leadership in today's uncertain times and addresses budding managers aspiring to become tomorrow's leaders.

This how-to-become-a-leader book is different from others, even contrarian. It does not advocate management based on information alone, because it recognises that complete information is rarely available for leaders to arrive at decisions. Gopal draws on ingenious insights and lessons from Nature to emphasize the importance of imbibing, developing, listening to and trusting intuition—increasingly becoming a differentiator in senior circles—to develop the confidence to take that leap of faith which every risk-bearing decision entails.

Today's leadership skill set, Gopal observes, has moved away from the coldly analytical, aggressive and thrusting, towards the humane, inclusive and intuitive. Good leaders, he advocates, overlay the known facts with their gut feel and instinct, which they consciously develop through keen listening (to a company's 'infra-sounds', as he calls it), reflection, contemplation and mentoring. Managers who neglect this side of their personality end up becoming 'bonsai managers', as Gopal labels them somewhat ingeniously.

Good mentoring is so very important for creating leaders, and the book rightly urges companies to create structures to institutionalize mentoring. I have often said that I wish that the close relationship I developed with Mr J.R.D. Tata in his later years had happened sooner, so that I could have been a wiser manager in my more formative years.

Every company, the book observes, has its code of change, a little like a combination lock which protects the company culture. The effectiveness of any change agenda is governed by the ability of the leadership to understand that code, crack it, and leverage it. All change is painful, but if you match the speed of change with the code, then you can minimize the pain and advance the change agenda effectively. My own experience in the Tata group bears this out.

Gopal concludes that just as nature favours effectiveness over efficiency, in management also you are most effective and are behaving 'naturally' when you let values motivate your decisions. When you do that, you expend the least effort and you unfailingly accomplish what I have often commended with heartfelt enthusiasm—a good night's sleep.

I am pleased to recommend this book, in particular to aspiring entrepreneurs and managers seeking to emerge as tomorrow's leaders. The book is a worthwhile read for a wide group of leaders in the corporate sector.

RATAN N. TATA

Chairman, Tata Sons Ltd
Mumbai
4 February 2007

ACKNOWLEDGEMENTS

There are so many I should thank for supporting this modest effort of mine.

My family (wife Geeta and children Anugraha, Anirudha and Anila and my brother, Naru), were constructively harsh about the required improvements. Without their candour, I may not have been as driven as I became. It is important to acknowledge their stellar contribution!

My dear friend, Sudha Raghavendran, inadvertently revealed her interest in literature and in editing—and got roped in to do a huge amount of work, which she did very cheerfully. She was terrific in the detail she could go into, and in the breadth of her ideas. She spent so many hours over the script; I cannot repay her.

Thanks also to my colleagues, Ravi Arora and Christabelle Noronha, who invested personal time to read an early version and suggest changes, as also to Ajay Kumar, a journalist turned colleague. My executive assistant, Neeti Chopra, was a huge ally. Her ability to comment incisively and to pull out information from the net were most helpful.

My friends Ambi Parmeswaran, Gurdeep Singh, Chandrakant Mehta, N. Muthuswamy, Bittu Sahgal, Dinesh Daftary, Shanker Menon, and Anil Dharker, who offered valuable inputs at early stages.

Art Kleiner, a professional writer, asked me a few hard questions, the answers to which caused me to recast the book substantially. I should add that the faults and weaknesses are entirely mine. Art Kleiner has only been a long-distance advisor; none of the lapses in the book should be associated with him.

Theresa Sequeira, my secretary, who relentlessly reworked the many versions. She never once asked me whether there would be more. Her patience and cheer were exemplary.

To my publisher, Krishan Chopra, I owe a special word of thanks. He would always interact in such a way as to egg me on, to believe in myself, without ever revealing whether he thought I was getting anywhere! He made extremely constructive suggestions without even inadvertently being intrusive.

Towards the later stages, it was a relief to hear him say 'I think it is coming along well.'

I am deeply obliged to Mr Ratan Tata, who graciously agreed to write a Foreword in spite of his punishing schedule and crammed diary.

INTRODUCTION

The title of this book serves as a warning that managers can become like stunted plants. Just as artificial constriction can cause a plant to develop into a bonsai, so too it is with managers. Although for the Japanese creating a bonsai was an art, and the ornamental plant a thing of beauty, for the purposes of our book a bonsai manager is one whose growth has not run its course, as he has not been able to flourish by drawing sustenance from his natural environment.

The absence of intuition—or its inadequate use—has the effect of constricting a manager. If he does not overcome those blockages and stays in that condition for long, he becomes a bonsai irreversibly. As a result, bonsai managers are not able to work at the top end of their potential.

No one sets out to become a bonsai manager, just as no plant is created by Nature to be a bonsai. Managers become bonsai through their own acts of omission and commission.

A manager can develop to his full potential by learning to be intuitive, inclusive and humane—the kind of skills that are not taught. These are also difficult to teach. This book is not a substitute for formal learning of all that is logical and analytical in management. It actually complements formal learning; it is, hopefully, a winning overlay.

The theme of this book is the intersection of two circles— Nature and Management. The chapters contain anecdotes from Nature and my own experiences in the worlds of business and management—some everyday, some intriguing, some surprising, offering reflections on the known, the perceived, the imperceptible and the hidden vistas of human nature, mind and managerial behaviour.

Several years ago, as a young, travelling sales manager in Hindustan Lever (now Hindustan Unilever Ltd), I spent the night at a forest rest house at Dandeli. This little town nestles in a picturesque part of the Western Ghats in northern Karnataka. As I settled down to sleep, I began to notice the sheer variety of sounds in this quiet place—a series of clicks, buzzes, shrieks, whistles, croaks and caws—that I had never heard in the city. I developed a naïve curiosity about the world of animals and insects. This curiosity caused me to collect facts about Nature little known to lay people. I learnt that such communication methods among birds, animals and insects constitute an amazing language system. It is quite mind-blowing. For example:

❀ The sounds of all birds of a particular species may sound similar to human ears. However, this is not so with the birds themselves. Baby birds use one call to tell their parents that they are hungry and another one to say they are frightened.

❀ Crocodiles hide their oval-shaped hard eggs amidst nests of vegetation and rubbish, hidden from the sight of predators. When ready to emerge, the young reptiles chirp, or emit a sound from within the shell. Upon hearing this alert, the mother digs out the egg and helps the young come out.

❀ A vervet monkey categorizes its predators and gives suitable signals to other vervets. For a leopard alarm, the vervet climbs on a tree. For an eagle alarm, it dives into the thick undergrowth. For a python alarm, it stands upright and scans the environment.

Biologists studying various kinds of living creatures do not agree as to what constitutes communication among animals.

But animals do communicate and signal each other as part of the preservation and nurturing of the species.

About a decade ago, I started to see a curious connection between such facts from Nature and anecdotes from my professional career in management. I began to share these 'Nature-and-management' stories at in-company training courses. Encouraged by a positive reception, I gradually expanded the audience to include outsiders, i.e., management associations, students and managers in other companies.

By now, I have presented these anecdotes in a PowerPoint format to over 10,000 people. I have felt encouraged by the invariably positive response to this presentation.

This is what generated the idea that these anecdotes might be shared more widely; that they just might help younger managers to prepare better for the emerging demands of future leadership. This book is such an attempt.

Lifelong learning

I have had a rich and enjoyable career in management for forty years. It seems just the other day that I took the double-decker bus from Warden Road to Churchgate in Mumbai to join Hindustan Lever as a trainee in the newly set-up computer department.

When I began my career in India, management schools in India were just coming up. Within the Indian context, the management curriculum and teaching were perceived as flaky compared to more established disciplines like engineering and economics. Hindustan Lever recruited me as a trainee without my having a two-year MBA. It was too good an offer to pass up.

Within the first five years at Hindustan Lever, I was put through many short duration courses on finance, industrial engineering, marketing, brand management and so on—what we would call the business functions of management. There were so many that I must have been a resident of the training centre 'Gulita' for about 10 per cent of my working days during those early years; it felt like much more.

Since then, I have attended advanced programmes in India, Europe and the US. Through these wonderful programmes, I have learned what could be taught.

More importantly, through my work experience, I have become sensitive to what cannot be taught, e.g., dealing with human nature, the complexities of employee behaviour within organizations, charting out an agenda for change. If a manager has failed to learn those lessons, it proves to be costly. More often than not, managers fail because they have not learnt such things. And these cannot be taught.

The future manager's challenges

The future manager will face challenges different from the ones prevalent when I started because the world around has changed dramatically—incredibly dramatically.

The centre of gravity of the world used to be the west. Companies were discrete entities and were run quite independently, not as though they were part of an inter-dependent ecology of companies and institutions.

In societies representing half the population of the world, ideas like freedom of speech and democracy were not very well understood—the Soviet Union, eastern Europe, China, Africa and the Middle East. People in such countries were told what to do by their political rulers. Such programmed behaviour impacted those societies and the way in which groups of people got things done. Their world of management was quite different from that in the west.

In western Europe and America, the management world in the 1950s and 1960s was preoccupied with control rather than freedom, with tightness rather than looseness, with direction rather than participation, and with productivity rather than creativity. The management books of that time exemplify this—notably, Peter Drucker's *The Practice of Management*, William Whyte's *The Organization Man*, Alfred Sloan's *My Years with General Motors* and Jay Forrester's *Systems Dynamics*. Operations Research and other such techniques were developing as potential panaceas for forecasting and for reducing the uncertainties of business through engineering and mathematical methods.

Managers used to be taught logical thinking and analytical techniques in management courses. By mastering these, it was thought that they could tell their people what to do and lead them successfully. Leaders needed to know more than their people and demonstrate that they knew more than them.

In today's context, it may seem unbelievable that this was how companies were run. Donald Peterson, a former CEO of Ford Motor Company, has described the atmosphere in the company when he joined in the 1940s. It was a top-down approach with a lot of emphasis on giving orders and exercising control. There are still companies operating in this mode, but it is generally regarded as old-fashioned.

Today, the centre of gravity of growth has shifted from the west to Asia; billions of people have entered the market economy and have experienced some degree of democracy and free speech. Companies and people across borders are interconnected through information, entertainment and employment in ways that could not be imagined earlier.

These developments have impacted leadership in all walks of life, including management. They have changed the fulcrum of leadership skills from the thrusting, the dominantly analytical and logical, towards the inclusive, intuitive and humane. This has had implications for managers in all parts of the world.

Watching the shift from the analytical and directive style to the intuitive and participative style, I have been fascinated by the outcomes. For example, while the old, hierarchical companies have had to programme and work very hard to promote teamwork and team rewards, the new technology companies have culturally evolved with the mantra of collaborative working, often across borders. Managers in these technology companies don't know anything different!

Modern managers need to comprehend this change and what it means to their leadership. Profound changes in the world have redefined managerial leadership. Now leaders are required to lead differently.

Managers lean naturally towards the analytical

The reason why managers lean towards the analytical rather than the intuitive is because the analytical can be taught. Besides, patterns of career progression within companies also encourage this trend; people advance in their careers most often for being analytical, not for being intuitive! Analytical skills offer skill differentiation in the initial stages of one's career; because these skills can be taught, they can be acquired by any willing student and what is available to any diligent learner soon ceases to be a sustainable differentiator.

It is not that analytics are unimportant or undesirable. They are essential. Top managers acknowledge that while taking decisions, they do place reliance on analysis and data, but ultimately they are guided by their intuition. Experts and colleagues can analyse and comment. However, there is a limit as well as a limitation to analysis because of time, costs or techniques; that point is loosely referred to as the point of 'analysis-paralysis'.

Managers know the limits of analysis, yet they transgress those limits and make mistakes. A common reason for managerial mistakes is that successful managers tend to repeat solutions that worked for them earlier or those that they think worked for other people. This is a valid approach when the problem and its solution are 'technical' in nature, e.g., how to improve machine performance in a factory, or how to calculate the present value of a business from cash flows. In these 'technical' situations, both the problem and the solution are known.

Where 'human' factors are involved, neither the problem nor the solution is clearly known. The adoption of an earlier successful model may or may not work unless the context and circumstance of the two problem situations have been taken into account. Successes in one human context do not necessarily transfer well to another context.

That is why Mumbai cannot be developed or run like Shanghai which, after the Chinese government opted for market-led growth in 1992, became the showcase of its modernized economy. For, no matter how many sighs emanate from recent travellers to the latter, Mumbai carries a lot of historical baggage which democratic processes and the probing media will not allow to be simply swept under a carpet of silence.

Increasingly, managers work under a great deal of pressure to perform. As a result, they often do not consciously separate the problem on hand into 'technical' and 'human' categories.

Pressured with performance targets, they quickly analyse the situation, identify the issues and problems, and plunge headlong into the implementation of their solutions. In the process, they generate and receive masses of data to acquire all the rational opinions and analytical information available. But when they take that crucial call, it is often on the basis of unclear data that their mind is yet to filter and interpret.

- ❖ Should we or should we not acquire that company?
- ❖ When everybody advises against this project, should we persist or abandon? Will posterity see me as the idiosyncratic genius who ploughed a lone furrow or as a huge disaster?
- ❖ When the competition adopts 'dirty' tactics, should we match or follow an alternative path?

❖ Is the entry into this new line of business an act of folly or foresight?

❖ When an exceptionally competent manager wants to leave, should we walk the extra mile to hold him back?

This was very well caricatured in a mid-1980s advertisement for Columbia University's executive programme; it showed a lone executive looking out of a window with the caption, 'You've surrounded yourself with people who are paid to give you good advice. And they do…Then the ball is in your court.' It is a tough call for leaders—and invariably, believe it or not, it comes down to the leader's gut feel and intuition.

Intuition at work

Business history and entrepreneurship is full of stories about leaders who trusted their intuition.

The great Indian industrialist of the nineteenth century, Jamsetji Tata, had bought some marshy land near the Nagpur railway station in 1874 at a low price. He floated a company called The Central India Spinning, Weaving and Manufacturing Company. When asked to subscribe to its shares, a local Marwari banker refused to invest in support of 'a man who was wasting gold by sinking it into the ground'. This person later admitted that Tata had put earth into the ground and pulled out gold.

In the 1950s, Ray Kroc decided to buy the McDonalds brand because 'my funny bone instinct kept urging me on'. Against all odds, his company expanded to become one of the icons of fast food, not just in America but all over the world.

In the late 1980s, ignoring all the market research evidence, Bob Lutz, then president of Chrysler, went ahead with the Dodge Viper car model. This was an outrageously powerful, eye-searing roadster launched at a time when Chrysler was down and out. Bob Lutz felt that the company had to take a lot of chances because it would go out of business if it did not.

So he did a lot by intuition and 'cut out all the crap normally associated with a new product'.

There are less famous, though equally apt examples from the Indian marketplace.

In the 1950s, Brooke Bond, the leading tea company, wanted to sell to the lower income consumer. After reducing packaging and other costs, their sales people made an intuitive observation—lower income households did not have cooking gas at home, so lighting the kitchen fire meant wood or coal. That meant a lot of effort and cost just to boil some water for tea. Hence the men went away early in the morning to the nearest 'hot tea shop' (HTS in Brooke Bond terminology) to enjoy a ready-made cup of tea. The cost per sip was higher than home-made tea, but it made sense to the consumer. Based on this intuition, Brooke Bond developed their HTS distribution system—and it was to stand them in good stead for decades.

In the 1970s, international companies were targeting lower income customers to use shampoo to wash their hair. Their market research and logical analysis confirmed that the price was too high. So their effort was to reduce the price per litre, principally by focusing on achieving lower packaging costs. An entrepreneur, trusting his instincts, figured that the cost per litre was not relevant; the unit price was the key factor. He launched a sachet of a few millilitres of shampoo for a single wash at Rs 2 per sachet. The cost per litre of this product was higher than the bottles, but the unit price was affordable. Velvette shampoo captured the market; others soon followed.

All the above turned out to be great decisions. Nobody has a magic formula to develop intuition, but is there a common thread?

Knowledge, intuition and wisdom

Knowledge is what you know you know. Knowledge can be taught, you can acquire it from external sources.

Intuition is what you do not know you know. Intuition is what cannot be taught, you learn it on your own. At the core of intuition is a set of understandings that the owner just does not know about.

When knowledge is integrated with intuition, it becomes wisdom.

Both knowledge and intuition are valuable for leaders in their decision-making process. Is one more important than the other? Is one more desirable than the other? Not really, they are complementary in nature. Intuition plays a key role by filling in the blanks when there is not enough information.

The role and value of intuition increases as a person rises in the organization and finds that he has to solve more complex issues. In fact, such senior leaders are paid for their intuition: their knowledge is taken as a given.

Intuition does not always just 'happen', it can be developed. The absence of intuition at crucial times is one of the reasons for the surprising failure of top leaders, who have already established a reputation of success.

On the other hand, intuition has to be learnt, and the way one uses it can be a huge differentiator. The absence of such intuitive qualities may explain the increasing management failures we see around us. However, there is a problem that managers face. It is not easy to teach intuition. It is not clear what exactly intuition is.

Intuition will be a key differentiator for excellence in the future, equal to or more than even in the past.

Intuition is a vast storehouse of knowledge that we possess and do not know that we possess. American psychologist Frances Vaughan pointed out that at any point of time, we are conscious of only a small part of what we know. There is below that conscious part a bank of knowledge we all have. But we can access that only when individual separateness and ego boundaries are transcended.

In the practical world of the manager, human ambition,

motivation and social relations play a very important role. These are difficult to teach, they are the agenda one learns by oneself.

In every part of the world, people learn lessons on difficult-to-teach subjects such as good conduct and morality through fables and mythology taught by their forefathers. That is why many cultures have a rich tradition of parables, stories and mythology to help common people relate to complex subjects like character, honesty, hard work, sincerity and so on.

In management too, anecdotes and evocative stories can help managers learn about human nature and reflect on it. Such stories can be on many themes such as historical characters and literature. That is why you have books like *Shakespeare on Management* or *Lessons on Management from Alexander*.

As a theme, Nature—animals, insects, geology, plants—appeal to most people. Nature inspires awe and evokes emotion; that is why we are wonderstruck after watching Nature-oriented television programmes.

The six simple messages of this book are:

❀ Intuition does exist and it is very important for the manager, especially at the more senior levels of leadership

❀ Analysis and intuition are not substitutes of each other, they are complementary

❀ A manager can develop intuition through viewing issues holistically, with the 'surrounds' of the issues, and not in isolation. He should observe and learn from the peripherals of his vision, hearing, experiences and relationships

❀ The manager's intuition is enhanced through varied experiences and relationships, contemplation and reflection

❀ A manager can develop his intuition by exploring and sensing beyond what is visible and audible

❖ The leader needs to think about issues at the 'edges of the spectrum of the obvious'.

The book is organized in five sections.

Section 1 is a discussion about analysis and intuition. It contains a relevant incident from my experience.

Section 2 is a pragmatic view about how the leader's intuition works. This pragmatic approach may serve a useful purpose, considering that science has not quite got to the bottom of this 'mystery' of how exactly intuition works.

Why is success in management dependent on a balance between analysis and intuition? How do we learn what is not taught to us? How can we develop intuition?

Section 3 is about building intuition through undergoing varied experiences and having varied relationships.

Change is the essence of learning, and learning comes through varied experiences and relationships, including some which are beyond the obvious.

Why do many managers develop into stunted managers? Why does learning get accelerated through more sharing? How does a manager get coached instead of waiting for a coach to turn up? Why is comfort to be shunned and how can threats to comfort actually be used to advantage?

Section 4 is about building intuition through contemplation and reflection.

Leaders are so busy, so awfully busy, that they fail to pause and reflect.

They need to remind themselves of their own mortality and build sound succession. After all, the success of the organization must be sustained. They must understand subtle points about group dynamics and how people cooperate and what makes them competitive. How do we get the collective smartness of the people in the organization to work? Are resource constraints a positive or a negative? Change means pain, but are there ways to reduce the pain?

Section 5 is about building intuition through sensing and perceiving beyond the obvious.

Leaders need to sense, feel and touch; they need to hear the barely audible echoes in the organization as they implement their change programmes; they need to understand that status and power dim intelligence, so they could become victims of their own smartness. Leaders are trained to be efficient, but efficiency and effectiveness may require different approaches. Is efficiency in solving problems more important than effectiveness?

A final word about why narrating personal anecdotes is important.

History is usually written from the rulers' point of view. The 'subaltern' view of history tries to get away from this and present events from the viewpoint of the lower levels rather than that of the elite. In some anecdotes narrated in these pages, I have been at the subaltern level, and in some, at the upper level.

Personal anecdotes about events that occurred and about leaders and their leadership have two characteristics.

Firstly, they are narrated from my perspective. The same event or set of facts could appear different when viewed from another perspective. That is why other players may have different interpretations of the events.

Secondly, there is the inadvertent human tendency to romanticize past events when compared to more recent ones. The past being a rich array of events, such historical anecdotes can teach many lessons, though some may even appear to be contradictory.

This book provides anecdotes to help the reader reflect. It is about a different way to think about these subjects and draw a few memorable lessons. This book is not about technical skills, it is about emotion, intuition, relationships and more. The messages can be helpful to young career builders as well as mid-career managers.

Indeed, if I may suggest with humility, they can be of interest to anybody concerned with people, emotions and group working—that is, almost everybody! After all, there are very few fields of human endeavour that are devoid of human relations.

R. GOPALAKRISHNAN

Mumbai
25 February 2007

SECTION I

ANALYSIS AND INTUITION

The intuitive mind tells the thinking mind where to look next—I wake up in the morning wondering what my intuition will toss up to me like gifts from the sea.

—Jonas Salk

1

REFLECTIONS ON ARABIA
INTUITION FROM THE EDGES OF ANALYSIS

Sometimes, logic and analysis tell us something different from intuition. I had such an experience in 1991, when I was posted as the head of Unilever's newly-formed company in Arabia. The purpose of my narration is to share an anecdote from which some ideas can be developed. The experience itself is not at all unique and almost every reader would know of a similar episode.

One key business challenge was to enter the Arabian detergent market against a very dominant and well-entrenched competitor, P&G Arabia. Rather unusually, at that time, Unilever had virtually no washing detergent business in the Arabian peninsula, though very successful brands in personal wash, skincare and tea had been established over several decades.

Ever since detergent powders began to be produced commercially, they have been made through a process called spray drying. The structure of the finished powder is like a balloon—a light globule puffed up with air. The cleaning and other chemical agents are held within that globule. The cardboard boxes in which such products were packed were large in size due to the fluffy nature of the powder inside.

During the late 1980s, a revolution in detergent offerings occurred in Japan: the long-standing big boxes were replaced in substantial measure by compact packages. The construct of the powder detergent market in Japan changed in a very short time.

In this new format of the product, much of the air in the 'globule' was removed and the resultant powder was more compact and dense. Apart from occupying less space on the retail shelf, compacts had other advantages: they needed less capital costs for production, less paperboard for packaging, less warehouse space in the distribution system, and more tonnage could be loaded on transport trucks.

Such packs had recently been introduced in Europe; as of 1990, they seemed to be gaining some ground at the expense of standard, big-boxed detergents. How much of the sales of the standard detergents in Europe would be replaced by the compact was an open question. Would Europe go the Japan way?

Being a late entrant against a formidably entrenched competitor, Unilever would definitely have to be audacious. For at least three years before I joined the company which was to execute the project, the planners had worked on the basis of launching a compact. Such a product would provide a point of differentiation with the traditional products already in the market, apart from offering distinct consumer benefits. Such differentiation was essential if any dent had to be made against a powerful and well-entrenched P&G. All of this was very logical, and I could not fault the thinking. In fact, there was a lot of market research to support the validity of such an approach.

I was a first-time company CEO (chief executive officer), that too of a company in a foreign country. I felt a huge pressure on myself to be successful, and that meant getting the launch right. As I went through the persuasive market research and the well-argued business case, my gut instinct began to tell me the opposite of the analysis: that the product was unlikely to succeed and that the route contemplated was risky. I could not explain why, but I felt it in my bones. Arabia was not at all like Japan or even Europe!

As part of my induction into the company and the new country, I had walked around the bazaars in Jeddah, Riyadh and other cities to observe how consumers behaved. I was obviously seeing things from a new and different perspective. I had observed that Arabia had huge spaces in the shops, on the roads, in the homes, in fact, everywhere—quite unlike Japan. As I walked around Arab markets, I felt that consumers liked everything big—cars, kids' toys, clothing, housing, furniture and so on. The saving in packaging or transportation costs in a detergent seemed irrelevant in a cheap energy economy. Yet, the research was not saying these things clearly. I had long discussions with my senior colleague Alex Abraham, who too was new to Arabia. Like me, he was torn between the analysis available and his intuition. The question we both faced was, what do we do with this intuition?

I was assailed with self-doubt. Could all the bright managers who had formulated the plan have missed something so elementary? Or was it I who was failing by believing what I wanted to believe?

Let's hark back four centuries in history. Until his dying day in 1601, Danish astronomer Tycho Brahe was absolutely certain that the sun and the stars revolved around the earth. He had produced a lot of data to support his viewpoint. The truth was that he was a prisoner of the prevalent notion that the sun goes around the earth; therefore, each time he saw the data, it confirmed the same to him.

Yet, some years later, using the same data of Tycho Brahe, his German assistant, Johannes Kepler, proved exactly the opposite, i.e., that the earth revolved around the sun. The devil was in Tycho Brahe's assumptions, whereas Johannes Kepler tested the opposite hypothesis.

Centuries ago, Aristotle had advised that to keep an open mind, bend your mind in the opposite direction first, as a carpenter might do with a piece of wood before using it.

We all tend to interpret data through the prism of the dominantly prevalent view about how the future will turn out.

In this context, it is important to recall the hype around Japan in those days. The country was the flavour of the times. It was viewed by the world as an icon, a miracle. Whatever happened in Japan would be commented upon as 'leading', whether in electronics, in cars, or even in matters like management style, long-term planning orientation, and government-industry co-operation. It so happened that compact detergents too came to be seen as a big innovation. The economic case for compacts was, of course, quite compelling; hence, many in Unilever believed that the days for traditional detergents in Europe, indeed in the whole world, were numbered. According to the prevalent view, compacts were a technological discontinuity in the evolution of the washing industry.

There was a battle between my logical self and my intuitive self. To my intuitive mind, there appeared to be too many risks in entering with a compact product. Since there was no spare capacity for producing the new-fangled product, the fledgling company would have to invest in building the required production capacity in order to launch the product; if the product failed, we would have compounded our problem by having an idle factory! On the other hand, there was plenty of spare capacity around to source the standard detergent from third parties, and to launch it in the market with much lower risk.

Alex Abraham and I felt the strong urge to share our assessment with the regional director and the global detergents director. However, we felt diffident to do so. What might they think of us, arguing something on gut feel in the face of a lot of analytical data?

Finally, I took courage in both hands and set up a joint meeting with them in Unilever House at London. They heard me out carefully. If they accepted what my intuition was saying, the painstakingly constructed Unilever plan spread over three years would have to be set aside, and a sort of fresh start made. They were prepared to do so. But was I right? If they rejected my view outright, they would be ignoring the instinct of the local manager.

After a great deal of debate, the regional director said, 'Let us go ahead with belt and braces. We can modify our plan. Let us outsource from a third party and launch a standard detergent first (not originally envisaged), and follow it up within eighteen months with an own factory-produced compact (as originally planned).' If the truth be told, it was a compromise, accurately captured in the expression, 'belt and braces'. To me, at that time, it seemed a fair compromise. That was what we did.

The outcome after four years carried some lessons. The standard detergent we launched in Arabia achieved the target marketshare. My instinct that the compact detergent would be a very small part of the volume was proven right; the compact's marketshare was negligible. Compacts as a category achieved well under a sixth of the market volume even after several years. In a market like Brazil, concentrates had made very little headway. Indeed even in Europe, compacts had captured only about a fourth of the market in the mid-1990s.

Meanwhile, the compacts factory that we had built in great haste was ready for production, posing a new issue to be addressed. It was now a solution looking for a problem! The outcome of the 'fair compromise', which seemed reasonable to me at the time we took the decision, was staring at me.

The overarching lesson for me, of course, was that paying heed to my intuition arising from observation, applied common sense and reflection, was right so far as the product was concerned. Compromising on the building of the factory was wrong!

This interplay between analysis and intuition is intriguing and I have reflected on this experience a great deal.

What could have happened

What gave me that 'feeling in the bones' about compact detergents? I was certainly not the only person with such a gut feel, but such people were a minority in Unilever.

Certainly, it was not any special cleverness or foresight on my part. There are several other situations I can think of where I should have felt things in my bones, but failed to do so!

Thinking about this episode retrospectively, I realize that a state of mind got created which was conducive to intuition—dreaming, contemplation, reflection. The senses for receiving information (hearing, seeing and feeling) got heightened.

A combination of other factors may have been at work quite unconsciously—an open mind, a positive attitude, willingness to risk and expectations.

Like anyone who takes on a new and stimulating challenge, I had accepted my new job in Unilever Arabia with three companions: context, motivation and self-awareness. The manner in which each of these played out probably had something to do with that contrarian intuition.

Context

Perhaps I had a positive attitude and an open mind as I approached the new issues facing me. I was almost like an explorer planning his first journey. I was on a quest to understand what would work and what would not against so formidable a competitor.

Unilever had arranged for me to meet and talk to several colleagues across countries, people who had had live experience of battling with P&G in the market. Some experiences were of success, others less clearly so. I found that all the experiences were narrated by marketers, who had a starting volume and marketshare. Their battle was to hold marketshare or add a few points of share. I could not help feeling that theirs was a different context from the one I was placed in.

I wanted to talk to one who had mounted an assault from the bottom of the cliff, with no starting volume. He should have audaciously 'climbed the steep and formidably high cliff' to attack the 90 per cent plus marketshare of P&G. I could not find such an experience in Unilever, and that made me feel humble.

P&G was attempting precisely that against a powerful HLL in India and a dominant Unilever in Brazil, Chile and Argentina. Luckily, I could rely on my old network of Unilever colleagues. Susim Datta had become the chairman of Hindustan Lever in Mumbai, and Gurdeep Singh was the technical director of the detergents business. A colleague and contemporary, Nihal Kaviratne, was posted in London in a senior role, covering markets in Latin America. So it was easy to access lessons from the defence put up by HLL in India and Unilever in Latin America.

Although I had been travelling to the Middle East for twenty years before I took up my role in Unilever Arabia, I realized how little I really knew.

Thus it was not difficult to have an open mind. An unfettered and positive mindset, I think, helped to think beyond the obvious.

Motivation

I had become a director of Hindustan Lever prior to taking up this assignment. It was tempting to think of oneself as an 'accomplished and tested' manager. Equally, it was clear to me that, in rational terms, just a wee bit of whatever I had learnt in India would be helpful for the Arabian assault. I was anxious about my new job, to be honest, if not a bit scared!

The desire to succeed in the assignment was very strong because I was a first-time company CEO. I made copious notes of all sorts of observations and pored over them for long hours. I was assailed with self-doubt on whether doing such things was a waste of time. This desire fanned the sense of intuition. I was inherently a believer in intuition, and such faith itself perhaps caused me to search for things beyond the obvious. For some reason, I continued to dawdle.

Self-awareness

I had been moved from my comfort zone in HLL to a situation where I had no choice but to take a few planned risks. For example, there was some risk in asking for a meeting with two main board directors, both of whom had supervised the preparatory work thus far, to share a counter-intuition and to ask for a change of plan! Likewise, it was a bit of a career risk to argue in support of the business case and the consequent significant investment before the apex special committee of Unilever just four months into the new job. There was no place for diffidence—and, in hindsight, that required me to be very self-aware.

Quite often, it was in the early mornings that I would withdraw my mind from the events of the previous few days and meditate on the most recent conversations and incidents. I was so totally immersed with the new and strange issues facing me that I often felt a heightened sensory experience. I was hearing and seeing things very differently and sensitively.

I should not give the impression that I was in a sort of trance; that would be an exaggeration. But I was quite alert and self-aware. I deployed my heightened self-awareness largely because I could trust the Unilever environment, which I knew so well. It was the huge support of the top leadership in Unilever that made this awareness possible, it was no heroism or clairvoyance on my part.

So, based on this and other experiences, and some reading and reflection, I have visualized a pragmatic mental model of how intuition works and perhaps how we can develop it.

This is the subject of the next few chapters.

SECTION II

THE LEADER'S INTUITION

What lies before us and what lies behind us are small matters compared to what lies within us. And when we bring what is within out into the world, miracles happen.

—Henry David Thoreau

2

WHAT INTUITION IS
THE IDEA OF THE 'BRIM'

Intuition is mysterious

Whether we call it intuition, extrasensory perception, insight, or any other word, when we see things that other people do not see, we refer to it as intuition. Everybody knows what intuition is, yet it is so difficult to explain. It is thought to come in a flash or a dream.

During my college chemistry classes, I heard the story of how nineteenth-century chemist Friedrich August von Kekule saw the benzene ring in a flash.

'I turned my chair to the fire and dozed...the atoms were gamboling before my eyes...my mental eye could now distinguish larger structures of manifold conformation...all turning and twisting like in snakelike motion...as if by a flash of lightning, I awoke...'

Likewise, there is the well-known story of how Archimedes jumped out of the tub exclaiming '*Eureka*' when he figured out what volume of water is displaced when a weight is immersed into water.

In reality, intuition need not necessarily come in a flash. All of us have intuition.

Spirituality recognizes intuition as the product of an attitude of letting life flow naturally.

Psychologists say that intuition is habitual, and that if we listen to our inner voice as a habit, we will become more intuitive.

Science knows a lot about how the brain functions, but is still unable to answer what exactly intuition is and how it works. It has been proven that altered states of consciousness and deep relaxation cause the brain to produce 'alpha and theta wavelengths'—which is good for intuition to function.

It is also known that intuition is enhanced by certain factors:

- ❖ Receiving information—sensing, seeing, hearing, smelling
- ❖ An open mind, including a belief in the power of intuition
- ❖ A strong desire to achieve or overcome, and a positive attitude
- ❖ An attempt to remove oneself from the outside world and self-awareness
- ❖ Willingness to take risks, supported by common sense

So while we know we have something called intuition, we are unsure how it works and how we can develop it. All that we do know is that to develop intuition, we must learn what cannot be taught. To learn what cannot be taught, we need an idea about how the brain is organized to learn.

It is a bit like a complex combination lock.

The brain as a combination lock

Think of the brain as a combination lock. Suppose you have to unlock a combination lock of four digits, and you do not know the code, how will you go about opening it? You will begin at 0000 and go on through until 9999. At some point of this trial and error method, you will get the click, the 'aha' feeling of having unlocked the lock.

To make the situation more complex, imagine that you have to do the same with a hundred-digit lock. Further, assume that the code of that lock varies by the hour of the day. Clearly, the trial and error method will not be very practical in terms of time. You will necessarily have to tinker with the lock over an extended period of time, register patterns, recall those patterns and establish your own intuitive way to unlock the combination lock.

There is a sequence in Dan Brown's novel *The Da Vinci Code* which suggests how complex complexity can be. The main protagonists Sophie Neveu and Robert Langdon find a cylindrical device called a cryptex, which contains a secret. The cryptex has five rotating parts; each part can be set at one out of twenty-six possibilities. Sophie explains to Langdon that the only way to access the information inside is to know the proper five-letter password. And with five dials, each one with twenty-six letters, that is twenty-six to the fifth power—approximately 12 million possibilities.

It was impossible to approach the problem logistically and sequentially. The riddle was solved through well-judged answers to clues that came their way as the story unfolded. They used a combination of intuition and analysis.

The human brain is even more complex than the cryptex referred to in the novel. However, in the matter of getting locked and unlocked, the brain does behave like a combination lock.

For something to enter and reside in the brain, this

personalized lock has to be opened. What opens the mind of one person may not open the mind of another. And for each person, there are much more than the 12 million possibilities referred to in the novel!

The only thing you do recognize is when your mind has been unlocked. When the mind has been opened, you get the 'aha' feeling—we say 'the penny dropped for me'. You can get the 'aha' feeling out of some story, emotion or experience that you have uniquely related to. That is why it is important to be exposed to stories, experiences and emotions; you never know when you will get the 'aha' feeling, and that moment is not the same for all people. Once you get the 'aha' feeling, there is some chance, that that lesson will enter and stay in your brain.

Knowing that there is an 'aha' feeling when the combination lock opens is nice, but the question arises: how is this combination lock structured and how does it work?

Unlike animals, the human brain has three parts

The brain is under 3 per cent of the body weight but consumes a quarter of the energy used by the body. It is a very interesting piece of equipment.

The expression 'hare-brained' has been used for a long time to describe a person whose ideas are not so well thought through. Supposedly, such a person behaves like a hare, which darts about without thinking. As it happens, there is a part of the human brain that resembles a hare's, and functions like that!

There was a neurologist and anthropologist in the 1800s called Paul Broca. He was a brilliant brain anatomist and made important investigations on this subject. His work was one of the early indications of two facts: first, that specific brain functions exist in particular locales of the brain. Second, that there is a connection between the anatomy of the brain and what the brain does.

Though far removed from the world of neuroscience and psychology, I have found it interesting to understand in a layman's way something about the structure and functioning of the brain through a crude model. I was helped by my doctor friends, Dr P.R. Parekh and Dr R. Rao, and by psychology professionals Amrita and Noah Bruce.

A scientist, Paul MacLean, chief of brain evolution and behaviour at the National Institute of Mental Health in the US, called the brain 'triune'—three-in-one. He conceptualized the brain as having three inter-connected evolutionary levels.

Imagine that you hold a modest-sized cabbage in your hand. It is well layered with complex structures overlaid in a pattern of great beauty and hues. On top of that, place a small lemon, and over that a common green pea.

Now hold all these with a set of wires and glues so that they are 'wired' and all three pieces are held together. Turn the structure upside down so that the pea is at the bottom, the lemon in between and the cabbage on top. Place the whole, wired structure into the empty skull of a human being (if you can get one!) and connect the wiring to the rest of the human system. You have a crude metaphor of a human brain—in terms of approximate proportions, rather than colour or physical shape.

In the 'pea' part of the brain, the basic life functions are controlled. It supports things like breathing, heartbeats and so on. Suppose you are on the treadmill and the heart has to pump more. This 'pea' is the brain part that swings into action. Without proper functioning of this 'pea', life functions would cease.

There is a medical condition in which a person may stop breathing while sleeping. If it happens for long, the person may die. This condition is linked to the destruction of cells in the 'pea' brain. That is why all living creatures have this 'pea' brain, whether they are reptiles, mammals or humans. Evolution folks refer to this 'pea' as the reptilian brain; the technical people call it the brain stem and cerebellum.

Then you have the small 'lemon' part, which evolution people call the paleo-mammalian brain; to the technically inclined, it is the limbic system. This was present in early mammals and, of course, is in human beings. This supports basic emotions such as fear, love and hunger. So when you see a threat, you have the instinct to flee. When you feel hungry and see food, you have the desire to eat. Pigs, horses, cats and such animals have this 'lemon'.

Finally, you have the 'cabbage', or neo-cortex, which is present in a rudimentary form in mammals. In humans, it is uniquely well-developed, that is, the 'cabbage' is large, complex, and nuanced. Though early mammals possessed this part of the brain, it is far more important to human functioning. A human without the neo-cortex is virtually a vegetable. This allows humans to do all sorts of things.

This cabbage part of the brain is the repository of complex emotions. For example, it can hold multiple and opposite emotions simultaneously. That is why you can hate someone's guts, yet appear polite and loving towards him. An animal cannot do that. It either loves you or hates you. Dogs are loved because they cannot feel one way and behave another way towards you; they always appear faithful in exactly the same way. Not true with human beings! In this respect, dogs are better off without a frontal cortex or a huge neo-cortex.

It is in the 'cabbage' that complex analytical processes are done by human beings—thinking in a logical and sequential manner, working out the alternative action options available and choosing the most appropriate one, figuring out what might happen in the future and preparing for it and so on.

This 'cabbage' is the point of human distinctiveness; it is also the source of our over-braining, worries, anxieties and indecisiveness. You can appreciate the huge intensity of work in the brain.

If you hold only the 'lemon and pea' parts of a human and pig brain in your hand, you can hardly tell the difference between the two! It is quite sobering to reflect on this. Evolution scientists believe that each layer came on top of the other as the species evolved—from reptiles to mammals to humans. That is why they appear almost in a row, each one overlaid on the earlier part, reflecting the way the brain might have evolved.

Different circuitry for analysis and for intuition

The three parts are wired up in a complex way, so the 'electric currents' can flow in many ways. From a lay person's perspective, this multiple wiring causes human responses to be of an instinctive or analytical type.

Although the brain structures are similar in all people, the wiring in the brain works differently for different people. An instinctive response comes out of a different brain circuit as compared to an analytical response. Different currents are generated and run through different wires, depending on what the brain is engaged with at a point of time.

The analytical type is uniquely human—how to develop options, choose from among them and act on one thoughtfully. The human brain can receive external stimuli, it can evaluate, analyse multiple angles and figure out which is the best option. People with a strong data-driven mind are interested in the realities and facts that their senses have picked up explicitly. People operating in this mode and with this kind of mind tend to be best with detail, they prefer solid routines and process, they emphasize targets and plans, and they trust authority and experience. This is the mindset that all societies coach their people to develop.

The instinctive type includes the survival variety, for example, how to escape danger; or the emotional variety of like or dislike; or the type that comes out of past experiences almost without thinking about it. People with an intuition-driven mind are more interested in the possibilities than in the predictions, they like to listen to what comes from the unconscious, and they emphasize vision and purpose and are less driven by process and routine.

This is illustrated by the different behaviour of an animal compared to that of a man in an experimental situation. A squirrel can only receive stimuli and respond without logic or analysis at that point of time. It cannot anticipate a future problem, let alone respond to it. So if a squirrel runs across a narrow platform towards a food source, it will do so irrespective of whether the platform is at ground level or at a height of 100 feet. It will still run across without a concern about falling off from a height.

Human distinctiveness lies in the possession of an analytical brain. If the narrow platform is at ground level, the instinctive brain says 'Go' and the analytical brain agrees. However, if the platform is raised to a height of 100 feet, the analytical brain will point out the dangers of running across the narrow platform at such a height and dissuade the instinctive brain from saying 'Go'. The consequence is that while the squirrel may still run across, the human being is unlikely to scamper across the same platform.

The durable Brain's Remote Implicit Memory (BRIM)

There is a sort of 'email ID' in the brain. This is what I call the BRIM, standing for the Brain's Remote Implicit Memory.

The letter R in BRIM stands for 'remote'.

The part of the memory called the remote memory stretches very deep into your psyche and childhood—your village, your grandfather's house, the smells of mother's cooking, and the stories that granny told you. This remote memory is very durable. That is why a person may forget what happened last week, but can recall early life events with great clarity. A study of the deterioration of brain cells also shows that the remote memory suffers less than some other parts.

The letter I in BRIM comes from 'implicit'.

In the implicit memory, you hold *processes*—such processes manifest themselves as skills and habits; these are housed in the implicit memory without your being aware of it. When you have practised over and over again, then the 'routine' gets encoded in this implicit memory. After that, you access from this memory without even being aware of it: how to ride a bicycle, how to swim or how to change gears in the car, the kind of stuff that you do not know that you know, and certainly, have a lot of difficulty in teaching others.

It is in the explicit memory that you hold *facts*. You know that you know. For example, you know that you know your son's date of birth. You know that you have to speak at a function next week.

BRIM is the common area between the remote and implicit memory in the brain. To develop strong intuition, this email ID must be accessed for messages stored there.

There is evidence that the BRIM exists

You know that the BRIM exists because you use it all the time. You drive from home to work each morning, using your BRIM. You feel expectant about grandma's food after a long time because your BRIM has stored that experience.

When Shoaib Akhtar's cricket ball comes hurtling at Rahul Dravid at 150 km per hour, Dravid responds with his instinct. He certainly does not estimate the trajectory by computing the ball speed, wind direction, angle of throw and other such matters of physics.

Art Kleiner, writer and author, interviewed two commentators who have written extensively about the Toyota Production System for *Strategy + Business* magazine. One of them, Daniel Jones recalled, 'When we first visited them,

Toyota was completely incapable of articulating its first principles. They could tell you all the techniques they used, but not the rationale behind them. They had lived that way for two generations. And they were surprised that the rest of the world did not work that way too.' This is a great example of stuff residing in the BRIM of the Toyota engineers. As a matter of fact, the BRIM activity is true not just of managers but of all people.

An American consultant called Gary Klein studied nurses, firefighters and other professionals who have to make decisions based on imperfect information and under pressure. He refers to them as 'experts'. He found that when experts decide, they do not have a systematic and logical way of arriving at the correct option for action. They size up a situation rapidly, and drawing upon their intuition and experience, they act quickly. The quality of their decisions under such conditions of high stress could be assessed only much later; it seemed to depend on their training and their intuition.

Instinct does not lend itself to analysis

An important feature of instinct (or intuition, I use these words interchangeably) is that it does not lend itself to analysis. You need both instinct and analysis precisely because they are different and complementary. When they get mixed up, it is quite a muddle.

Philosophers say that the centre of the mind's thinking is not in the conscious process, that is why it is good to let it function in a natural and spontaneous way. True ingenuity is manifest when the natural functioning of the mind is not blocked by formal methods and techniques—too much of which produce the bonsai manager. This is illustrated by an amusing verse about the centipede.

The centipede was happy,
Quite until a toad in fun

Said, 'pray, which leg goes after which?'
This worked his mind to such a pitch,
He lay distracted in a ditch,
Considering how to run.

Soon after I learned to play golf—unfortunately the lesson never seems to get over—I recall standing at the first tee box at my golf club. Apart from my group, the next group was waiting, so I had seven pairs of eyes watching me. I knew all the right things to be done to get a great drive off the first tee. The principles were firmly embedded in my mind, the pictures from the golf book were indelibly etched in the brain and, above all, I could recall all of them with great clarity. Do you think I got a good swing?

I play tennis with a competitive guy over weekends. Sometimes, he plays invincibly and I just cannot outplay him. During the change of sides, I appreciate his game and inquire about what it is that he is doing that day which makes him so good. He thinks about it and gives me some analytical explanation. During the very next set, his game deteriorates perceptibly!

Marlin Eller was Microsoft's lead developer for the Windows operating system during the 1980s. Stories have been written about this successful development being the outcome of a far-sighted, well-thought-out strategy. Marlin Eller has, however, expressed a completely different point of view. He says that the view from the trenches resembled white water rafting, swerving widely from one end to another, just avoiding the rocks and keeping out of trouble!

Business and psychology teacher John Eliot recounted an incident from the 1976 Winter Olympics at Innsbruck, Austria. Alpine skier Franz Klammer was racing against the defending Olympic champion, Bernhard Russi of Switzerland. The accepted technique to win was to stay low and keep the skis gliding flat in a straight line. Franz Klammer attempted it very differently in that race. He skated hard out of the gate and whipped around the corners wildly, just missing fences. His coach thought Klammer might be killed as he veered around the sharp corners so dangerously. Klammer beat Russi by a small margin to the wild cheers of spectators.

The cheering journalists and spectators wanted to know how he did it and what was going through his mind as he swerved past each of those corners. Franz Klammer simply said, 'Nothing. I was just trying to get to the finishing line fast.' It is true to say that top performers perform at the magical moment with their intuition—their own brain does not know in any analytical sense what they did right.

There are many stories published of successful people who probably do not quite know how they did whatever they did. The media or some analyst writes up an ex post facto account which makes the whole process appear orderly and systematic, even though the reality was not so at all. The media puts a beaming CEO on the cover and explains how he did some wonder within his company. The magazine got a story and the CEO got an ego boost. So here is what probably happened.

This exercise required the CEO to present what he did as the outcome of a series of orderly thoughts and plans, which was probably far from the reality. Upon seeing his story on the magazine cover, the CEO may start to believe that indeed he did do it. Soon after, his fortunes seem to head south because he begins to analyse and present what he does intuitively. That is the reason conservative leaders say, avoid getting on to the cover of a magazine, it can destroy you! Perhaps such stories aggravate the ego. But it could also be that the cover stories and awards require them to brain about what their brain does not know. The result is that they over-brain, and then there seems to be only one way to go: south.

I recall that as soon as the definitive book *In Search of Excellence* featuring outstanding companies was written by

Tom Peters and Robert Waterman in the early 1980s, some of those companies started to decline. For example, Eastman Kodak, Amdahl, National Semiconductor and Wang Labs all slipped in their rankings. I have also found that coincidentally as soon as some companies win the prestigious Malcolm Baldrige Award for Quality, they veer off course. For example, Motorola and General Motors' Cadillac division.

Top performance in the arts and sports—as well as in management—comes out of the instinctive brain, not out of the 'sensible, rational and analytical brain'. The normal mode of action takes place in the analytical brain. At the moment of performance, which is usually stressful, the highest part of the brain is not your friend. You cannot rely on the analytical brain; you have to rely on your instinctive brain.

That is what I mean when I refer to the analytical brain and the instinctive brain at the moment of performance.

So the message is that at the crucial moment, trust your instinctive brain, and don't use your top quality analytical brain! It is exactly the opposite of all that society teaches you.

Enrich the BRIM. You can think of it as 'flashbulb' memory. This is the part of the memory that the brain refers to in the jiffy just prior to responding to the situation on hand. Instinct works on this accumulated memory. Embedding something in the 'flashbulb' memory or BRIM is very valuable for developing and strengthening instinct.

The next chapter is about how intuition can be enhanced and the role that emotion-rich stories can play.

3

DEVELOPING INTUITION THROUGH THE 'BRIM'
THE VALUE OF ANECDOTES

A mental model of how intuition works

As mentioned in chapter 1 with respect to my Arabian experiences, our minds engage with our surroundings in an immersion mode and in a reflective mode. There is a difference between the two modes.

Immersion

All of us are immersed in our work and routines, some superficially and some deeply. The degree of immersion may vary, but not the fact of immersion. Incidents that occur during the course of our work are like pebbles that hit the surface of the mind. Each incident leaves some impact, small and negligible in most cases, but large and permanent in a few cases.

The deeper the immersion with the work and the more emotional the involvement with the incident, the sharper the pebble marks left on the mind surface by that experience. Very deep and emotion-laden experiences enter the BRIM and sit there in the form of anecdotes. In short, emotions help to etch events and incidents more deeply in our memories.

Gabriel Garcia Marquez wrote the story (*Chronicle of a Death Foretold*) of a man who returned to the village where a violent murder had occurred several years ago. The man met the villagers and all of them had a recollection of the murder. The detail and sequence in which they stored the 'facts' and recalled them varied. The relations and close friends of the man remembered things which others did not. There was no doubt that the emotions generated by the murder left a clear— if inconsistent—impression in everybody's mind.

The connection between emotion and recall is further exemplified by another experiment, conducted by two professors at Irvine, California. Two experimental groups were told a similar story. One was told in a fairly unexciting, factual and sequential manner, the other had some emotion-laden material. After several weeks, both groups were tested for recall. The emotion-laden group could recall the sequence far more vividly (although not accurately) through the professors' metaphor of a 'flashbulb memory'.

Reflection

When we are engaged with some subject in a reflective or contemplative mode, then relevant anecdotes bubble up from the BRIM as extra-sensorial insights.

Philosophers have long recognized this. That is why, when complex issues arise, philosophers prescribe immersion and contemplation, whereas psychologists and academics prescribe analysis. As modern psychologists would state it, immersion should lead to contemplation, which should lead to happiness—in management, indeed, in life as a whole!

Management magazines make a hero out of the quick-thinking, decisive leader. In reality, particularly with complex problems, it helps to slow down deliberately, and to reflect and contemplate. This helps managers build more confidence in their intuition and recall lessons when they have to make decisions without full information.

For managers, analysis and contemplation are both important. Acquisition of knowledge and analysis are easier to do. Everybody learns to do these, though admittedly, the quality of their practice may be variable.

On the other hand, the art of contemplation is far more difficult to teach, learn or practice. How can managers contemplate? Just close their eyes and think? Of what? That is not very practical or helpful to the average operating manager. Here is a suggestion.

Contemplate on the 'surrounds'

While observing or reading, our natural tendency is to focus on the 'issue', to absorb and analyse it, but not what surrounds it. What surrounds the issue may be broad and large, and often, is relevant for the viewing of the issue within a context. In short, viewing an issue within a context, gives one a different perspective from viewing it in isolation or more narrowly. Some examples follow.

Those who have read *War and Peace* will remember more clearly the lives of the five featured families, who go through birth, childhood, marriage and so on. Less clear in the memory would be the backdrop: Napoleonic Europe, 1805–20.

Another example: if a large, black dot is drawn on a white sheet of paper, and you ask people what they see, most would likely answer, 'A black dot.' Only a few might say, 'A white space with a dot.'

Try this experiment. Draw two straight lines at an angle as you would to depict a funnel—broad and opening out at one end and closer and convergent at the other end. Within the space thus created, draw two vertical lines of identical length. One line should be placed near the broad end, so it will have a lot of funnel space above and below it. The other one should be placed at the converging end so that there is little funnel space above and below the ends of the vertical line. Now hold the paper at a distance and ask people which of the vertical lines is longer. Many would look at the paper and observe that the line at the convergent end is longer.

These examples confirm that context influences the perception of the issue.

In management case situations, the broader industry and company context of a particular success or failure story, the employees' motivations and interests, and such other 'surrounds' deeply influence the story or research being written. Although some factors may be correlated, their causality (one causing the other) cannot be assumed.

Managers suffer from a paucity of time, so they grasp case outcomes in haste and even transplant them into their own situation. If the transplant fails, they develop a healthy cynicism for the idea. In reality, ideas should qualify as 'theory' only after there have been 'cycles of observation, followed by classification of phenomena, followed by development and testing of hypotheses'.

That is why the surrounds are what the contemplation should be about. Expressed differently, the contemplation should be not just about the rose, but its bed of soil as well. In this manner, true value is extracted out of the act of reflecting—on how the success or failure happened, and becoming sensitive to the context in which things worked or did not.

Often leaders and managers fail to do this. If they could do so consciously, then the value from the reading and contemplation will enter their BRIM, and sharpen their intuition. Surely that has value!

So emotion promotes a flashbulb memory and a flashbulb memory promotes instinct.

Intuition through practice and immersion

The BRIM is enriched in two ways, through practice and immersion.

The first method of enrichment is through *practice*, which means doing the same thing so often and, hopefully, so well, that you don't know that you know. That is the way Sachin Tendulkar swings his cricket bat, without thinking and without knowing how exactly he achieves whatever happens after the swing. Practice embeds processes into the implicit memory.

The second method of enrichment is through *immersion*; this means experiencing emotions and involvement so deeply that they enter your remote memory and stay there—often forever. Sachin Tendulkar probably watches and analyses videos of his own action, of great moments and matches played by others, talks to his coach and so on. It is a busy day for him, not very different from the day you have at work. He is totally and emotionally immersed in his profession.

Achieving total immersion is very important to developing intuition. The process of immersion may appear 'wasteful' to an analytical mind, but it is the key to enriching the BRIM. In each profession, people figure out how to achieve total immersion.

Managers must also find a way to achieve such immersion; travel, talking to people, books, and seminars are all ways to do so. Staying rooted—mentally and physically—would inevitably make them bonsai.

The amazing power of immersion: Leela Chitnis

I quite enjoyed the story recounted by the niece of India's top film star of the 1940s, Leela Chitnis (*Indian Express*, 9 October 2005).

Leela was the antithesis of a film star. She was the daughter of a professor, skinny and gawky; due to weak eyesight, she wore thick glasses. While still at college, she fell in love with an urbane gentleman who was fourteen years her senior, Dr Gajanand Chitnis. He was the editor of a Marathi magazine. He was also involved with the Marathi stage as a writer and director of plays. Unfortunately, Dr Gajanand Chitnis was not economically successful. The shy and self-conscious Leela, now with two children, started accompanying her husband to the rehearsals, helping with the costumes and the sets in order to earn a bit of money. She observed the goings on; something must have been lodging in her BRIM all the time. One day, the heroine of the play failed to turn up. Leela was thrust on the stage only because she had attended the endless rehearsals.

As her niece recounts, 'Now from the recesses of her brain, she dredged up the dialogues.'

She must have acquitted herself very well. Very soon roles poured in. Then she signed for her first film. In 1940, when Lux, the 'beauty soap of the film stars' sought models, Leela was the first to be chosen. Soon thereafter, she became the leading Hindi film star.

Such is the value of immersion as also the benefits of chance!

Another story is a contemporary one about Steve Jobs, co-founder of Apple Computer.

Steve Jobs delivered a commencement day speech at Stanford in June 2005, in which he stated, 'What I stumbled into by following my curiosity and intuition turned out to be priceless later on.' After dropping out of college, he decided to take calligraphy classes to learn about serifs and sans serif typefaces. He found it 'fascinating and beautiful in a way that science could not capture'. It had no practical application in his life, not one that he could visualize. Ten years later, while designing the first Mac, it all came back to him—it helped him to design the first computer with beautiful typography, multiple typefaces and proportionally shaped fonts. He concluded his narrative with, 'You have to trust something—your gut, destiny, karma, whatever.'

These are real stories about intuition, which 'resides' in the BRIM by deep immersion.

The need for and the value of immersion is observed in many fields. When Indira Gandhi was a child, she witnessed and heard the drama of the national movement constantly. Was it a surprise that she acquired a tremendous instinct for politics in her later life?

In the 1950s, Indian tennis star Ramanathan Krishnan grew up in a 'tennis household'. His father T.K. Ramanathan was a player of considerable merit. Is it any surprise that he grew up with tennis in his genes? And, in turn, he imparted it to Ramesh Krishnan, his son. Such immersion is relevant to management also.

Some managers take pride in stating that they do not read management books or attend seminars. Of course, some books are avoidable and so are some seminars. However, the better ones are the 'waters' in which managers can immerse themselves in order to enrich their BRIM. Such immersion has a major role in strengthening the managerial instinct.

The manager's mind is like a sponge which can absorb water, but you can never be sure how much and which kind of water. Just as you would place the sponge under a running stream, in the rainfall, out on the meadows, in just as many water-bearing places as possible, the mind and its memory too must be exposed to management anecdotes and leadership stories. Even a bonsai, incidentally, is never kept thirsty—in fact, it is watered with sprinklers to simulate rain.

Reflection scoops out the anecdotes

In the 1940s, the Indian statesman and politician C. Rajagopalachari wrote a series of weekly chapters on the great Indian epics, the Ramayana and the Mahabharata. These were finally put together as an enduring book.

K.M. Munshi, the editor, wrote in his preface,

> *The Mahabharata* is not a mere epic; it is a romance, telling the tale of heroic men and women...it is a whole literature in itself, containing a code of life, a philosophy of social and ethical relations...through such books alone, the harmonies underlying true culture will one day reconcile the disorders of modern life.

To this day, the book sells very well. Its longevity demonstrates the value and durability of stories and emotion.

Think of the best lessons you have learnt about soft subjects like character, self-esteem and honesty. Almost always, the lesson is associated with an anecdote from your own experiences or an interaction with somebody you respect or a story told by somebody.

There are traditions of storytelling in India that have evolved over the centuries, for example, the *jatra* in rural Bengal, the *upanyasam* in Tamil Nadu, and the *harikatha* in the north are regional expressions of education and entertainment rolled in one. This is so in other countries too.

Even to this day as dusk settles in Marrakech, storytellers emerge in the market square of Jamaa El Fna, holding the attention of several hundreds each evening. Your memory invariably carries a narrative, in which some idea is interlocked with an emotion.

The drama of human emotion is a great preservative for ideas, because both the idea and the drama get indelibly etched in your mind—the selflessness of Hanuman, the righteousness of Yudhisthira, Aesop's hare and tortoise, the love of Heer and Ranjha, and so on. The strong connection between learning on the one hand and anecdotes and stories on the other is because *an idea is united with an emotion.*

That is why stories are a very important way of teaching

and imparting knowledge, especially on fuzzy and complex subjects. When it comes to ethical and religious studies, subjects such as good character, good citizenry, and good social values and so on, storytelling is effective.

Stories are not a management fad

A big part of a CEO's job is to motivate people to reach certain goals. To do that, he or she must engage their emotions, and the key to their hearts is a story. And successful CEOs know that they cannot thrive by selling pipe dreams or by communicating via spin doctors. They must engage with their managers, looking them in the eye and say, 'We'll be lucky as hell if we get through this, but here is what I think we should do.' And they will listen to him.

I have witnessed this during my career, and indeed practised it, especially in situations of turnaround: Etah Dairy, Lever Exports in Hindustan Lever, Unilever Arabia, and some of the Tata companies with which I have been associated. Getting the best out of the people who know the business well is so very important—yet one needs to do so at a time when they are least motivated to open up and share their views.

In the May 2004 issue of *Harvard Business Review*, Stephen Denning wrote an article entitled *Telling Stories*. In his workplace at the World Bank, his function was knowledge management.

Like many managers, he too believed that analytical was good; anecdotal was bad. All of business thinking and training is about being rational, analytical and logical—almost as though, once the logic is clear to someone, he will do the obvious! Yet, every manager knows that is not true.

Analysis may excite the mind, but it rarely offers a route to the heart. Not surprisingly, Stephen Denning found it an uphill task to persuade his World Bank colleagues to accept knowledge management through his logical PowerPoint presentations. He then told them a 150-word story about a health worker in Zambia. It brought out a human perspective, packed with emotion, about grassroots level problems as perceived by the worker. He was amazed that his audience at the World Bank was now 'connecting'!

Denning learnt the value of the story for sure, but he learnt one more important lesson—that the story or anecdote must be told in a minimalist way, even lacking texture and detail, if it is to attract the attention of managers. This is so because managers in their workplace mindset and attitude have little time and patience for long, 'maximalist' stories with a great deal of embellishment and detail.

Hollywood's top screenwriting coach, Robert Mckee, is a Ph.D. in cinema arts. His students have written, directed and produced winning films like *Forrest Gump*, *Erin Brockovich*, *Gandhi* and many others. Mckee feels that executives can engage listeners on a whole new level if they toss out their PowerPoint slides and learn to tell good stories instead, because 'stories fulfill a profound human need to grasp the patterns of living—not merely as an intellectual exercise, but within a very personal, emotional experience'. In a story, you not only weave a lot of information into the telling but you also arouse your listener's emotions and energy. Storytelling is related to management.

But why anecdotes and stories about animals, plants and Nature?

Nature provides fascinating anecdotes

The world of animals has an evolutionary linkage to man; Nature has always been inspiring and emotive.

There is fascinating research about how favourable human beings feel to savannah grasslands as compared to rainforests and deserts. People in the age group of eight to eighty years were shown pictures of various such environments and were asked which one they would prefer. The young ones, with unconditioned minds, invariably preferred the savannah, the environment of our ancestors millions of years ago. The children's psychological make-up seemed to carry some genetic memory about their evolutionary homeland! The great Africa specialist, Richard Leakey, has commented that the vast majority of people who come to Africa feel something they feel nowhere else...they feel they are home.

From time immemorial, Nature has caused emotion and wonderment in man's mind. That is why watching television channels relating to animals and Nature leaves one with memorable impressions. What is memorable may vary from person to person, but almost everybody is strongly influenced by watching Nature at work.

Ethology is a subject that teaches us to look closely at the lives of animals around us (plants, insects, etc, included for my purpose) and to examine more objectively our own behavioural pattern. Some specialists even believe that ethology should form a serious line of study in the school curriculum. In the kingdom of plants, insects, birds, mammals, reptiles, there is some orderly form of chaos, or chaotic form of order. There is an amazing balance between the realities of life in each species—communication, mating, socialization, survival and reproduction.

There are many beautiful things to discover in Nature. There are perhaps as many horrid things that happen too. Any owner of a home pet realizes how much he learns and discovers every week. Some people love Nature, its perils and battles, its struggles and its magic. Others get completely put off by the aggression required to survive and the ruthlessness directed at other species. However, it is good to recall that both the beauty and the horror are judged by human standards, something that the ethologist would not do. But in every sense, there is poetry in Nature, a poetry that combines an idea with an emotion.

Ethologists have found extraordinary facts about the behaviour of animals. In their television series and book, Gerald and Lee Durrell have brought a lot of these to life. They have found that animals too use a type of language, which does not resemble human language.

Different species can use pretty sophisticated means of communication among themselves, ranging from the language of tails and ears among canines, scent trails laid down by caterpillars, electrical discharges of fish to duets by gibbons. Their lives are probably as complex as our own and their skills are, within their context, perhaps as extensive as ours.

More importantly, we can see some of our own behaviour patterns mirrored in animals, leading to the sober realization that in a sense, humans too are animals! The Durrells acknowledge that the proper study of mankind is indeed man. But predictably, they applaud the many behavioural lessons that men can benefit from by a study of animals!

American writer Walt Whitman's lines in *A Song of Myself* are apposite:

I think I could turn and live with animals; they are so placid
    and self contained,
I stand and look at them long and long.
They do not sweat and whine about their condition,
They do not lie awake in the dark and weep for their sins,
They do not make me sick discussing their duty to God,
Not one is dissatisfied, not one is demented with the mania
    of owning things,
Not one kneels to another, or to his kind that lived a
    thousand years ago,
Not one is respectable or unhappy over the whole earth.
So they show their relations to me and I accept them,
They bring me tokens of myself; they evince them plainly in
    their possession.

4

LEARNING WHAT IS NOT TAUGHT
THE NATURE OF MANAGEMENT

The myth of the proven manager

As they develop their career, the kind of mistakes that managers make is truly amazing; even more amazing are the mistakes made by successful managers after they have reached the heights of glory. They range from ignoring feelings of consumers or employees to acquiring the wrong companies despite advice to the contrary. When you discuss case studies at the training courses, you cannot help wondering why such 'dumb' things were done by such accomplished and experienced characters as depicted in the case!

When someone talks about a 'proven manager', do not believe him. There is no person who fits that description. You have to prove yourself day after day, every single day of your career. However, we tend to forget it, partly because we are constantly assailed with this talk about proven managers.

You don't believe it? Talk to a headhunter. He will persuade you that he can find you proven managers. Read the job advertisements in the morning newspaper. Often, they seek proven managers with a track record. The concept of the proven manager is deeply embedded in aspiring managers as well as potential employers.

There is a peculiar characteristic about human affairs, and this is true of management as well. When you are successful, it makes you feel that you know a lot and that you have a lot of experience. This may well be true. But soon, you start believing that you know almost everything worth knowing—and your behaviour starts to reflect this attitude. It is then that the matching opposite characteristic manifests itself, i.e., just as you begin to solve your next problem with the well-tried technique from your rich repertoire of 'ideas that have worked', everything begins to fail. Have you, then, become a bonsai manager?

It is a bit like any sport, as soon as you have got it right, something happens to remind you that you have not! Indeed, it is a lot like the story of life itself. You never know whether you have got it. And you spend a lifetime trying to understand what is going on!

Management is among the most sought-after professions in the world today. There are many questions relating to management education and training. What is the value of a formal management education? How do you develop a top manager? How come a successful manager is well-regarded one day and considered ineffective on another day?

Management as a performing art

One can study optics, chemistry and mechanics through a syllabus to become a professional technologist. The key attribute of the scientific process is that the outcome will be the same no matter how many times that experiment is performed.

From this perspective, clearly management is not a science. Given a set of inputs, the outcomes are not always the same; the outcome is strongly influenced by the circumstances at the moment of performance. Management closely resembles sports or a performing art.

To dramatize the point, consider a world-class tennis player. You cannot be a top tennis player only through a classroom curriculum and some intensive practice; you have to develop a strong sense of instinct, timing, and mental composure to cope with moments of great tension.

Vijay Amritraj once arranged a fun tennis game for some of us to play with Bjorn Borg at the CCI (Cricket Club of India) courts in Mumbai, and that brought back memories of a great match played by Borg during his career.

Borg's father, Rune, was an accomplished table tennis player and he won a tournament when Bjorn was nine years old. Senior Borg's prize was a tennis racket, which started young Bjorn on his journey. He reigned as the world's supreme player through the 1970s and early 1980s.

There was a memorable Wimbledon final in July 1980 between Borg and McEnroe; both were in peak playing forms. McEnroe was in a devastating form, having served as many as fifteen aces in his semi-final against Jimmy Connors. Borg had already surpassed Rod Laver's record for the maximum number of consecutive singles wins at Wimbledon.

During the finals, Borg was leading two sets to one at the end of the third set. In the fourth set, Borg broke McEnroe and had two match points. If he won even one of them, the Wimbledon crown would be his, once again. McEnroe cheekily attacked Borg's serves, and managed to save both the match points and then, levelled the game score. McEnroe went on to win the fourth set after as many as seven nail-biting and tense tie-breakers. And finally came a very, very gripping fifth set, which Borg won 8-6. It was one of the most dramatic finals that Wimbledon had seen. Borg relied on his instincts, held his calm, and played through that magical moment of performance!

Consider another performing art, music. The rendering of songs in Carnatic music involves a feat of doing eight things simultaneously. These consist of continuous adherence to shruti (the basic pitch), mastery over laya (rhythm), remembering accurately the sahitya (lyric), deeply understanding the meaning, playing out the bhava (emotions), the correct pronunciation, a comprehension of the special features of the raga and finally, the correct use of gamakas (ornamentation). An all-time great like M.S. Subbulakshmi became renowned not merely because of her complete mastery of the technical aspects, but also because of her ability to blend these eight elements together with intuitive harmony.

In all the performing arts, a successful artiste has to coordinate a unique set of skills and intuition at the moment of performance, but the magic truly comes when inspiration combines with skill to make for a great performance.

It is the same with leadership in management, but with one big difference. The sportsman or musician's magical moment is clearly known, it is the match moment or the concert moment. However, for a business manager, the magical moment of performance is fuzzy. The reality is that when he goes to work each day, it is not to play his match; it is for the most part mere practice. He has minor moments of decisions, which define his performance. However, the manager's magical moment comes when he is faced with the big decision point.

Such a decision-moment comes up onto him; he may well be unaware that the decision-moment which faces him is quite so crucial. In this respect, this is so unlike the performing artiste who enters the performance-moment with great awareness of the moment. It is a huge difference.

Managers can be taught many things in a course

When institutions teach management techniques and concepts, they appeal to the analytical brain. When the student manager graduates from there, he feels that he knows a lot about management. Otherwise, why would he go there in the first place? So management education does have its value. However, management practice is much more than the acquisition of such knowledge or the MBA diploma.

As he manages in real life, the manager must analyse, but he must also synthesize; he must know about and be aware of the strengths of people around him; as he will always realize but rarely admit, he will never know enough, not at any time during his career. When the chips are down, he must lead with truthfulness and credibility; and when the going is good, he must alert his team to the impending challenges so that complacency is consciously avoided.

He must be a master of psychology without possibly ever having studied the subject. He must at all times be rational, but his rationality must have a core of emotion, which is the essence of all human motivation.

As acknowledged by experienced managers, effectiveness comes through good judgement, good judgement comes through experience, and experience comes through bad judgement!

Management courses do not really teach the student soft skills, yet graduate the student with the sense that he is a well-equipped manager, ready to face the real world. In every walk of life, to be useful, acquired knowledge must be enriched with experience; only then can experience become wisdom.

Yet two-thirds of the one lakh Indian students of management have no work experience. The curriculum cannot convert them into managers. Yet, youngsters believe that such courses 'make' them managers. Recruiting companies also woo them and pay them such a huge salary that the student cannot be blamed for thinking that he is a 'terrific manager.'

These arguments should not cast any doubt about the usefulness of a management education: it is very valuable for training young people in business functions. But that is all that it is. A manager is much more than a trained resource in business functions.

Managers have to learn some other kinds of things by themselves, often from other managers, or risk becoming bonsai.

Managers can learn some things only from other managers

Who will help managers learn all these things? Successful leaders teach others to be leaders. They view teaching as one of their major jobs and they spend a lot of time doing it. I have met Roger Enrico, the former chairman of PepsiCo only twice on a one-to-one basis; he was a most charismatic individual and on both occasions, he was fully engaged, intellectually and emotionally, for all of the forty-five minutes I was with him.

Suman Sinha, the retired former Pepsi India chief, who was so successful in building the Pepsi business in India, says that the time Enrico spent with his top executives was phenomenal, all to coach and mentor them. Suman Sinha considered such coaching to be highly value adding to all involved and he was most admiring of Enrico's value as a coach, mentor and a passionate teacher. I asked Suman to describe Enrico's style of coaching. He related the following episode.

Suman was invited by Enrico for an interactive learning session with five other PepsiCo senior managers, to his ranch in Texas. The senior managers were selected by Roger, with general management, finance, marketing and technical backgrounds. In his group, Suman recalls that he had Mike White, John Cohil, and Donna Hudson, all of whom went on to hold very senior positions in PepsiCo. They were all asked to bring a write-up on one idea, which would be applicable to

PepsiCo business worldwide, and yield maximum benefit to the company on a sustainable and long-term basis.

The one-week interactive session started at breakfast at 8 a.m., when Roger briefed them on the business issues that he proposed to discuss that day. After breakfast, Roger played a videotape of his interview with some of the most well-known business leaders, like Jack Welch. He had posed the same issue that they were to discuss, to those leaders, and the tape played their views on how they would handle that particular issue. Roger would then seek the views of the group, give valuable insights and add immense experience-based examples to the discussions. By lunchtime, they would arrive at some clear, conclusive options on how a particular business issue could be solved and handled.

The afternoon was spent discussing the paper with each participant's idea of improving the operations of PepsiCo. Every day they took one idea, discussed it for five to six hours and fine-tuned it. Roger would then ask the originator of the idea, to write down a one-page article as if it were to appear in *Time* magazine, describing the idea and how PepsiCo could implement and benefit from the idea.

After dinner at 7 p.m., Roger and the group would sit by a flowing river on his ranch, and discuss PepsiCo operations, products, marketing ideas, financial innovations, almost anything till 2 a.m. or 3 a.m., while drinking Sambukas which Roger loved, or anything else that the others wanted. These seven or eight hours every evening were most educative, with everyone sharing experiences, ideas, innovations and indulging very informally in out-of-the-box thinking.

On the fourth day, Roger took them horseback riding across the mountains—a four-hour ride to a lovely mountain stream, where he taught them fly-fishing. They returned, very tired, to a bonfire, where Texan musicians were singing and playing the guitar. The informality and team-building experience were awesome.

The group was so overwhelmed by this learning experience and coaching approach, that they asked Roger, how he found the time, once a year, to spend coaching six senior managers. In his humble way, he said, 'This is my way of getting to know six senior people very closely, become their friend, and be available to them for solving any of their problems.' He added, 'Where can I get six excellent practical ideas to benefit PepsiCo?' Roger's coaching style and approach were both unique, probably not followed by any other CEO, and made a very long-lasting impact.

Such leaders constantly update and refine their views as they acquire new knowledge and experience. And they store them in the form of stories that they use not only to guide their own decisions and actions, but also to teach and lead others.

When leaders discuss their career experiences, they do not approach it as 'teaching'. Yet, you learn.

The basic principles of management do not change, except for occasional embellishments and insights, but the way that the facts interlock and change colour to make patterns is unique to each situation, indeed to each manager. That is why management is a subject in which new interpretations seldom displace old ones. Management principles are tenets, at best philosophies, and certainly not discoveries in any scientific sense.

A great manager realizes that the energy to manage actually comes from the dark side. It comes from everything that makes him suffer—difficult trade unions, unreasonable competitors, change-resistant middle managers, poor top teams and so on. As he struggles against these 'negative' powers, he is forced to live more deeply, more fully.

A great manager is a person who has realized that he is mortal, i.e., he can make mistakes and he will not be in that position or job in some years. As a result, he develops compassion for others.

Pain is the precursor to personal growth, managers should not dread it, and they must learn to embrace it.

How do you teach these kinds of things—nurturing talent, developing succession, relationship building and teamwork? You do not. They are learnt by the persons themselves. These kinds of lessons are constantly sought by aspiring as well as practising managers.

SECTION III

INTUITION THROUGH VARIED
EXPERIENCES AND RELATIONSHIPS

Experience is not what happens to a man, it is what a man does with what happens to him.

—Aldous Huxley

5

THE STUNTED CROCODILE
LEARNING FROM VARIED EXPERIENCES

Stunting by limiting and constricting

When I attended a Unilever conference in Zimbabwe, the host company had arranged a boat trip down the Zambezi river. One of the destinations was a crocodile farm. I did not find the farm visit appealing, though it was instructive. I learnt that the growth of a crocodile could be stunted by confining the animal to a small enclosure soon after it emerged from the egg.

I also learnt that long ago, in the early stages of evolution, crocodiles used to be 15 metres long. The longest of today's crocodiles is only half that length. Crocodiles eat many small animals such as fish, birds and turtles. When a crocodile has torn a chunk of flesh off its victim and is swallowing it, pressure is exerted on the thin, flexible roof at the back of the reptile's mouth. This squeezes the tear glands which are just above, causing tears to well up in its eyes. Hence the cynical expression 'crocodile tears'.

This stunting of a crocodile by restricting its space intrigued me and I asked my friend, noted environmentalist Bittu Sahgal of *Sanctuary* magazine about it. He dismissed the very idea of such a thing being done deliberately, but sent an inquiring email to his friend at the Madras Crocodile Farm. The subject mentioned on his email reflected his disbelief, 'Strange Verification Required'. Within a short time, back came the reply, 'Bonsai crocs are well known and they are created just as you mention, in enclosures too small for them! Rom Whitaker knew of a mugger reared at the Madras zoo for possibly 15–20 years and it was a little over a metre long. It should have been closer to 3 metres.'

A stunned Sahgal forwarded me the email with the comment, 'It seems you were right, though why anyone would want to do that is absolutely beyond me.'

Actually, there is a commercial reason for it. Wealthy people, it seems, love to take their guests around their vast home compounds which have ponds with bonsai crocodiles. It would not be very convenient to have full-size crocodiles in the ponds of your home compound!

Like with many species, the growth of the crocodile depends on the external temperature and the amount of food it consumes. However, the space available to grow and the threats that the animal has to encounter also have a great influence.

If stunted crocodiles could be created, can there be stunted human beings? The physical growth of a young child raised in a one-room tenement in Mumbai would not be stunted as compared to the growth of a child raised on a sprawling farm in the countryside. But the mental growth could be stunted.

Can there be stunted managers?

How a manager becomes stunted

A stunted manager is one who is operating and working at a level which is well below his potential. He himself is the best judge of this, because he can sense such a condition better than anyone else. He would probably exhibit certain characteristics and attitudes which would indicate to other people that he is working in this manner.

He may, for example, come through as a person who is not very involved or very happy with his work. Worse, he may have given up trying to change this position and may have reconciled to it. This would make him look like a 'tired' manager who does not have the motivation to do something about his situation for many possible reasons.

The disinclination to change the environment around him could be because he is more concerned with security than with satisfaction. It could be that he finds it too much of a bother to seek change. It may be that he is low on self-esteem and is worried about the consequences of trying to alter his situation. Reasons such as these cause him to continue with his unsatisfying predicament to the stage when this very situation becomes normal for him.

At some point of time, his characteristics and attitude become somewhat irreversible. Reviving his managerial learning and motivation becomes very difficult, or not worth the effort on the part of the organization. This is when he can be considered to have become a permanently stunted manager— it is the stage beyond which it is difficult to make him 'grow' again in a managerial sense. Such managers can be seen in large as well as small companies, multinationals and the public sector, almost everywhere.

The message is that the 'space' in which a manager grows is extremely important. This space around his job is defined by the manager by four perceptions.

- ❖ The nature of his industry and company
- ❖ The type of work he does and his role within his organization
- ❖ The people relationships he is involved with, and
- ❖ The threats or obstacles he faces and has to overcome.

If the space in which the manager operates and grows is limited, if his emotional and mental exertion are low, then his development gets stunted. If he stays in this stultifying situation for long and does nothing to change his circumstance, then he can become a permanently stunted manager!

Just as the growth of the crocodile depends on the diet and the space available, the growth of a manager too is influenced by his 'mental' food (reading, training, and people challenges) as well as the experiential space (new experiences and tough assignments that disturb him from his comfort zone). Nobody sets out to become a stunted manager. Yet stunted managers do exist, in large numbers.

Because of inadequate challenge and learning arising from working at the grassroots of company operations, young managers can get stunted in their growth at a very early stage of their career. The truly big and successful managers are set to solve problem after problem, they are constantly challenged to swim upstream against the tide so that they learn and grow fast.

Like many senior managers, I have sometimes had to counsel an aggrieved manager who felt sensitive about being passed over for a promotion. Indeed, on several occasions, I myself have needed counsel from a superior or mentor during my own career.

Once, I had to meet a manager who had spent twenty-five successful years, all in the foundry. He felt slighted because the company had decided to promote a colleague to be the next general manager. As far as the aggrieved manager was concerned, the colleague was not even a peer.

'Why is that so?' I inquired.

'He was five years my junior at the engineering college,' came the reply, crisply logical and beyond debate as far as he was concerned.

'But that was twenty-five years ago! Surely it is not relevant any more,' I persisted.

'It is,' he shot back. 'Even in the IAS and the Army, they recognize seniority throughout the career. They recognize not just the batch number, but also the rank in the examination for initial entry into the service. Thus a person with third rank can get promoted to Chief Secretary ahead of a person with thirty-third rank, even thirty years after the IAS examination,' he pointed out.

So far as he was concerned, the company had done him great injustice. What did he lack?

These are very difficult conversations to have.

I tried to minimize the importance of seniority in such decisions within the company. It is a socio-cultural thing in India whereby managers continue to think of seniority in a somewhat absolute sense, perhaps because society equates age and seniority with wisdom and competence—completely wrongly!

I explained the broader exposure of the other person and how it had prepared him for the new role as a general manger. He had rotated through several functions such as purchasing, manufacturing, planning and so on during his fifteen years' service. The manager, however, was unconvinced because it was not his fault that he had not been rotated.

I told him that he too had a career, he could be the competent head of the foundry; but he was determined to be a general manager. I failed to persuade him.

The question is, how should one think of varied experiences that add value? My observation is that mobility for the sake of mobility or changing jobs and companies merely because that is perceived to be a faster route to the top are quite counter-productive. The aspiring manager needs to think through how each varied experience actually adds value.

There is no formula, experience is unique to each individual and his aspiration. Basically, he must be willing to find the zone of his calling.

How variations of experience add value

As soon as a manager feels that he is in a zone of comfort, he might start to think of how to get the next variation of experience. Variations of experience disturb the equilibrium of the environment in which the manager works. The new experience and environment cause the manager to retain his curiosity to learn afresh, and inculcate a sense of humility about how little he really knows. It is this combination of curiosity and humility that fosters in the manager the attitude of being in a continuous developmental mode.

I advise young managers to seek out experiences with multiple challenges, in multiple geographies, and perhaps even spread over multiple domains—that too, early in their careers. Care is required that rotations and multiple job exposures should not be overdone. A solid three- to four-year stint in each role, performing four or five varieties of tasks within the first twenty years would be a good guideline for the person aspiring to be a general manager.

The 'work' that a manager perceives he is doing is defined in his mind by four dimensions.

- ❀ First is the *function* in which he is working, which could be in areas like personnel, marketing, logistics, and finance
- ❀ Second is the *organization* in which he works; it may be a family business, a multinational or a public sector company. It is the organization that provides him the

human network of relationships and the emotional environment of work

❀ Third is the *domain* or industry in which his company is operating, which may be anything from steel and chemicals to software. Some are fast-changing (software), some are volatile (commodities or derivatives trading), some are intense with long hours (business process outsourcing and hospitality), and some others are (wrongly) thought of as 'messy' (steel, automotive and chemicals). It all depends on how one views it, there is no one reality

❀ Fourth is the *location* of his work, which may be in his home city or home country, both of which are usually emotionally comfortable to him, or he may be working elsewhere.

It would be pointless to seek change in all these parameters constantly. Any hope that such variety would provide growth would be false. Such change will merely produce a rolling stone which has gathered no moss. There are many such managers, whom one has seen, some have been through ten corporations in twenty years of service.

For a large part of my career, I worked in one domain (FMCG) and one company (Unilever). Geographically, I have had to work out of Mumbai, Chennai, Delhi, Bristol, Jeddah, and Bangalore; now it is back to Mumbai again. I did not live in the same house for more than four years during the first thirty years of my career! In terms of functions, I have been in IT, marketing, sales, exports, corporate communications and then general management.

The gain from so much change was that I was constantly challenged to unlearn the past and learn something new; I was moved out of my comfort zone all the time. There was never a dull moment. Each day was pregnant with new learning, new vistas; a sense of boredom or ennui was never encountered.

Geographical and functional change are not, however, essential as illustrated by the story of my friend Prem Mehta, who rose to become the very successful CEO of Indian advertising behemoth Lowe Lintas. Prem had studied for his MBA in Mumbai and then joined an appliances company, selling typewriters and calculating machines. He was bitten by the advertising agency bug after three years, and joined an ad agency. He then joined Hindustan Lever as an area sales manager. This was when he and I worked together. Although he valued the exposure at HLL, he could not reconcile himself to the constant transfers and relocations that an HLL marketing career involved. So he did something about it, he went right back to something which he enjoyed a lot—advertising, this time at Lintas. After some years of more varied experiences, he was appointed CEO and later chairman of the company.

The point is not about how to achieve the success that Prem Mehta earned. This anecdote illustrates how he sought growth and challenge, and in the process, he became successful. He got varied experiences that suited his needs, and those were different from, for example, mine. He learnt how to get satisfaction from his job in a different way from others, and he averted becoming stunted.

The need for renewal stays with a manager throughout his career, not just in the early part. Prakash Tandon had become the first Indian chairman of an international company (HLL) in 1961. About the time I joined it, he had been chairman for only seven years and was about fifty-seven years of age. Yet, he said he felt the need for a change. He recalled that he was becoming increasingly conscious of how easily the answers came to him and the facile temptation to repeat what had once worked before. He reckoned that if he continued as chairman of HLL till his retirement in 1971, there was both the danger that he would become stale and that Unilever's Indian subsidiary would miss the infusion of new ideas. So, he averted the bonsai syndrome by retiring ahead of his time, and moved on to the public sector, where he enjoyed a very successful second career: initially as chairman of State Trading Corporation, then as chairman of Punjab National Bank.

Developmental challenges come in many forms

Within the company environment, some opportunities are planned by the employer. If that happens, it is terrific. However, one should not depend on that alone. After all, it is the manager's career, and he shouldn't be just an ornamental plant—a bonsai! Then there is the possibility that the manager is watchful for opportunities within his organization or even outside. This prompts a manager to seek a more complex or difficult challenge.

However, developmental opportunities do not arise only within the organization where one is working. There are developmental challenges that are external to the company and come completely disguised and unrecognizable. At the time it happens, it will look neither magical nor developmental to you. That emerges only in hindsight. They can arise in non-work situations too like in a club, a building society or an NGO with which a manager might be associated.

When these common things happen to us, it never strikes us that they could shape or influence us in some way. It is what we learn and make of those that determine whether they have succeeded in shaping us or not. The challenges into which managers are sent can be experienced at the workplace or even personally. Both influence the shaping of the manager.

That is why it is important to recall Huxley's statement that experience is what you do with whatever happens to you.

I would like to share a couple of my own experiences.

When I was sixteen in Kolkata, my family moved to another city. Since I had to stay back to continue my studies, my father assigned me the tasks of settling a court case regarding the house, auctioning the furniture and depositing the sales proceeds in the local bank. This was not what my peers were doing, so I did it a bit reluctantly. I had to build a relationship with diverse characters like the lawyer, the auctioneer, the court officials; above all, it imposed on me the task of gaining a rudimentary understanding of the issues involved and figuring out the best solution. Telephones between Kolkata and other cities did not work too well in the early 1960s, so the frequency of parental consultation was minimal.

But I learnt a lot out of that experience—responsibility, taking charge and understanding complex matters sufficiently enough to act. Such opportunities are commonplace in everybody's life and there is much to be learnt by grasping those diligently rather than dealing with them casually or as a burden to be discharged in the least engaged way.

Many years later, I was the regional sales manager of Hindustan Lever for north India. I was quite kicked about my career progress and was probably in need of a lesson in humility—of course, I did not think so at that time.

The company had launched a detergent powder and I was working with a local salesman, Narinder Sood, on the retail beat in Jalandhar. All of twenty-seven, I said to the fifty-five-year-old experienced salesman that his merchandising and product displays could be better. He was a union leader; he was reputed to be a bit impudent. He politely requested me to demonstrate the higher quality of work I was seeking.

I had three choices. I could take umbrage and pull him up. I could let the matter pass, almost as though it had just not happened. I could take him up on his 'challenge'.

I felt I had to seize the gauntlet he had thrown and spent the next two hours in the bazaar, doing sales calls, merchandising and product displays. My work was certainly not superior, but that was not the point of the experience. He probably wanted to test whether I would dirty my hands. Later he demonstrated appreciation of my effort and became a warm colleague.

I learnt from this experience that for any leader, the wellsprings of humility lie in the field with the men one is privileged to lead. If you cannot do what you ask your men to do, if you cannot experience their pain and pangs at their workplace, you cannot develop empathy for them. You cannot lead them successfully. You can develop empathy through mobility. Here is how Tata Consultancy does it on a company-wide basis.

Tata Consultancy: How global mobility creates space

Tata Consultancy Services (TCS) is a truly global company in that it builds global mobility into its career path planning. At the Global Workforce Summit convened by Worldwide ERC and the *International Herald Tribune* at Warsaw in June 2005, S. Padmanabhan, executive vice-president and global HR head for TCS, noted that he had travelled to fifteen countries in twenty-three years. Here is a summary of his presentation, reproduced from the October 2005 issue of *Mobility* with the permission of Worldwide ERC.

> To establish a background for his discussion, Padmanabhan outlined some statistics and demographics. TCS has experienced phenomenal growth in the amount of people it employs. In one year, TCS grew from 30,000 to 45,000 employees, and the company anticipates adding another 10,000 this year. Ninety-five percent of TCS's business comes from outside India...hence, global mobility is a key part of career-path planning for executives working for the organization...at any given time, approximately 22,000 people are either ready for mobility, in the process of moving, or on assignment.
>
> About 1,500 associates are non-Indian nationals operating

in China, Hungary, Ireland, Uruguay, Brazil, Canada, and Australia—locations where technological skills are high, university systems are very good, the telecommunication infrastructure is well-developed, and governments are friendly toward human and currency mobility. Based on these criteria, TCS has identified Poland, the Czech Republic, and Russia as emerging locations.

Padmanabhan noted that mobility of non-Indians presents a greater challenge for the company than Asians, who he describes as "very mobile". Americans move a lot, but predominantly within the United States. Mobility among Western Europeans is very low for reasons related to pensions and culture issues. He also said Western European management schools are recruiting Asian students, which creates an excellent talent pool for organizations seeking to recruit leaders for their operations in the Asia-Pacific region.

Padmanabhan also said that nearly 22 percent of TCS associates are women. Mobility of women is very different from that of men, he observed, noting that women are not quite as mobile as men are (although this is changing). Cultural attitudes toward the role of women in child-rearing and family life play a role as women move through different life stages. TCS is finding that more and more women are being sent on short-term assignments to balance career and family needs.

Historically, companies produced their goods and services locally and sold them globally. Truly global companies now produce, buy, and sell globally, said Padmanabhan. This results in more local hires and growth of local management talent. To increase local talent, TCS works to make sure that local hires become globally mobile, as well...TCS creates career plans for each individual that consider all three factors in the space of 15 years.

"The person's personal development is driven through experience in different geographies, experience working with different customers, and experience working with different technologies," said Padmanabhan..."The sum of the development of all the individuals equals the growth of the company, which depends on the cumulative knowledge of our people," he said.

How variety and space created chairmen

Job rotation and variety are in the bloodstream of top-class managers. The rotation may be into many functions and geographies for a general manager, or may be into new challenges and new skill-building for a top-class functional manager. It matters little whether the manager seeks to be a general manager or a functional manager; the principle is the same so long as he is out to be top-class in his chosen field— whether he aspires to be a general manager, or a head of the laboratory or a chief of operations.

There are two well-recognised leaders from the corporate world whose career paths illustrate how they were systematically moved from one challenge to a greater challenge as part of their development.

Jurgen Schrempp was the accomplished and controversial chairman of Daimler Chrysler, which was Daimler Benz before Chrysler merged into it in a $36 billion deal in May 1998. He was one of a family of five, money was tight and all of them were squeezed into a small flat with only two bedrooms. He joined Daimler in 1967 when he was twenty-three, servicing truck customers on warranty issues and repairs. Seven years later, he grabbed an opportunity to work in South Africa, where Mercedes had a major operation. He found a great tutor in a salesman-turned-chairman Morris Schenker. Young Schrempp worked right at the heart of the market operations— making service calls, fixing trucks, and enjoying every bit of it.

Schrempp caught the eye of Daimler's chief financial officer, who pulled him out of the relative comfort of South Africa. He was sent to run a new truck division in Ohio, USA. He stayed there two years, and sold it for a price which top management appreciated. After doing that, Schrempp was promoted and sent back as chairman of the South Africa operation. He bloomed there, and became not only a leader but a presence and a force. Some factions of the African National Congress demanded that Daimler shut down its offices and factories in protest against unequal treatment to blacks.

Schrempp stunned everyone by refusing. He said that he would offer equal pay to blacks and whites at Mercedes— preposterous by the standards of those days. He was brought back to Stuttgart as head of the Mercedes truck division. Soon he was noticed by Alfred Herrhausen, the supervisory board chairman of Daimler, who selected Jurgen in 1989 to head DASA (Daimler Benz Aerospace). Five years later in 1994, Schrempp was appointed CEO of Daimler. As Jurgen Schrempp grew professionally, he was challenged by increasing levels of problems to be solved, and he was placed in larger and larger roles. Never was his experiential space limiting, thus avoiding the possible bonsai syndrome.

Another fascinating story is that of Roberto Goizueta, the exceptionally successful chairman of Coca-Cola in the 1980s and 1990s. His story demonstrates that everyone's life is filled with experiences that are traumatic, frustrating or exhilarating. These are sources of valuable learning and those who learn benefit from the experiences.

His grandfather Marcelo migrated to Cuba from Spain. He was successful in founding a sugar and real estate empire. Roberto was a young boy when his grandfather retired, so the two could spend long hours conversing. Roberto acknowledged that he had learnt a lot from his grandfather. Roberto studied chemical engineering at Yale and joined Coca-Cola in Havana as an entry-level chemist. In 1959, when Fidel Castro took over Cuba, the Goizueta family fled to the US with $40 in cash and 100 Coca-Cola shares. Roberto's subsequent career demonstrates that it is possible to learn and prosper even after you have lost everything.

Goizueta recalled later that if you are willing to go out on a limb, it is possible to create opportunities. He felt that Fidel Castro had taught him to be fearless about taking risks. This attitude of risk-taking allowed him to introduce successful products such as Diet Coke and caffeine-free Coke. It also encouraged him to think completely out-of-the-box and take a huge risk by changing the formula of the basic and long-successful Regular Coke. When he found he had created a disaster, he quickly changed tack to recover, doing what his grandfather had taught him: focus on the things that matter!

It took Roberto a little over twenty years to become the chairman in 1981. He returned the company to a singular focus on the drink, disposing of Columbia Pictures and other unrelated distracting businesses. More importantly, he took risks with products and sold his managers the idea of Coke's minuscule share in the total fluid intake of consumers! He advised his managers, 'Don't wrap the flag of Coca-Cola around you to prevent change from taking place. It is extremely important that you show some insensitivity to your past in order to show proper respect for the future.' His grandfather taught him to work hard and stay close to the business. Fidel Castro taught him that nothing is insurmountable.

Through a long career, it is important to feel energized and rejuvenated. It is not nice to have an 'Oh God, it's Monday' feeling, barring the odd week. A proven way to get that great feeling of 'Thank God it's Monday' is a challenge in the profession, often through job rotation. It also has the advantage of rapid general management development.

Job changes appear interesting while reading about them in management magazines and books. But they can be disturbing, both for the individual and the family as they might involve change in location as well as function. A former CEO of Ford Motor Company, Donald Peterson, recounted how mobility influenced him positively and also created some stresses.

He joined Ford in 1949 in the product planning department after studying for a Stanford MBA degree. He recalled his good fortune in having joined a corporation that offered multiple career opportunities within one company. During the first two decades, he seemed to have a new job every year and a half. In fact, in hindsight, he felt that he had moved too fast, too soon.

Then around the middle of his career, when he was about fifty, he was shifted to the Ford truck operation as vice-president and general manager. In those days (and perhaps even now), trucks were not considered glamorous, cars were. So the people in the truck division evolved as a better knit team—they seemed to feel: what the hell, we are truckers, let us enjoy being truckers, and let us make a jolly good truck. Peterson was deeply bothered that much as he enjoyed the work, he felt his career was at a standstill. He was assailed by doubts on whether he had been bypassed. Such psychological pressures, apart from physical dislocations, add to the sense of uncertainty and self-doubt.

He overcame the stress by contemplating questions such as, 'Am I enjoying my work?', 'Am I adding to my professional value and experience?' and 'Am I working for the joy or the reward?' In due course, things became clearer—fortunately for him in a favourable way, when he was appointed CEO.

How more space accelerated the growth of fish

I would like to close this chapter with a Nature story from West Bengal.

On one occasion, as I discussed this subject at Kolkata, a member of the audience drew my attention to an experience in Bengal. According to him, more space increased growth, more than one had imagined.

There is a local delicacy, katla fish, and its growth was accelerated by increasing the space for growth. The

Ramakrishna Mission at Nimpith, Sunderbans, had been guiding the village farmers on land shaping in the early 1980s. The farmers were accustomed to harvesting only one rice crop when the monsoon brought rains. This provided a limited source of income, apart from being risky due to dependence on a single crop. What could they do about it? The farmers were advised to dig a pond on 20 per cent of the land and spread the excavated earth on the rest.

As a result of better topsoil on the 80 per cent land, there was an improvement in productivity of paddy. As a result, this land produced as much rice as the 100 per cent used to earlier. Further, the hole that had been dug in the 20 per cent collected rainwater, making it a natural pond. This pond could grow a second crop, katla fish. Into this pond, the farmers were taught to place baby katla fish just before the monsoon. As the rains arrived, the ponds filled. Katla fish could grow to a certain size in limited ponds. However, when it rained a lot, the ponds overflowed.

The fish could swim more vigorously over longer distances. They found that such fish attained in three months the same size as they had earlier attained in nine months, a threefold increase in growth rate. Fish droppings also became a natural fertilizer for the land. The veterinarian in charge of agricultural development had the following explanation to offer: each species has a biological limit to growth, based on genetics. In a limited space, the physical exertion is lower, so growth is lower.

Therefore, young people should be put through varied experiences of location and function. If possible, different industry experiences too can help. If a youngster remains stunted for long, he may become permanently stunted.

6

THE SNAIL AND THE LOBSTER

LEARNING FROM THREATS

The threatened snails that grew bigger

This chapter emphasizes the obvious: that threats keep a species alert and adaptive.

The obvious, however, is not always so.

Think of how junior staff responds to leadership initiatives, or how unions respond to management initiatives. In India, there is so much comfort among the staff of public sector undertakings and government departments that they oppose disinvestment in any form. Too many people want to keep the status quo.

Business commentators like to use the metaphor of a fast-moving tiger or cheetah for companies. But believe it or not, the lowly snail lends itself to comparison too!

The snail is an animal with a soft body that is covered with a coiled shell. It likes moist weather. When the weather becomes dry, the animal responds by exuding a slimy substance. When this liquid dries up, it seals the snail inside its shell. It literally cuts itself off from the world. When it moves, it does so with a muscular action of its foot, but the muscles actually move in a backward, wave-like motion. So it moves forward by exercising its muscles backwards!

The snail has an enemy in the lobster, for it forms the latter's favourite diet. From the slow snail's point of view, the lobster is a fast mover and is quite horrendous. It has five pairs of legs; the top one near its head is like a powerful pair of pincers that can grab its prey and hold it viciously. It is a fighter, and in case it loses a limb or a claw in battle, it grows a new one in its place.

Science magazine had a report about how the growth patterns of a particular variety of snail were significantly altered by the presence of predatory crayfish, a type of lobster. When the snail grew in an environment free of the predator, it began to reproduce when the shell size was just 4 mm. Its lifespan was about four months. Then the experimenter introduced the crayfish predator.

The snail had to have some response to this threat because life could not carry on normally any longer. First, it had to use some method to avoid the crayfish and second, prepare how to respond if it did meet its enemy.

The snails now postponed reproduction till they were twice their size (8 mm instead of 4 mm) and their longevity increased to twelve months from four months. The threat actually improved all growth parameters.

The scientists hypothesized that when faced with the threat, the snail reallocated its resources away from early reproduction towards growth and community survival.

The comfortable crocodiles that became lethargic

The converse is also true, that in the absence of any significant threat or problem, complacency sets in and even 'normal' behaviour fails to manifest itself. The *International Herald Tribune* reported on 25 October 2004 a fascinating story about crocodiles imported into China from Thailand.

Crocodile meat is eaten in China. To make it affordable, the Chinese forestry department eliminated the steep duties on imported breeder crocodiles in the mid-1990s. Crocopark Guangzhou bought nearly 40,000 crocodiles from Thailand in 1997 and 1998, filling the holds of five chartered Boeing 747 cargo jets. It was an attractive commercial deal for the Chinese; the Asian financial crisis had made the Thai sellers panicky and crocodile prices collapsed.

The hope was that low wages and highly skilled farmers, as well as the well-developed road and port infrastructure, would rapidly convert China into a competitive producer of crocodile meat, purses and other goods. The logic must have seemed impeccable.

What happened thereafter was that these crocodiles experienced some difficulty in adapting to the cooler climate of China compared to that of Thailand. The male crocodiles started eating more in late autumn and early winter than they did in Thailand. They became so plump that they lost their sex drive when the mating season arrived in spring! Impotence, obesity, runny noses all conspired to make the Chinese dream difficult to realize.

How fish stay fresh when threatened by sharks

Take another example. The Japanese have always loved fresh fish, but the waters close to Japan have not held much fish for decades. To feed the population, the fishing boats got bigger and went farther than ever. The farther the fishermen went, the longer it took them to bring in the fish. If the return trip took more than a few days, the fish were not fresh. The Japanese did not like the taste.

To solve this problem, fishing companies installed freezers on their boats. They would catch the fish and freeze them at sea. Unfortunately, the consumer could taste the difference between fresh and frozen fish: the frozen fish fetched a lower price. So fishing companies installed fish tanks on the ship. They would catch the fish and stuff them in the tanks.

After a little thrashing around, the fish stopped moving. They were dull and tired, but alive. Unfortunately, the Japanese could still taste the difference. They liked the taste of lively, fresh fish, not sluggish fish! Finally, they hit upon an idea.

They added a small shark to each tank. The shark did eat a few fish, but the rest of them were challenged and kept on the move by the shark. The Japanese consumer got the freshest possible fish.

In Nature, threats cause adaptation

When faced with a threat, two key responses are involved— first, an adaptation to survive, and later, a reallocation of resources. Quite often, the adaptation to survive takes the form of deception when the animal learns to pretend what it is not. The same principles apply to organizations and it is instructive to trace the parallels between Nature's ways of coping and the way organizations and individuals do!

The simplest form is camouflage.

Butterflies and moths often have colours and textures that make them indistinguishable from a leaf or a tree bark. There is a reptile called the Malaysian flying gecko, which lies flat and immobile on a tree trunk, and is almost impossible to pick out separately from the tree trunk.

There are managers who criticize company policies privately, but when the boss is around, they speak vehemently in favour of the same. They are like the chameleon that changes its colour to harmonize with the background.

A second form of deception is mimicry.

For example, some tropical spiders are similar in appearance to the ants on which they feed. There are colleagues who pretend to be part of your group as peers in private conversations, but end up carrying tales to the seniors, who have their own reasons for not discouraging such behaviour. It is like the predator that adopts a form which lulls its prey into believing it is something else.

A third form of deception is simulation.

A prey animal may simulate a tactic to remind the predator of a previous bad experience. A drone fly can buzz like a honeybee to keep away trouble. A group of long-standing employees, who do not wish to change their way of working, may 'warn' the enthusiastic, new head about the bad results from a previous attempt to introduce change.

Yet another form of deception is to develop misleading props. There is a butterfly that has wings with big eyes on them to scare away its enemies. It reminds me of a manager I know who would always be seen with the boss, thus conveying the impression that he was close to him!

Lastly, deception may be resorted to on a group basis.

When threatened by a snake, squirrels gang up together and display aggressive behaviour. The squirrels do this by making their hair stand erect, flagging their tails, bobbing their heads, and kicking up sand to scare off the snake. In a similar manner, the manager who does not want to lay off 'his' people in a corporate rationalization exercise may get them to write a representation directly to the bigger boss.

Imitation, flattery, excessive zeal to agree with the boss's opinions, all these are the organizational equivalents of using deception to survive. One can write a whole book on real-life experiences, but that would be superfluous because it is a daily occurrence within every manager's observations—and his own skill-set, I should add! Some people seem to last a whole career virtually using this tactic alone!

Managers instinctively do not like uncertainties and threats; in fact, they are trained to minimize or avoid them! They strive hard to achieve comfort, free of threats and uncertainties. The mere act of approaching that goal produces a bunch of unintended consequences such as poorer instincts and slower growth.

This is the paradox of life itself. The truth is that threats provide the positive balance and are essential for a healthy business. In Nature, there is a constant struggle in every organism: to eat without being eaten, and to ensure that genes are being passed on to succeeding generations. Companies too need to do this with great efficiency.

Survival is never assured in Nature

No animal behaves as though its existence is assured even for a day. Each morning, every animal figures out how to survive the threats in its environment, and how to get its quota of food for the day. Similarly, managers should figure out how not to become bonsai.

The African gazelle need not learn to run faster than a leopard, it needs to run faster than the next gazelle to survive.

It is only the human being who assumes that his survival is more or less assured, whether it is his job in a company or his life in the community. By understanding how animals respond to ever-present threats, there are memorable lessons for managers.

There is copious management literature on how to annihilate competition and formulate a unique strategy that helps to create an uncontested market space. There is nothing wrong with these ideas except that, when taken too far, they become counter-productive.

This is reflected in the corporate world too: for instance,

in the way corporate heads carp at unions or resent their own middle management as blockers of their transformation agenda. When it comes to competition, they try to prevent it; if this is not possible, they explore ways to annihilate it by some means. They exhort colleagues to develop the killer instinct. The metaphor of war is used to get their juices flowing.

There is also the imagery built up of multinational or big firm competition being predatory, that those forms of competition will wipe out Indian firms, and that they are therefore undesirable.

All such approaches have a modest degree of validity, a great deal of emotion, but above all, an unwillingness to see the flip side, that is, the benefits of fierce competition in reorienting the resources of the firm. A good manager must learn to consider these threats as actually desirable, because they keep managers on their toes and constantly renewed; they are essential to the firm's ecological balance.

In fact, if you look at Nature or organizations, you find examples of both—great growth and vigour when there are threats, and a lethargy and absence of vigour when there is comfort!

The Brooke Bond leader who wanted a healthy Lipton

Unilever acquired Lipton in a global deal in the early 1970s. In India, Lipton India was a serious competitor to Brooke Bond India in the branded tea market with a share about half of Brooke Bond. For a number of reasons, Lipton India had become a problem company for Unilever by the early 1980s.

My former boss, Bipin Shah, was specially selected to go into this troubled company to fix its problems. Bipin was a consummate turnaround artist with a very fine commercial sense and a terrific intuition for business. The challenges he faced were considerable. Even while he was at work, in a global deal, Brooke Bond too was acquired by Unilever in the mid-1980s. However, Brooke Bond continued to make life difficult for Lipton India because the companies were run on a stand-alone basis and at arm's length. So this is the story of two fierce rivals for over sixty years, who suddenly found themselves as sons of the same parent due to some global moves.

Lipton's marketshare was stagnant, its cost structure was bloated, it was a single-product (tea) company, its cash generation was stressed; and Brooke Bond was not making Lipton's life easy in the marketplace. Brooke Bond had twice the volume of Lipton, had healthy cash generation and commanded the market.

In the early 1980s, a Unilever director, T. Thomas, decided to call on C.S. Samuel, the chairman of Brooke Bond. His private agenda was to assess the probability of survival of Lipton—selling out must have been a distinct option from Unilever's perspective. Such a conversation would not normally have been easy, but in this case, it became possible because Thomas and Samuel had worked together at Hindustan Lever in the 1960s. Thomas had been a technical manager and Samuel an accountant.

Thomas and Samuel have separately recounted this meeting to me several years later, and both had identical versions of what transpired. Samuel understood the predicament of Lipton, which was candidly outlined by Thomas. After all, his company was partly responsible for some of the woes of Lipton, though some other woes were, in his opinion, self-inflicted. He could not help in any meaningful way, Samuel asserted.

But for sure, Unilever should dismiss the option of selling out its stake in Lipton. 'For its own long-term interest, Brooke Bond needs Lipton to be a strong competitor, so Unilever should invest in seeing how to strengthen Lipton,' he commented. A rather strange attitude, one might have thought, because one can imagine CEO Samuel doing a delighted jig at the misery of his main competitor.

But Samuel realised that the complete removal of 'the Lipton crayfish' would stultify the 'Brooke Bond snail' too. So, he took a long-term view, enlightened self-interest no doubt, but nonetheless far-sighted.

Lipton survived and grew, so did Brooke Bond. Finally in 1994-95, when I was working in Saudi Arabia, Lipton was merged into Brooke Bond. One year later, I returned to India to lead the merged company. Tea volumes and margins were under great pressure, partly due to a downturn in the tea industry, but also due to the emotional mayhem that goes with such mergers. The most common comment I heard from managers was that in the absence of any competitive threat, the new company had nobody to fight with. I could not possibly encourage such a discussion as the merger was by then a fait accompli; life had to go on.

In a major drive of volume expansion, the new company notched up 30 per cent more volume within three years, giving up some margins in the short term in the hope of a long-term growth of volume and marketshare.

Meanwhile, another crayfish called Tata Tea was emerging; by the early 1990s, Tata Tea began to pose some challenge to the two dominant branded tea players, Lipton and Brooke Bond! That is yet another story.

I will always wonder what might have been the outcome if Lipton and Brooke Bond had not merged in 1993!

A Toyota leader who worried about a weak General Motors

Once when I narrated this Brooke Bond–Lipton story to a friend, he thought it was a bit far-fetched.

In May 2005, I read a story in *BusinessWeek* about the perilous state of General Motors (GM) and Ford. Their combined marketshare in the US collapsed from 65 per cent in 1982 to 47 per cent in 2004. All three Japanese car majors— Toyota, Honda and Nissan—had opened factories in the US during this period. Commentators felt that the cash pile with GM would allow it to stay the course for only a few years more. Without a sharp course correction, GM would be on the path to disaster.

The report quoted a statement by Toyota chairman Hiroshi Okuda, 'I am concerned about the current situation GM is in.' Okuda went to the extent of thinking aloud about the possibility of raising prices to give GM breathing space. Later, there was such a howl from Detroit that Okuda backed off. Auto lobbyists in Washington indignantly said that they were not looking for handouts or trade restrictions, a very different stance from the protectionist war cry of the 1980s.

Perhaps after consulting his public relations adviser and thinking it through, one month later in June, Okuda expressed his real fear, that if financial troubles worsened at GM and Ford, there could be a protectionist backlash! This unusual incident—that a competitor could think of helping a sick rival—certainly confirms that conversations like the one that Thomas and Samuel must have had with regard to Brooke Bond and Lipton do indeed occur.

A scientific institution which had lost vigour

In the book *Ideas That Have Worked* (Penguin India, 2004), astrophysicist Jayant Narlikar wrote about some challenges he faced while working in scientific institutions in India.

Narlikar, a talented astronomer, went abroad for study and research. He worked as a research student with noted astronomer Fred Hoyle at the University of Cambridge. In 1972, Narlikar returned to India to work at the prestigious Tata Institute of Fundamental Research (TIFR). This institution had been set up with scientist Homi Bhabha's grand vision in 1946 with a generous endowment from the Tata Trusts.

However, by the 1980s, Narlikar found that conditions at TIFR had declined sharply. He felt that, over the years, he had become restless at TIFR, where life as a research scientist was perhaps too smooth to generate challenge. The success of the west's scientific momentum was due to the fact that one generation of motivated research scientists replaced another. He found that in India, research institutions were isolated from the mainstream of students. He felt that the insistence that university dons carried a heavy burden of lectures with research relegated to a negligible level ensured that the sciences held no research attraction for students.

He saw the scientists in the institution as 'comfortable snails' with no 'predatory lobsters' of students to challenge and renew their work. In January 1988, when Professor Yashpal, chairman of the University Grants Commission, asked Narlikar to take on the directorship of a new Inter University Centre for Astronomy and Astrophysics, he jumped at it and moved on from TIFR. Proving, once again, that top class talent needs to be challenged and renewed.

Hidden resources get stirred when threatened

It is a paradox that we strive hard to achieve comfort, free of threats to survival and growth. But the mere act of approaching—let alone attaining—that goal seems to produce a bunch of unintended consequences such as less growth, poorer instincts and generally speaking, less preparedness for a fuller life—as the example of the snail demonstrated.

That is why organizational leaders have the unique challenge of constantly stirring the pot to prevent their managers from becoming complacent. Every organization tries to 'destroy' the competition, but without competition of a minimum quality and threat, the organization will atrophy.

An example from the detergent market is worth mentioning. Capacity limitations were prevalent in the 1970s and 1980s, and Hindustan Lever was producing to its full licensed capacity. Its market entry was Surf, a high priced, top-of-the-line brand, selling to the consumer for Rs 20 per kg. There were several lower priced detergents in the market, the most notable being Nirma.

In 1973, when I was responsible for detergent sales in the western region, I recall being asked to do a survey of 'an Ahmedabad-based small-scale manufacturer called Nirma'. I recall reporting with the naiveté of a novice that I could not quite comprehend its operation and cost structure. However, this company was doing big things in the Ahmedabad market and could easily replicate it in all of Gujarat.

Karsanbhai Patel had started making detergent in 1969 in the backyard of his home in Ahmedabad. He mixed the powder by hand in a 100 square feet shed. He worked eighteen hours a day. He himself procured raw materials, mixed them and then he went around shops selling the product. Since it was priced so low, he found he had a success on his hands. He moved to a bigger facility at Vatva, an industrial suburb of Ahmedabad. He branded it 'Nirma' after his daughter Nirupama. He targeted the poor localities and rural consumers, who would benefit from the low price.

The volume of the HLL brand Surf was not eroded but the share of Surf was eroded over fifteen years from 1973 to 1987. Apart from some bluster and tactical responses, HLL felt it had limited options to respond to brands like Nirma that retailed at one-third the price of Surf.

The limitation of options was due to a highly restrictive production environment imposed by the government's licensing system. If HLL responded through price cuts, it would reduce the profits per tonne of limited licensed capacity. Developing new, low cost brands would eat into the same limited capacity; anyway, the company had not been successful with such attempts. Outsourcing of production was not legally permitted as the company was considered a foreign company and had certain regulatory restrictions.

The consequence of all this was a steady erosion in marketshare (not necessarily of company profits!), a huge irritation within the company with these 'snipers' like Nirma and a steady growth in these competitors' cash flows and brand success. Around 1987, Chairman Ashok Ganguly felt things had gone too far. At about this time, I joined the board as exports director. I had no functional responsibility for detergents; it was run by two talented and experienced colleagues on the board, Susim Datta and Shunu Sen.

I recall my very first half-yearly board conference. I had conjured up this image of a wise and genteel group that would have esoteric discussions on long-term issues.

Instead, Ashok Ganguly opened that meeting with a bluntness and workmanlike approach that puzzled me. Vice-Chairman Susim Datta and Marketing Director Shunu Sen had what I thought was a serious look on their faces.

I heard urgency in Ashok Ganguly's voice. 'We are in deep trouble, gentlemen, and *we* have to get out of it because we are the guys who got into it. It is time for some plain speaking amongst ourselves,' he said.

There was just a plain admission of responsibility and a call for collective action. Quite a sobering start to a first meeting, many more of which I was to participate in over the next few years.

What Ganguly was doing was to recognise the crayfish amidst the snails literally, and ask all of us collectively to stop pretending that there was no problem.

He and Vice-Chairman Susim Datta redirected the company's rich resources and talent from developing convincing excuses to finding aggressive solutions. A crack project team code-named *Sting* was set up to meet a challenging brief. It was, in hindsight, a terrific exercise in how leadership can actually redirect resources within a company to meet the needs of survival and growth, where it sees the threat as the biggest opportunity.

The birth and subsequent success of Wheel detergent bar and powder became a part of Unilever folklore in the next few years as Datta and Ganguly led the effort from the front. In the 1990s when Susim Datta was chairman, Gessy Lever extended the concept to Brazil as part of Unilever's efforts to spread best practices across the world.

Wheel is now the single largest brand in the Hindustan Lever portfolio, with sales of over Rs 1,000 crore! Of course, Nirma too has gone from strength to strength, but in a somewhat different trajectory than earlier. New detergent brands entered the market at a price point even lower than Nirma (they did a Nirma on Nirma!), thus prising open the consumption market dramatically. Nirma invested in backward integration: the company began to manufacture the raw materials it needed to strengthen its competitive position.

Embracing the unknown is risky, but can produce winners

What actually happens within the company when such threats are addressed head-on?

It is human nature to seek a comfort level where the future can just evolve in a gentle and predictable way, even though the rational part of those same people's brains keeps telling them that the future is not what it is supposed to be. Among the most important tasks of leaders is to disturb the comfort of the known and to actively embrace and tackle the discomfort of the unknown.

In management, think of the care taken by several top-class companies for talent development.

For entry-level managerial assignments in Tata Administrative Service (TAS), McKinsey and Hindustan Lever, these companies recruit the best from the best institutes. They constantly pit these people against each other during the course of their work, and the best are kept the best by being put under the constant pressure of being 'deselected' through aggressive internal processes.

In short, they are like the snails among crayfish. They learn to reorient their intellectual and leadership resources towards survival and growth. Leadership is produced out of such pressure, just as a diamond is nothing but carbon that has been placed under great pressure!

Former Harvard business school professor Jeffrey Rayport, narrates an instructive story of an exam he took during his student days. In his sophomore year, he appeared for an unusual zoology exam. The students were presented with what appeared like a stuffed bird, covered almost fully with a cloth. All that the students could see were spindly legs, claws and an inch or so of feathers hanging out of the sides of the cloth covering. They had four hours to write their views on the bird, its migratory pattern, its mating habits and a whole host of such details.

Well, the exam must have been a challenge. As he became a professor of business later, he realized that charting the course of a business or a career under extreme conditions of uncertainty is not unlike writing an exam about a stuffed bird you cannot see.

So, he says, 'Don't squander the chances to make a difference in the world because of the comfort of inaction...Listen to your passions...And then do something truly great.' When such an opportunity is embraced, then the adaptive capacities of the organization come into play.

In simple words, this is the ability to grasp a context, see an unstructured issue within that context, and think up unusual, even experimental, solutions which might solve that problem. It also means converting adversity into opportunity. It is an attitude thing.

How Harvard produces winners

I found it interesting to learn about how Harvard, for example, acquired such a huge reputation for producing 'winners'.

There was a study called *The Grant Study*, which examined the lives of 268 Harvard undergraduates from 1939 to 1942. These alumni were chosen because they were thought to be the ones who would go far in life.

Subsequently, an analysis of the data was done by George Valliant, a psychiatrist. He averred that an ongoing process of challenge, adaptation, and learning prepared these individuals for more escalating challenges, and a virtuous spiral of experiences made for the best leadership development.

The people who aged most successfully, Valliant found, were those who had a great adaptive capacity and continued to learn new things. They looked forward with eagerness and optimism, rather than dwell on the past. This is the type of organization that leaders try to create, a dream organization.

A quotation which is relevant here reads as follows:

Be thankful for the troubles of your job. They provide about half your income. Because if it were not for the things that go wrong, the difficult people that you have to deal with, and the problems and unpleasantness of your working day, someone could be found to handle your job for half of what you are paid. It is a fact that there are plenty of big jobs waiting for men and women who aren't afraid of the troubles connected with them.

And facing such challenges head-on helps a manager grow from strength to strength—no bonsai effect here.

7

BLUE TITS AND ROBINS
LEARNING THROUGH SHARING

Social propagation promotes knowledge sharing

Managers acquire knowledge and intuition in many ways; while mobility is one, social propagation is another important source. In the practical, managerial world, socialization is not taught; one needs to learn by oneself. How does one benefit from socialization? The story of the blue tit illustrates this.

There is a charming story about two English garden birds, the blue tit and the robin, in Arie de Geus's book *The Living Company*. The robin has an orange-red forehead, throat and breast. Its back, wings and tail are olive-brown. According to English legend, this bird picked a thorn from the crown of Jesus Christ as He was on His way to Calvary. As the bird carried the thorn in its beak, a drop of blood fell from the thorn to its breast, dyeing it red! The robin has a cheerful carolling song consisting of repeated short notes that alternatively rise and fall. The blue tit too is a summertime visitor and a songbird familiar to the British. It is related to ravens and crows.

The UK had a long-standing milk distribution system whereby milkmen in small trucks delivered bottles to the doorstep. Early in the 1900s, these milk bottles had no caps. The cream would rise to the top and the birds had easy access to the cream. Both species of birds tapped this rich food source by picking the cream from the bottle tops. The cream was much richer than the usual food sources of these birds and hence, both birds underwent some adaptation of their digestive systems to cope with the unusual nutrients.

By the 1940s, technology had progressed. Milk bottles had an aluminium seal. This closed access to the cream to both species. The effect on these species of the denial of cream, however, was very different.

Within a decade or so, the entire population of blue tits had learned how to pierce the aluminium seals. Regaining access to this rich food source made the blue tit a better survivor than its peers. However, robins as a species never figured out how to pierce the foil; occasionally, a lone robin would master the art, but unlike the blue tit, the knowledge did not get passed on to the other robins.

So how come the blue tits went through an institutional learning process and the robins failed? Professor Allan Wilson, a zoologist at the University of California at Berkeley had a hypothesis.

Professor Wilson's subject of research concerned the accelerated learning of a species within generations. He had developed the hypothesis that it was the *behaviour of a species* rather than external environmental changes, which was the major driving force for evolution!

According to this theory, accelerated evolution occurred in species with three characteristics: one or a few members get an idea (innovation), then they share the idea with their colleagues (social propagation) and finally, they all try the idea out in different circumstances and locations (mobility). In the jargon of the professional, *innovation* is the capacity either as individuals or as a community to invent new behaviour and to develop skills that allow exploitation of the changing environment; *social propagation* is an established process to transmit a skill from an individual to the community through direct communication and socialization; *mobility* is the ability to move around and use the new skill collectively.

Put simply, learning was accelerated when members of the species *behaved* in a particular way rather than through changes in the way of teaching or the material taught—and that behaviour was simply to talk to each other and learn. How elegantly simple!

Professor Wilson applied these ideas to these songbirds. In spring, blue tits live in couples until they have reared their young. By early summer, when the young blue tits are flying and feeding on their own, the birds move from garden to garden in flocks of eight to ten. These flocks remain intact, moving together around the countryside.

In contrast, robins are territorial birds. A male robin will not allow another male to enter its territory. When threatened, the robin sends out a signal that seems to say 'keep away from here'. Robins tend to communicate with each other in an antagonistic manner, with fixed boundaries that they do not cross.

The lesson for company managers

Every February, about 300 top managers from around the world would gather to listen to presentations by the two chairmen of the British and the Dutch holding companies of

Unilever. This event was internally referred to as the OBJ, short for Oh Be Joyful, though it was not very joyful sometimes when the chairmen had tough messages to communicate. About fifteen years ago, I attended such a conference in London.

At that time, Unilever was grappling with the issue of the balance between centralization and localization, particularly in its more traditional markets. Unilever operated its many companies around the world like a 'flotilla of ships', as Chairman Niall Fitzgerald often described it. Its great strength was the autonomy given to the local subsidiary to do what is right for its own market.

This well-tested strength was challenged in internal debate because more centralized corporations seemed to be stealing a march over Unilever. Competitors like Procter and Gamble had entered Unilever's traditional markets in Europe or Asia with a version of a product and marketing mix which had been developed and successfully established elsewhere. They saved substantially in costs this way. Further, they achieved this market success through a much lower-cost organization, since their organization was pan-European or pan-Asian—unlike Unilever, which had multiple companies in each country.

In India, for example, there were seven companies: Hindustan Lever, Lipton India, Brooke Bond, Tea Estates, Doom Dooma Tea Company, Ponds India, and Stepan Chemicals. So it was a significant issue.

Chairman Michael Perry put it across forcefully that senior managers needed to be vastly better at sharing experiences and knowledge and at working collaboratively across countries if Unilever was to grow in a rapidly globalizing marketplace. He felt that the basic strength of local capability, embedded in the Unilever DNA, should remain intact; however, he wanted to see more collaborative, cross-border working for the overall benefit of the corporation.

He concluded his address with the expression, 'If only

Unilever knew what Unilever knows!' to signal that collectively we know a lot, but somehow we are not good enough at sharing it. Unilever was reasonably good at it, but managers needed to make further improvements. I started thinking about knowledge management in a rather basic way, not the more pedantic version displayed nowadays. What promotes knowledge transfer, especially knowledge on soft matters with an intuitive content?

The songbird's story contains learning for companies. Any company is bound to have a few innovative people. But merely having such people in an organization will not lead to institutional learning. Without question, the organization must allow them to innovate individually; in addition, it must actively encourage and promote institutional learning through the flocking of its managers. Flocking depends on two of Allan Wilson's criteria for learning—*mobility of people* and *an effective mechanism for social propagation*.

How managers transfer implicit knowledge

A refreshing example about the generation and transmission of knowledge within companies appears in *The Knowledge Creating Company*. The authors, Ikujiro Nanaka and Takeuchi Hirotaka, point out that no single Japanese company ever dominated a business the way American companies such as IBM, GM or Sears once did in their respective markets. Why?

'As rulers of their own fiefdom, these companies sat comfortably on their laurels...Certainty, not uncertainty, became the norm,' they write. A bit like a well-fed robin, one might say!

In the implicit memory, you hold knowledge that you do not know you know. In the explicit memory, you hold knowledge that you know you know. The same principle emerges in the field of knowledge management.

There is a difference between explicit knowledge (available

in books, CDs, etc.) and tacit knowledge (available in managers' minds). Academics treat this subject with a lot of jargon. Put simply, explicit knowledge is visible in the same way to many people. Tacit knowledge is not visible, one ferrets it out.

Tacit knowledge has to be experienced, felt and emotionally absorbed; unlike explicit knowledge, it cannot be imparted intellectually. So, tacit knowledge has three characteristics.

First, it is difficult to express and heavy reliance is placed on figurative language and symbolism; second, an individual should want to share his personal knowledge with others; and third, the new knowledge is born in the midst of ambiguity and redundancy. In short, tacit knowledge is transferred through socialization—the very same idea which emanated from evolutionary biologist Allan Wilson after studying birds! Westerners tend to emphasize explicit knowledge; the Japanese tend to emphasize tacit knowledge.

Professors Nonaka and Takeuchi use Honda and Matsushita as examples of how tacit knowledge is converted into explicit knowledge.

How Matsushita developed a unique Home Bakery

To a bread-maker, a home bread-making machine can be as challenging as making great chapatis. In every house in India, the making and serving of soft chapatis is valued, depending as it does on the quality and freshness of the *chakki atta*, (freshly ground flour from the mill), the kneading of dough and the *tava* (griddle) operations.

Matsushita, an Osaka-based appliances company, was trying to build a breakthrough home bread-making machine in the late 1980s. It centred on how to mechanize the dough-kneading process, which was essentially tacit knowledge possessed by master bakers. The first cycle of development brought together a team of employees from R&D, mechanical design and software development departments.

They used all the available explicit knowledge to design a prototype machine. The machine produced bread which was raw inside but with an overcooked crust. The team was stuck—clearly unacceptable. For the dough kneading, the actions of a master baker and a machine were x-rayed and compared. Yet, no meaningful insights were obtained.

Ikuko Tanaka, head of software development, knew that the best bread came from Osaka International Hotel. To capture the tacit knowledge of kneading skill, she and several engineers volunteered to apprentice themselves to the hotel's head baker. Making the same delicious bread as the head baker's was not easy and no one could explain why.

As the division chief noted, 'If the craftsmen cannot explain their skills, then the engineers should become craftsmen.' Over a year of such apprenticeship, the team noticed that the baker was not only stretching but also 'twisting' the dough—this turned out to be the secret for making tasty bread as it had an influence on the gluten development in the dough. The team came up with product specifications, which replicated the head baker's stretching technique. The subsequent success of the Matsushita Home Bakery has been written about extensively.

Matsushita's Home Bakery was introduced in the market in February 1987 at 36,000 yen. It sold a record-setting 5,36,000 units in its first year. It hit the top of the list of Mother's Day gifts. Its success was so extraordinary and rare in the mature cooking appliances market that *Fortune* magazine featured the machine in its October 1987 issue. Six months after market introduction in Japan, Matsushita began exporting Home Bakery to the US, Germany and Hong Kong. According to Matsushita, in the US, the entire market for an automatic bread-maker expanded to as much as 1 million units, as new competitors entered the market.

From a learning perspective, however, the message is that Ikuko Tanaka learned the skill through socialization: observing, imitating and practising the actions of the head baker, rather than through reading memos or manuals. She then translated the kneading skill into explicit knowledge.

Examples in magazine articles and books may sometimes appear remote. I came across two live examples during my own work experience.

How Quilon serves top-class Indian cuisine in London

Sriram Aylur is the chef at London's well-known Indian restaurant Quilon, managed by the Tatas' Taj hotels group. It is named after a quaint town of Kerala and was opened in 1999. Sriram himself hails from a village not far from Kozhikode, another town in Kerala. Sriram's culinary skills and innovations have made Quilon a brand in London.

Not only does the restaurant attract a top class crowd of diners every evening, but the brand is used to market ready-to-cook meals manufactured in London and sold through the chain of stores Waitrose. All this happened in the last few years since Adi Modi, Tata's top restaurateur lured Sriram to London.

I met Sriram in the mid-1990s before I joined the Tata group. At that time, he was the chef at Karavalli, the Tata restaurant in Bangalore which is famous for Kerala cuisine. I had a Unilever visitor, Antony Burgmans, then foods director of Unilever, and later the chairman. I headed Brooke Bond Lipton in Bangalore.

Antony Burgmans wanted to meet people who really understood Indian cooking traditions and eating habits and could innovate. Sriram's was the most unusual interview Antony and I did. 'Every year,' he told us, 'I go away to a coastal village for two weeks. I live with a village family; I spend the whole day watching what they do, how they do it. In the evening, I make some notes. That act itself raises some questions in my mind, so I watch and note again next day. In this way,

I get recipes, traditional ones, not just the ingredients and proportions, but the whole process and atmosphere of food preparation. These two weeks provide me invaluable insight because I come away with a formula, a passion, an approach and above all, a bunch of friends. It is these two weeks that help me to be creative as a chef.'

Once more, I noted the process of learning through socialization—observing, imitating and practising the actions of someone who did it all instinctively!

You can imagine how impressed we both were.

'A real life case of converting implicit knowledge to tacit knowledge by socialization,' as the jargon would express it!

In later years, I found that learning was a never-ending quest for Sriram. He was fascinated by Japanese cuisine for its clean-plating and interesting flavours. He was impressed with French cuisine for its technique of cooking and cuts of meat and vegetables. He seemed to be on one big continuous binge of learning and innovation.

How socialization transformed a traditional Tata

In an interview with Ratan Tata (the *Tribune*, January 2005), Sailesh Kottary commented on the Tata Group experience in the 1980s with respect to innovation and entering new industries:

> Ratan Tata had publicly announced this plan which envisaged taking his group into sunrise industries such as telecom and biotechnology...not much was implemented within the group. That was because the House of Tata, under J.R.D. Tata, was traditionally run by CEOs who viewed their companies as private fiefdoms. These aging chieftains were therefore most reluctant to reshape their operations or risk new ventures.

It took several years before Ratan Tata could get hold of the group, reshape it from fiefdom companies into collaborative companies, who would work together by knowledge sharing, mobility and socialization! In an epilogue to R.M. Lala's book *The Creation of Wealth*, Ratan Tata expresses the challenge and its emotion thus:

> We were rightly called a loose confederation of companies. Therefore the task was to transform this loose confederation into a synergetic group of companies with a unified direction. And that is the task I have undertaken in the years that I have been in this position. Very often in undertaking this kind of role, your objectives are not well understood. You are seen to be disruptive just for the sake of change. You are seen to be exerting your will when for forty to fifty years individual companies operated entirely independently.

The story of how Ratan Tata transformed the Tata Group is told in chapter 12.

Sharing does not diminish what we have

In 2003, after my daughter graduated from Duke, we as a family took a holiday in Coachela Valley, Palm Springs, California. An engaging taxi driver, David Fajardo, drove us around on a few occasions. He was full of joy and energy, never seeming to be weighed down by any concern, at least during the five days we were there. One of his remarks struck me as very relevant to organization as well.

He said that his grandmother in Barcelona had taught him to always share; there is a lot of joy in sharing. Imprinted into his BRIM was the granny's message, 'You cannot give what you don't have. You cannot have what you don't give.' So it is with organizational knowledge.

In fact, when you think about it, technology has moved all of society from a sense of finiteness to infiniteness during the last quarter of a century. Earlier, when you shared, your stock of the 'goody' diminished. Not so any more.

Professor Nicholas Negroponte of MIT has pointed out that earlier, society was preoccupied with 'atoms', but currently is interested only in 'bytes'. Atoms are limited in nature, so more people means more sharing. A kilogram of cake for one person translates to half a kilo each for two persons. But bytes are unlimited. Data on a disc can be multiplied a million times without losing anything—for example, a music recording. Sharing costs nobody anything any more. The notion that sharing will diminish the giver is less and less relevant. That is the trend of modern technology.

All organizations try to promote socialization in order to improve learning: seminars, conferences, workshops, conventions. These provide a forum, a platform, a chance to avoid becoming bonsai managers.

Individual managers must bring with themselves an inherent curiosity which permits them to observe and learn others' innovations. They should not wait for some big boss to create the 'right' conditions. It is in their power to do so in their own domains.

When they return to their workplace after corporate conferences, they must create a departmental atmosphere which encourages, indeed demands, social propagation of ideas and managerial mobility to try ideas in different locations and circumstances.

8

THE FALCON AND THE ARAB
LEARNING THROUGH COACHING

The building of top-class leaders through mobility and socialization has been discussed. Coaching is yet another powerful way through which top-class leaders are built. In this chapter, the words 'coaching' and 'mentoring' are used interchangeably.

I have been travelling on business to the Arab world since the mid-1970s. Those were the days prior to the amazing economic and social developments due to big oil wealth in the Middle East. There were many traditional souks and markets, and there was immense pleasure in walking around these souks, conversing with shopkeepers in a relatively unhurried manner.

I was struck by the Middle Eastern fascination for falcons. A picture of the ferocious-looking bird seemed to be synonymous with Arab traditions and culture. My travels reinforced my curiosity. Why would anybody try to train a bird so ferocious, and what exactly was involved in the training?

The instructional training involves getting the bird to return to its perch on the falconer's fist after the hunt is over. Various devices are used for the process. A hood covers the eye of the bird, keeping it calm. Small bells are placed on the bird, helping to locate it if it is lost. While sitting on the falconer's fist, leg straps are used to restrict the bird's movements. A great deal of skill is required for the trainer to be able to train this bird.

There is an emotional connect between the falcon and the falconer

I came across a news report datelined Kyrghistan, September 2005 that dozens of tourists from as far as the US and Japan were travelling to this picturesque region to take part in a festival dedicated to birds of prey like the falcon and the golden eagle.

Ishenbai Kydyrov, now a businessman, but hailing from a family of bird trainers said, 'Sometimes it seemed to me that my father could speak the eagle's language so deeply that they understood each other.'

I learnt that the training of a falcon in Arabia takes three weeks, just half the time it takes in other countries. It requires a great deal of patience and commitment.

I also learned about a 'relationship' between the bird and the falconer. I was a bit nonplussed about how there could be a 'relationship' with such a ferocious bird. But it turned out that there is one, an essential one.

I wondered why the Arab way of training was so much more efficient compared to other ways. Could it be of relevance to management learning?

An Arab friend would express amusement at the fact that elsewhere it took more than twice as long to achieve the same training. He would speculate that they may subject their birds to instructions very systematically but there may not be an intimate relationship between the trainer and the bird. His speculation may or may not be true.

The falcon never parts company with its master. The trainer carries the bird wherever he goes, communicating with it all the time in one way or the other—feeding it, stroking it, even holding conversations it!

For me, the central issue is whether learning gets greatly accelerated when the explicit forms of instruction are accompanied by a 'relationship' between the trainer and the trainee? Of course it does!

The emotional bond between the two, called coaching or mentoring, accelerates training greatly. Management literature is full of this theme. But at a practical level, what are the elements of this mentoring that managers need to know? How does one find a mentor? How much time does a mentor have to spend with his protégé? How much contact is required with the mentor? After all, today's senior manager who would like to be a mentor cannot walk around with the trainee perched on his fist!

The elements of coaching

There must be trust, respect, commitment and faith in such a relationship.

Getting coached as well as coaching are both very satisfying. Coaching is one of the most important relationships in personal development. A coaching relationship between two people may be fleeting or prolonged, but one thing is essential—the pupil must want to learn and must seek a teacher in several people. The teacher may be proud of his protégé, but it is the pupil who gains more.

Even the origin of the word mentor is interesting.

In Homer's epic, Ulysses had to undertake a long and uncertain journey to fight the Trojan War. Ulysses had a young son, Telemachus, and he had to think about who would look after the growth and mental development of Telemachus when he was away. He decided to entrust the youngster to the care of his trusted friend, Mentor. Over the centuries, mentoring has come to symbolize the transfer of wisdom from one generation to another.

In modern management, coaching has come to be the subject of a lot of study by trainers and academicians. From an operating manager's perspective, it is important to have an understanding of the elements of coaching.

It involves an instructional as well as emotional relationship: recall how the Arab talks to his bird and strokes it. There is some sort of mutual respect between the two.

The pupil derives more than the tutor out of the relationship; of course, the tutor may derive some satisfaction—remember the pride of the Arab and his enhanced social standing when his bird is seen as an accomplished one. The bird derives food and security from its master.

Last, the mentor is not constantly demonstrating what has to be learned; rather he is creating a motivational environment. It is for the pupils to pick up what they think is helpful. The pupils must want to use their natural abilities.

I would like to narrate four stories, one is mythological and it exemplifies the trust aspect. One illustrates the aspect of respect and is about J.R.D. Tata and John Peterson; another is about Helen Keller and Anne Sullivan and shows mutual commitment; the last is about an American entrepreneur, Michael Klein and his grandfather Max, and it demonstrates the power of faith.

Trust in coaching: Krishna and Arjuna

In the Mahabharata, the Pandavas are shown to have fought with the Kauravas on a matter of principle.

Arjuna was the person on whose shoulders the morale of the Pandavas rested. His well-being heralded victory and he stood for all that was supreme in Pandava valour and glory. He had two biological older brothers, so he was not solely responsible for looking after the family. However, Arjuna was a little vain and sensitive, and felt he had nobody to look up to. Krishna filled this void. Krishna's style of mentoring relied on certain building blocks.

Krishna proclaimed his love for Arjuna publicly and attached the highest importance to his friendship with Arjuna. They spent much time together and Krishna took every opportunity to demonstrate his love for Arjuna. On one occasion, they both fought a battle which pleased Lord Indra. Lord Indra offered Krishna a boon. Guess what he asked for? He asked that his friendship with Arjuna continue forever! This built great trust in the relationship. Trust is the first building block in mentoring.

The second feature was that Krishna was always supportive of Arjuna but never interfered with his life. At no point did Krishna take the decisions or the actions required, he merely offered his advice to Arjuna. At any rate, Arjuna had a fragile personality, the kind that would not accept interference by someone else. Krishna ensured that after proffering his advice, he gave Arjuna his own space so that the protégé felt no sense of dependence on the mentor.

The third feature was that the relationship was one of cheer and warmth. Arjuna took his tasks very seriously and had frequent outbursts of temper. Krishna showed himself to be a friend and comrade despite the moodiness of his protégé, so that Arjuna felt free to open his heart to him.

The fourth feature of Krishna's mentorship was that when

required, he criticized Arjuna's decisions openly but never insulted or denigrated him personally. Krishna's focus was on the issue, not on the person. Thus, he was always non-judgemental.

The fifth feature was that Krishna never left Arjuna to fend for himself just because he had chosen a path which Krishna was not supportive of. When Arjuna's son Abhimanyu was killed in battle by Jayadratha, Arjuna vowed that by evening he would either kill Jayadratha or commit suicide. Krishna did not think this was a good idea, but he stood with his protégé to help him complete his difficult task. Lastly, when Arjuna faced a personal crisis on the battlefield, Krishna came to his rescue by propounding the Gita; it was not a mere sermon but a way of looking at the issues he was facing and helping Arjuna to resolve his dilemmas himself.

Respect in coaching: J.R.D. Tata and John Peterson

This fascinating story concerns the mentor of J.R.D. Tata, John Peterson, who was a Scotsman and director of munitions in India during the first world war. It is related in the biography of J.R.D. Tata, *Beyond the Last Blue Mountain* by R.M. Lala. After the war, Peterson was persuaded to resign from the Indian Civil Service and join the Tatas in Bombay.

When twenty-one-year-old J.R.D. Tata arrived in India in 1925, his father took him to Peterson's room. 'John,' he said, 'you know my son Jehangir. I would like you to look after my little boy.' J.R.D. recalled that a small desk was ordered by Peterson to be placed in a corner of his own room. Peterson never had a moment of privacy after that because every single paper going to his desk was routed through young J.R.D. (recall the falcon which was always next to the Arab!).

'I studied the paper before I sent it up. And I studied his comments before I sent them out. I must say that was a very formative and important time of my career. I learnt a lot,' recalled J.R.D. Tata many years later. Between 1926 and 1931, the Scotsman was a major influence on young J.R.D.'s life. He also kept his protégé out of trouble.

How much J.R.D. admired and respected Peterson was recalled by him through an incident. 'I was driving with chairman, Sir Dorab Tata, somewhere in Vienna and he criticized my mentor, Peterson. I turned around and said to him, "Dorabji, it is not right that you criticize one of your colleagues and what is more, it is not true."'

In 1929, just four weeks after J.R.D. had acquired his flying licence, the Tatas received a proposal to run a flight from Karachi to Bombay. J.R.D. was most keen to pursue the project. However, the Tatas were just recovering from a business downswing. Further, Chairman Sir Dorab was past his prime and was not too enthusiastic about new adventures such as airplane services!

It was John Peterson who came to the rescue of an enthusiastic J.R.D. by telling Sir Dorab, 'Let the young man do it. It doesn't cost too much.' Finally, Sir Dorab agreed, setting the Tatas and indeed all of Indian aviation on a glorious future course. No wonder J.R.D. Tata's feelings for John Peterson were so warm that he regarded him as a kind of father from whom he acquired many qualities.

Some of the elements of mentoring are illustrated in this story. There was a strong emotional bond between J.R.D. and Peterson, as is evident in the way J.R.D. thought about Peterson. Clearly J.R.D. got more out of the relationship, though Peterson too must have derived a sense of pride when he took it upon himself to plead with Sir Dorabji to let young J.R.D. start an airline. It seems as though Peterson wanted to let his young ward spread his wings—both literally and figuratively—and demonstrate his natural potential and abilities! And his ward did succeed; the Tatas set up Tata Airlines— later, the nation called it Air-India.

Commitment in coaching: Helen Keller and Anne Sullivan

This is a story with a different dimension to it. Unfortunately, the world has many differently abled children and there are schools for them. These schools impart instructions through techniques developed specially for the purpose. Some kids do not respond to these methods as well as others do. They require special treatment. There is the touching story of Helen Keller who rose above her disabilities to become internationally famous and help handicapped people lead fuller lives. This is a good illustration of a mentoring relationship.

Helen Keller was afflicted by a serious illness when she was less than two years of age. This shut off her ability to see and speak, and thus her connection to the world. For five years, she grew up, as she later said, 'wild and unruly, giggling and chuckling to express pleasure, uttering the choked screams of the deaf-mute to express the opposite'. When Helen was seven, her father consulted the Perkins Institution for the Blind in Boston.

A young lady, Anne Sullivan, was deputed from Boston to teach Helen. Anne herself had been nearly blind during her childhood, but a surgery performed on her partially restored her sight. There must have been a great empathy between Anne and Helen. Anne Sullivan was able to make contact with Helen's mind through the sense of touch. Gradually, the child was able to connect words with objects and within three years, she knew the alpnabet and could read and write in Braille.

Anne Sullivan stayed with Helen Keller for many years. Helen graduated from Radcliffe College with honours in 1904 and went on to devote her life to improving the conditions of the blind and deaf. It is well known that Anne Sullivan was the gifted teacher who unlocked the intelligence of the young, blind and deaf Helen Keller. Less well-known is that Helen Keller taught her beloved teacher Braille, when Anne Sullivan lost her limited sight.

Faith in coaching: Max and Michael Klein

When mentoring occurs in a family or an organization, it is a powerful process of learning, adaptation and transformation that is extremely personal to the individual. There is the story of Max Klein (*Geeks and Geezers* by Warren Bennis), who was a classic American entrepreneur. He left an unsatisfying job with General Motors to strike out on his own. He owned and ran the Palmer Paint Co. in Detroit very successfully. The head of his art department once proposed a do-it-yourself kit that would allow amateurs to create professional-looking paintings.

Max Klein implemented the idea and made a fortune. His own children, a boy and a girl, had no interest in business. So, Max decided to impart his ideas to his grandson, Michael. Among those ideas must have been his thoughts about entrepreneurship and how to be successful at it.

Michael was only five when his grandfather said to him, 'You are never going to get any money from me...but I'll tell you anything you want to know and teach you anything that you want to learn from me.' And a process began, a bit like that between the Arab and his falcon. He spoke to his grandfather for an hour on the phone every day until the latter died.

The youngster derived satisfying instructions and learning out of this interaction as he would recall later in life. So did the grandfather. Michael Klein went on to earn millions in the southern California real estate market while still in his teens! At nineteen, Michael Klein lost $20 million when the real estate market tanked.

He rebuilt another small software company into Transoft, which he sold to Hewlett-Packard in 1999. Michael Klein said that his grandfather was his mentor, a business school of one. On his part, Grandfather Max Klein said that he knew instinctively that he had things to learn from his grandson as well as to teach.

We learn from this story that teaching is not the sole function of the mentor. The protégé may also be a teacher, a guide to understand the mindset of the younger generation. This allows the mentor to continue to learn and adapt.

Modern forms of coaching

If you find yourself in an environment where there is no coaching, look for the problem within yourself. You will not find it within the organization, even if it is the 'perfect' organization for coaching. Which one is, anyway?

I have heard the lament from managers that their company has no 'proper mentoring system'. Conversely, some organizations have such elaborate coaching processes that you get the feeling that anybody and everybody can be coached so long as those processes are adhered to! I find these to be synthetic. Coaching comes within the eyes and between the ears of the pupil.

The traditional perception of coaching is of an extended and unique instructional relationship between two people. It is an old-fashioned view. We cannot lead our professional lives today with the nineteenth-century model of the traditional master craftsman-apprentice model in our minds.

In this old model, evident in both the stories of J.R.D. Tata and Helen Keller, the mentor and protégé connect early and work together for years. This is a difficult pattern to replicate in modern organizations. Nowadays, relationships tend to be shorter, perhaps more intense, and above all, more diverse. It is not just a young manager who needs coaching, even older and more experienced managers need it—the latter too can be in danger of becoming victims of the bonsai syndrome.

In the Tata Group, there has been the practice of attaching promising junior and mid-level managers to senior executives for a couple of years in keeping with the mentoring concept. Tata Administrative Services (TAS) officers like N. Srinath and Rajiv Dube worked as assistants to Ratan Tata, and later progressed to occupy senior assignments. Koushik Chaterji worked as an assistant to Ishaat Hussain, finance director of Tata Steel and later of Tata Sons, for several years before being positioned as the finance chief of a large company like Tata Steel. Neeti Chopra, another TAS officer, worked as my assistant before moving on to be the marketing chief of Trent.

A senior and experienced manager who changes his employer organization needs mentoring about the culture and ways of the new organization. I found this to be the case when I switched to Tatas after thirty-one years with Hindustan Lever. The ways of Tata were different from those of Hindustan Lever, as they will always be different between any two organizations. I chose two or three mentors (without telling them their role!) from whom I could learn the ways of the Tatas and how to get things done.

A mentor can be of any age. An older person who wishes to learn about computers or the new devices available nowadays can seek a young mentor as I did with my children. Besides, one can have many mentors. The creation of a coaching climate really rests with the protégé who can and should think of coaching as an input from many mentors, not just one or two. The inputs may come out of apparently casual and random conversations; the pick-up of the lesson is in the ear and mind of the protégé. Mentors can invest their time in reflective conversations.

This model about the protégé's listening and reflecting on conversations with multiple mentors is important as it makes it quite distinct from the 'old' model of craftsman-apprentice. Today's manager can and should derive coaching from many people. Often, it is apparently casual and unplanned, but always very rewarding.

Coaching can come disguised as casual advice

Quite often, the realization that it was a coaching experience dawns on the protégé many years later. A couple of experiences I had in Hindustan Lever illustrates this.

Prakash Tandon was the legendary chairman of Hindustan Lever when I joined as a trainee. He had the practice of inviting the trainees to lunch once a year or so. It was a terrifying experience for the trainees, but for him, it was probably a way of keeping in touch with the quality of new recruits and their aspirations.

On one such occasion, one of my trainee colleagues became rather expansive. Prakash Tandon said in his measured, clipped accent, 'Young men, your ears have twice the surface area of your mouth. And you have two ears as against only one mouth. It is good to listen four times as much as you speak.' The temporary consequences of this devastating rebuke apart, that bit of advice has stayed with me ever after—always keep your ears and mind open.

I felt a mentor had spoken to me, but only years later as I reflected on that episode; whether Prakash Tandon intended to mentor or not, I cannot tell, but I felt mentored.

Another experience I recall relates to a company proposal to move me to a new assignment within Hindustan Lever, involving relocation from Mumbai to Delhi. This was planned within just six months of a transfer from Chennai to Mumbai! I was miffed, it would cause inconvenience all over again to my family. I wanted to meet Marketing Director Jagdish Chopra.

He was elegant and polished, with a reputation of being a relationship-building manager. He had accomplished great things on the sales side of the business; as a result, he was a director at the young age of forty. The company was fairly hierarchical; it was not common to ask to meet the big boss, especially on a matter like this. Nonetheless, I asked for an appointment.

He was kind enough to see me despite my being a junior officer in the hierarchy. He listened to me very carefully, then explained at length that the proposed transfer was to a more difficult and complex role; that this would be a challenge to me, and further that it had been mooted by the chairman, T. Thomas.

He advised that arguing about the transfer could convey the wrong impression that I was running away from what was widely recognised to be a tough assignment. I finally did accept the move and was grateful for the advice I received at an important juncture.

In the normal perception, these interactions would not be thought of as coaching because they would be seen as pieces of one-off casual advice. I feel that there are many such once-off pieces of casual advice which collectively build up over time. That is why I regard these as examples of the organization and its senior people creating an environment, and the protégé listening carefully and reflecting on the conversations he/she has had. Such a company would produce very few bonsai managers.

How to recognise the relationship

I conclude this chapter with a delightful story, which illustrates how a correct mentoring relationship manifests itself. The recognition of mentoring usually does not necessarily happen at the moments of mentoring, rather they get to be so regarded after the passage of time and the realization of what influenced one a great deal.

In his autobiography, B.K. Nehru recalls his association in the 1930s with the most dominant personality at the London School of Economics, Harold Laski. Laski had high hopes of young Nehru attaining high academic distinctions. Once when Laski and Nehru were walking back along Piccadilly after a function, Laski made his expectation from Nehru quite clear. 'If you don't get a first, Nehru,' he said, 'I shall kick you from here to Aldwych.' Only a very involved mentor could say that to his protégé. It is almost like the angry Arab rebuking his ferocious falcon!

In 1948, after fourteen years, B.K. Nehru met Laski again, in fact, for the last time. During those fourteen years, Nehru had returned to India, joined the Indian Civil Service and served in the districts. He had acquired an understanding of the real India. This pragmatism did not quite connect with the teachings of Laski at LSE, Nehru felt. So, during their meeting, Nehru said he had a confession to make—that his ideas now were totally opposed to all that Laski had taught him over the years. In fact, none of the nostrums prescribed by western political thought provided solutions for the problems of India, Nehru declared to Laski. Laski's reply was that of a great mentor, 'What I taught you was to think independently for yourself. If the University of Life has taught you differently from what it has taught me, I am happy that I have been successful as a teacher.' The pride of Laski is self-evident from this episode.

As the stories above illustrate, mentoring is needed by all, irrespective of age or experience, from the new trainee in the company to the new managing director brought into the company from outside. However old one is, one can be a mentor to some and be mentored by others.

All it takes is to be humble about what one knows, recognise what one can learn from others and be willing to seek out opportunities. Like with the Arab and his falcon, it all depends on whether you connect with the person, on the building up of a relationship with a mutuality of benefits and satisfaction.

The onus lies with the seeker of mentoring more than the mentor himself. Nobody can mentor an unwilling or indifferent protégé; that is the hard truth. It is well worth the effort, but it is the relationship between the two people that creates the magic.

SECTION IV

INTUITION THROUGH
CONTEMPLATION AND REFLECTION

The opposite of a profound truth may well be another profound truth.

—Niels Bohr

INTUITION THROUGH
CONTEMPLATION AND REFLECTION

9

ARRIBADA OF THE TURTLES
RENEWING LEADERSHIP

The value of reflection and contemplation

Owing to the demands of changing markets, modern-day work pressures are great. Today's managers are caught up in the tyranny of time, and are always busy. This 'always busy' syndrome manifests itself through common symptoms.

Many feel the pressure to the point of being preoccupied and overloaded—physically, mentally and emotionally. This is accentuated by a self-imposed pressure to appear to be busy, and remain so. Modern gizmos aggravate the pressure felt by managers. This trend will continue into the future.

Unless the individual decides to take charge of himself and his life, his sanity and mental peace could suffer. To quote Albert Einstein, not everything that can be counted counts, and not everything that counts can be counted. If the individual is to take charge, he has to create enough mental and psychological space for himself. This is essential to allow his intuition to manifest itself and play a role.

In earlier chapters, the value of reflection and contemplation was mentioned. This book is not about how to reflect and contemplate; this is not my specialty. There are many techniques (solitude, long walks, breathing exercises, meditation) and many trainers, whether spiritual leaders or psychologists. Individuals can adopt what suits them, but it must have the consequence of creating space and pathways in their crowded and turbulent minds. This is very important to the development of intuition.

For as long as we can reach back into Indian history and philosophy, interest in metaphysical abilities has abounded. Mysticism and meditation were recognised and codified for centuries.

Elsewhere, interest in such subjects has been relatively more recent. For example, during the 1850s in Victorian England, associations like The Ghost Society at Cambridge and The Phantasmological Society at Oxford began to sprout. They established the existence of metaphysical abilities and the intuitive state. However, they could not identify what caused or enhanced them.

For very long, intuition has been believed to occur as a random chance. During the last fifty years, western researchers have been able to identify the process of the intuitive state, rather than merely reconfirm the fact that it exists. It has been established that certain processes can be created which are conducive to intuition, and instead of having a low chance of occurring, the chances of intuition occurring can be magnified five- to ten-fold.

Such western research suggests that examples of processes that promote intuition are dreaming, meditation and hypnosis.

This may be the reason why very wealthy western people turn to Indian gurus for achieving mental peace and equilibrium. We have come full circle. Once again, the west has discovered what India has known for long!

However, that is not the noteworthy point: what is, is that managers must find their own ways or processes of creating enough mental space so that the chance of enhancing their intuition is increased several-fold. I have found it useful to reflect on and contemplate the surrounds of an issue, not merely the issue itself.

In the next three chapters, three contemporary management themes are explored: whether increased resources are good or counter-productive, how to synthesize diverse opinions and get the best out of teams, and lastly, whether there is a way to transform while minimising pain.

Succession planning and how leaders are developed are the themes of this chapter.

If you do not expect to retire, you tend not to nurture talent

Those who know they have a finite tenure would be more amenable to systems of succession planning and leadership development.

Those who have no compulsion to retire or have no intention to do so may be less mindful about systems of succession planning and nurturing talent.

Here are four newspaper reports about happenings in different countries and cultures regarding succession.

On 3 April 2005, the London *Financial Times* carried a report about a large, well-known European telecom company. It was about the succession to Serge Tchuruk, the sixty-seven-year-old executive chairman of Alcatel. The company had stated that it would ask shareholders to extend the age limit for retirement of the chairman from sixty-eight to seventy.

Tchuruk was due to retire in May 2006. The report also quoted analysts' views that this would certainly be approved because the company had failed to resolve significant questions about who would succeed Tchuruk should he retire. One analyst said, 'We don't see anyone who can replace him. And Serge does not look like he wants to retire.'

In March 2005, a succession brawl unfolded in the Amul and National Dairy Development Board organizations. Without question, Dr Verghese Kurien is the father of the milk revolution in India, catapulting India to the world's number one producer of milk within a span of three decades. Yet he seemed to be involved in a public spat with his successor in one of his own organizational creations, and refused to step down from the chairmanship of another organization. A newspaper editorially asked that Kurien recognize he had overstayed and called upon him to step aside gracefully. Finally, when he failed to do so, he was removed.

On 6 December 2004, an *Asian Age* headline screamed 'India Inc Ducks Succession Planning'. The report referred to family-managed companies; it went on to make the controversial suggestion that the Securities and Exchange Board of India (SEBI) ask the owners of companies listed on the stock exchange to submit their succession plans.

On the very same date, 6 December 2004, the *Economist* carried a supplement on family businesses. It reported that all over the world, most family firms are facing up to their biggest problem: of avoiding a crisis as the business needs to transit from one generation to another. Family firms are more frequently confronted with intrigue and visceral hatreds, like medieval courts, and for similar reasons. Research shows that as few as one-third of businesses make the transition from one generation to the next. Succession is the ultimate test of a family business because parents do not like to give up the privilege of control.

As these stories illustrate, corporate succession is turning out to be a tricky issue. Many bosses dawdle on the way to the exit because, as the time approaches, they are significantly less willing to contemplate stepping down.

Although this subject had for long interested me, these reports triggered some deeper thinking.

How do you develop new leaders? How can there be a systematic way for seniors to give up control?

Strangely, leadership development and succession planning are subjects of a large number of seminars and papers; perhaps they are the hottest billing! Top managers pay a great deal of lip service and speak about succession planning as if it were the most natural and most important thing to be done. However, more often than not, there is a gap between the intent and the means to achieve it.

Failures occur for three reasons: in the worst case, not uncommon in occurrence, the company may have no structured planning system. At the next level, the company may have a system but its master plan goes awry because the planned successor quit. At yet another level, the successor stays, takes the top job, but disappoints by failing to deliver to the satisfaction of the board or shareholders, thus creating a succession void. All these cases reflect different kinds of failure in grooming successors.

In this chapter, I will concern myself with a system for top-level conversations on developing talent and building leaders. Here, I have relied rather heavily on my own experiences.

Developing management succession requires a sequence of protecting, nurturing and pacing. This is observed in Nature and organizations can learn from such observation. Therefore, ways to remind leaders of their finiteness and mortality need to accompany initiatives in succession planning.

As Nathaniel Hawthorne wrote, 'The love of posterity is the consequence of the necessity of death. If a species were sure of living forever, it would not care about its offspring.'

How the nurturing instinct increases with mortality

Many science writers insist that reptiles have no emotions as we understand them. They feel only pain and pleasure. They do not generally bond with each other and, except in rare cases, they do not care for their young.

The snake is a cold-blooded reptile. Most snakes mate, drop their eggs and go away. The young have to fend entirely for themselves, from hatching to growing up. The Australian green tree python is an exception—she coils her body around her eggs to raise the temperature, helping the eggs to hatch.

Another animal that illustrates this aspect is the turtle. Turtles have been the subject of poetry and mythology and I have read a reference to turtle nests in fourth-century Tamil literature! The turtle is thought to bring prosperity in some societies; these animals are on sale in a market at Amman, Jordan. People buy them and let them loose in their garden as harbingers of good luck.

Turtles are cold-blooded; their body temperature stays at around the same as their surroundings, air or water. There are no displays of protecting, nurturing and pacing of the young. The female turtle carries eggs which are fertilized by mating. A single mating can fertilize all the eggs of a female for several years. So turtles may not have a very rich sex life!

When the time comes to lay her eggs, the female turtle hauls herself out of the ocean onto the beach. Without the support of the water, the weight of her body presses down on her lungs, making it difficult for her to breathe. She drags herself laboriously to the top of the beach where the sand is just at the right level of dampness for incubating eggs but safe from flooding by the sea. She digs a hole in the ground with her flippers and then drops over 100 eggs the size of ping-pong balls into the hole. She then covers them with soil, sand, or rotting plant matter and smoothes the sand.

Then, the mother turtle waddles away from her eggs, never to return again.

The warmth of the sun hatches the young in due course and they dig their way to the surface on their own. The young then begin their journey to the sea, and various birds and mammals flock to the beaches for a meal. Few survive the journey to the water as the struggling babies are easy prey for predators. Even after reaching their natural habitat, the water, the struggling animals are easy prey for the fish.

So the survival rates are very low, estimated to be one in a thousand. Perhaps there are not many other species where the survival rate is so low. Yet the species has existed for 150 million years! It is entirely possible that the absence of the instincts of protecting, nurturing and pacing has been compensated for in Nature by prolific production with extremely low survival rates.

What sparked my interest in the turtle was a phenomenon that happens on the eastern coast of India every year. At three locations in Orissa, the largest being the famous Gahirmatha beach, the turtles come out in several hundreds of thousands each year for mass nesting. This happens in Latin America too, and it is called arribada, which means 'the rising up'. This describes how the turtle hauls itself on to the shore to lay its eggs.

This fantasy about the turtle not being nurturing to the young because longevity is assured seems relevant in the context of management succession!

Sequence of protecting-nurturing-pacing in Nature

My elder sister Saroja is very fond of animals. With respect to cats, she had observed how the mother cat stayed with her young to teach them how to climb, how to hunt for food, how to protect themselves, all this for a fixed period of time. Saroja had observed that thereafter, almost as dramatically as announcing that the apprenticeship was over, the mother cat stopped any form of nurturing and caring. The kitten would henceforth be on its own.

It was almost as though a switch had been turned off in the mother cat's mind. While cats do it this way, others do it differently; every animal has its own unique way of ensuring a healthy continuation of the species; this, after all is the essence of organizational succession planning. What is instructive is that there are three typical steps.

Protecting

Mating is the first step, before issues of protection and nurturing arise. Mating is an interesting ritual in the animal world. For instance, a mouse scampering around in a farmyard leaves a scent. This acts as a sexual attractant that is detected by another mouse. Scent is a common mating trail among species as diverse as mice, garter snakes and moon moths.

The mating step is somewhat like the process of recruitment into the organization. Impressive PowerPoint presentations, offers of attractive career opportunities and remuneration, and such processes attract management talent into companies.

Having been co-opted into the community of its species, new members must learn to survive and prosper before they become effective members. Almost all animals undertake some kind of protecting to help their young adjust to the new environment.

One of the most amazing examples of protective care is that of the crocodile. When the eggs are ready for hatching, the mother digs them out of the nest and gently cracks the eggshell to let the babies out. The young ones are very vulnerable to predators. The mother gently gathers the babies into the pouched floor of her mouth—not to eat them, as is sometimes assumed—and goes into the water where she opens her jaws to release the young!

In organizations, protecting is done through induction and alignment programmes; these help new recruits to know the people and the company, to recognize how to avoid dropping bricks and to respect the implicit behavioural expectations within the company. New recruits often underestimate the value of these efforts.

Nurturing

Baby birds use one call to tell their parents that they are hungry and another to convey that they are frightened. Community calls may warn of approaching danger. Even in a crowded colony, parent birds can single out the voices of their chicks, and chicks recognize those of their parents.

Companies too devise oral and written communication, such as codes of conduct, administrative manuals and so on. Through these, company members figure out the dos and don'ts of behaviour in the company.

Once a form of communication is developed within the species, it is used to nurture, teach, and coach the new or young members. Elephant calves thrive on long-term care. The mother suckles the baby for two whole years after birth. During this long period, the baby not only feeds well on the mother's milk, but also learns the finer points about elephant society, and picks up vital information about how to find the best places to eat and drink. Female elephants stick together in herds under a matriarch, around whom the herd bunches when there is a threat from, for example, a pride of lions. The experienced matriarch is the one who decides whether to flee or confront the threat.

All this resembles the efforts in a company to put people through formal training programmes, work under mentors and develop the managerial capabilities required to succeed.

Pacing

This refers to the progression of higher and more complex challenges which are given to the young to prepare for fuller roles.

It is the most important positive input for the enhancement of the species because protecting and nurturing merely maintain, it is pacing that enhances and keeps the vigour.

North America's grizzly bear cubs love the taste of salmon, but find it very difficult to grab these slippery things and put them in their mouths. The young intently watch their mother find a quiet spot and hook salmon out of the water with her claws. The young then fling themselves in erratic belly flops into shallow pools where salmon have gathered. Inevitably, the fish will escape, but this training goes on for two whole years almost like a set of increasingly difficult lessons. Finally, the young bear can intercept the fish even at rapids and waterfalls, thanks to the pacing and training given by the mother bear.

Protecting-nurturing-pacing in leadership development

The imagery of management development is of a sequential and logical set of developments and that too in a straight pipe, thanks to the use of expressions such as 'leadership pipeline'. The straight leadership pipeline concept is misleading; it is, in reality, a bent pipeline.

The development of leaders involves increasingly complex tasks being assigned in a calibrated manner. At certain junctures and times, there is a step change in the complexity of the tasks assigned. Those are what I call the bends, sharp bends, in the pipeline. Those bends constitute the most important part of leadership development and the building of succession capability.

Making it past those excruciating bends is what determines the success of the manager as well as that of the system. A further complication is the fact that the manager's recognition of the bend occurs much later; it is not as though he can see the bend coming ahead in his journey.

This is the reason why an organization needs a system and

a process for leadership development and succession planning. The conversations that occur during this process are hugely value-adding. The outcomes, as with many things in management, cannot be assured to be perfect, but the process is essential.

The fact that there is a system does not mean that there will be no aberrations. Mistakes will be made, they will happen. A system can only minimize the likelihood of a mistake, not eliminate it. On a lighter but factual note, aberrations in the succession planning of the Vatican are interesting.

The Vatican has chosen successors for centuries and a few mistakes have indeed been made. For example, in 855, Pope John VIII was elected, but there remained persistent rumours that the person was a woman! In 1378, a mob broke into the papal conclave during the election of Pope Urban VI. In 1492, Rodrigo Borgia was elected Pope Alexander VI in spite of his having fathered several illegitimate children!

But these are the exceptions. Orderly succession for the papacy has occurred for centuries, aberrations apart, and that has led to the longevity of the institution. In the end, it does not matter whether every step is followed in the succession plan. More important is the result, and the intent behind that result.

Example of a personnel planning system

During my senior years in Unilever, I was impressed to note the amount of time and effort spent by top management on identifying and grooming talent—getting familiar with names, faces, track records, strengths and weaknesses of the identified managers. Paradoxically, I could witness and experience this only when I reached higher levels and this helped me to shed the cynicism I had developed about Unilever's systems in my younger days. By this time, however, I found it difficult to persuade younger Unilever managers about the existence of a succession and career planning system—they were as unbelieving as I must have been in my younger days!

In essence, an elaborate Personnel Planning System had evolved over several decades. Unilever companies were required to follow a formal Personnel Planning Cycle, much like a Business Planning Cycle. After internal appraisals of performance and potential, companies would short-list the high potential managers into a taxonomy that was adopted internationally. This required a standard form with near standard data. Each year, senior managers from HQ would sit with the top team in the country and discuss these forms individually. It was not the forms, but the quality of discussion on each person that was notable. In this way, the name and reputation of a young man of thirty or thirty-five could be established in London without his ever being aware of a process which would make that possible. It was quite impressive for a company that employed 20,000 managers in over eighty countries.

In 1991, I went to Jeddah to head Unilever Arabia. My task was to pull together the existing Unilever businesses on the Arabian Peninsula and to establish a suitable engine to grow the consumer goods business to its potential. It was effectively a mandate to create an Arabian equivalent of Hindustan Lever.

Within twelve months of my assembling an expatriate, multinational team comprising sixteen nationalities, the Unilever chairman, Floris Maljers, visited the company. His central inquiry was about the steps I proposed to take to develop a local Arabic management team within fifteen years. How could I ensure that in 2010, there would be a Saudi national as chairman? Obviously, I had no answer, I had not even thought about it! However, I was quite struck by the foresight and concern from day one about the development of future leaders.

Careers don't develop the way you plan them

Young managers think that they must target their career path and 'be in charge'. The reality is completely different.

Dave Cote is the chairman of Honeywell International. I have met him twice: once, when he hosted me for lunch at Honeywell's headquarters at Morristown, New Jersey, in 2003. The second time was at Mumbai when he was on a business visit to India in 2006.

During our second meeting, we happened to exchange views on how careers are influenced by factors which cannot be foreseen, visualized or planned for. He had an interesting story to tell and agreed that it could be used to illustrate the point which led to our discussion.

Dave Cote used to work in GE during the 1980s, when Jack Welch was 'neutron-bombarding' the company. Dennis Dammerman, a trusted lieutenant of Welch, had been appointed chief financial officer in 1984 in succession to the very successful Tom Thorsen. At the time he was appointed, Dennis Dammerman was a surprise choice for the CFO's job; his mandate was to renew the finance function, which was rather set in its ways. Jack Welch balked at the wasteful bureaucratic procedures and the bloated number of data-obsessed staff at headquarters.

Thirty-five-year-old Dave Cote was in a relatively junior position, three levels below Dammerman in the finance department at headquarters. One of his tasks was to compile a detailed report of sales in every country in which GE operated—not for the current period, but the projected sales for the next five years. Dave inquired of his peers and immediate bosses why such a report was being compiled and to what use it was being put. The response he got did not provide him clarity, but was accompanied by the request to carry on doing it. 'While we have not used it in the past, we may in the future,' was the message.

Dave was puzzled, but did as was required.

One day in 1986, Dave received a telephone call to meet Jack Welch. He became quite anxious and thought furiously about what the meeting could possibly be about. A nervous young Dave Cote entered the chairman's room, armed with notes on every possible question that could possibly be posed to a young financial analyst by an aggressive and colourful chairman.

'So Dave, you look like a smart guy, why the hell do you ask our operating managers to forecast sales for the next five years; and anyway, what do you do with this data?' thundered Jack Welch.

'Well, that is a fair question,' replied Dave tentatively, 'I circulate it to the departments that plan for the future strategies of the divisions and perhaps it facilitates the planning and allocation of resources.'

The conversation continued in a predictable manner for a while longer and concluded with the chairman saying, 'I am going to get Dennis Dammerman here, and ask him why this kind of stuff is being done. How bloody wasteful!' Dave Cote was convinced he was about to be fired.

Upon exit from the room, Dave Cote immediately contacted Dammerman to tip him off. Dennis was quite calm about the whole thing, and seemed self-assured about how he would handle the matter. Dave kept repeating to Dennis that 'Jack was *really* upset,' and finally, Dennis got the message that this may turn out to be more than just a passing storm.

Soon thereafter, the practice of asking for and compiling such data was discontinued. The episode still bothered Dave because this outcome could have been achieved had the initial issue raised by him been squarely addressed. However, not being the 'I told you so' type of manager, he set about his other tasks, a bit puzzled and perhaps a bit wiser. He had still not been fired, so he kept a low profile!

Two months later, there was a company party to celebrate

the RCA (Radio Corporation of America) acquisition. From a distance, the chairman noticed Dave and beckoned him. 'So have you stopped producing that stuff?' asked Jack Welch as Dave Cote worried that a further inquisition might follow. A colleague, who was standing in the group, interjected, 'Jack, you should know that Dave was the guy who kept questioning the need for this report and had recommended stopping it.'

'Is that right?' asked an aghast Jack Welch, 'I did not know that. Nobody said that to me.'

That evening, in an appreciative and mentoring tone, Dave's boss, Dennis Dammerman said, 'Dave, you don't know how well you have emerged from this episode. The fact is that you wanted to stop it. Yet, not once did you defend yourself by saying "I told them so". Both these insights have gone down very well with Jack. Good things will happen to you.'

Some months later, Dave Cote was selected for a more senior position, which was three levels higher—a rare honour and privilege in GE. Let alone getting fired, he was promoted. For what?

Only Jack Welch would know for sure, but perhaps for being smart, at the same time loyal to his team. All that Jack Welch writes of this episode in his book (*Straight from the Gut*, Jack Welch with John Byrne, Warner Books, 2001) is:

> Unbeknownst to me, Dave had tried to shut the report down two months earlier. We got rid of that report for good that day. Dave got visibility and a series of promotions within the company, the last as CEO of appliances.

In 1998, Dave Cote moved on from GE to TRW Inc., and subsequently to Honeywell as chairman and CEO.

Negotiating a bend unknowingly

My own experience illustrates the sharp bend and the fact that the manager himself does not know that he is transiting through such a bend.

I joined HLL as a computer analyst armed with an engineering degree. I suffered from a common trait that many young people show; I had quite a lofty idea about technology, matched by a quiet and unexpressed disdain for functions such as selling and accounting. It was cerebral work that I had to do in the early years, I did it on my own and the challenge was of a personal and analytical nature.

With the passage of time and aspirations for career progress, my ideas changed. In the fifth year, I chose to move to an operational role in the sales function. The general sales manager was Bhau Phansalkar, who insisted that I should retrain all over again as a van salesman; he felt that I should aim to demonstrate my ability to lead a team of market salesmen who would be twice my age. At that time, I was quite miffed. What kind of challenge was this? Was I not smart enough to do all that and more? I did not appreciate why I was being subjected to this 'hardship'.

Many years later, I realized the significance, and thought of it as the first bend in the pipeline. Getting superior work done by frontline colleagues, motivating them, not talking down to them, securing their commitment to your goals, all these seem very simple. They are the muscle of a management role and the only way to learn them is by practice. One also realizes the complexity of human emotions and the need to take a genuine interest in people, not just talk about it. I did retrain as a van salesman, and learnt all those things that I had mistakenly assumed were so easy to learn.

About eight years into my career, a development occurred, which I regard as another bend. I was the branch sales manager in western India and my boss was a warm but tough taskmaster called Ranjit Talwar. In those days, production capacities were controlled and products used to be in short supply due to the licence regime in the country. A key task of sales managers was to serve consumers by achieving wide and equitable distribution of these short supply products—put simply, the task was to spread the shortage widely to minimize inconvenience to consumers.

A complaint was received that our cooking product Dalda, a brand leader by far, had been marketed for a higher than permitted price by one of our two Pune distributors. Talwar assigned me the responsibility to investigate and recommend a course of action. I was aware that such investigations rarely produce conclusive, cast-iron evidence. If true, there arises at the very best, strongly suggestive or near conclusive proof; I was aware that a fair decision on such a matter would send important messages to other distributors about the company's widely proclaimed commitment to an honest distribution system.

As it so happened, after my field work, I concluded that the distributor had indeed marketed the product at an unfair price. Further, the punishment was clear to me: his distributorship had to be terminated. But there was a major problem. The distributor had been a loyal soap distributor of the company for thirty-five years; the association of his firm with the company was over two generations, and had been started by his father.

He knew all the senior managers extremely well, including Ranjit Talwar and Bhau Phansalkar. And here I was, all of twenty-nine, recommending the termination of a distributorship which itself was older than I was! I was warned by colleagues that I would face severe questioning and pressure from seniors within the company. Some even advised taking a 'more pragmatic' stand.

To be frank, I felt scared and uncertain.

I was interviewed and asked many questions by Talwar and Phansalkar, and even the company's legal director, Shamdas Gursahani. I guess I must have sounded convincing without being rigid. To the credit of the seniors in the company, with a great deal of anguish, HLL did terminate the distributorship.

Contrary to the predictions of politics and pressure, it was a very professional process. But I did not know that would be so, and I felt I was taking a risk.

The distributor found his case weak on the real ground of investigation, so he escalated the matter as an issue of the company practising territorial restrictions on sales and restrictive trade practices to the detriment of the consumer. This spiralled into a case at the MRTP (Monopolies and Restrictive Trade Practices Commission) and the company fought the matter all the way to the Supreme Court as a matter of principle.

For me, there was huge personal development and learning. In hindsight, I count it as a bend in my own managerial development pipeline, a bend where I learnt that it is not only the functional competencies one needs to master, but also to stand firm with certain principles and standards whatever the threats or consequences.

One other incident occurred later in my career. On a hot, sweltering June day in my twentieth year of service, Chairman Ashok Ganguly called me and expressed the company's satisfaction with my work and invited me to join the company management committee as the exports director. I was forty-one years of age, not expecting it quite at that time, and understandably was over the moon. However, my elation was short-lived.

Three months later, a 'disaster' struck. The company had been exporting merchandise that was unfamiliar to its core business in household products, so we had recruited some specialist managers from these trades to bring in some domain knowledge. We had people with expertise in items as diverse as woollen carpets, leather and garments. It was quite a challenge to induct these recruits into the company culture, particularly the scrupulously honest practices and professionalism. These were not the hallmarks of the small operators who dominated such fields. Muktesh Pant, who later went on to occupy a high position in Reebok, USA, used to work as my deputy at that time in HLL Exports. Muktesh and I stumbled on the fact that one such specialist manager had swindled the company of Rs 1 crore, a lot of money in 1987, even for HLL. The evidence was fairly indicative, but not absolutely solid. What was I to do?

I went to my long-time mentor Bipin Shah, a director. He urged me to gatecrash into the chairman's room right away to inform him. Thereafter, the further course of action could be devised as a company rather than within my own department. It seems obvious, once stated, but it is not what most people would naturally want to do. The natural response would be to try and fix the problem. If avoidable, why involve others? I was very, very anxious.

What would people think of me, a new director with a fraud on his hands? Were my facts right? Had I alarmed everybody prematurely? I was in a quandary. But Bipin Shah had always advised me well, so I took courage and knocked on the chairman's door.

Ashok Ganguly was a warm as well as tough manager, a combination that could leave the bearer of bad tidings a bit in confusion. Which face would one see? My throat was dry as I told him what I had to. He raised his eyebrows sharply, looked at me with palpable shock on his face. As I was getting ready for a hollering, he suddenly seemed to soften. 'Gopal, sit down; have a glass of water,' he said. 'Now tell me again, what else do you know so far?'

It was a magical moment, because from perceiving him as a potential tormentor and judge, I saw him as an ally. Instead of being my problem, he suddenly seemed to become my possible solution. I learned that if a boss could support his subordinate when he has hit big trouble, surely there is a huge leadership lesson in it.

Over the next twelve months, the top management of the company's finance and legal departments helped me and

Muktesh Pant to unravel the mess, take corrective action and bring this sordid matter to an end. Regrettably, the company never got back the Rs 1 crore, so it could be regarded as the price at yet another bend to make a tougher senior manager out of me. As training goes, it was more expensive than the advanced programmes I have attended at B-schools.

How essential it is to invest in 'touch time'

Systems help, but there is no substitute for the investment of top management time on this issue. Top people should be investing a great deal of personal time on interfacing with people, remembering them and tracking their development and progress. Mere systems cannot achieve these essential ingredients.

In companies, processes and systems for leadership development are embellished with labels like talent management, career planning and 'drop dead' scenario: that is, what would we do if Mr X went under a truck tomorrow? Whatever it is that a company calls it, there have to be three ingredients. First, there have to be organized methods to protect, nurture and pace managers. Second, it also requires the tenure of leaders to be finite so that planning is forced. Third and last, there must be vigour and joy in anointing new leaders, not apprehension.

It is appropriate to conclude this chapter with the well-known story of how Jack Welch was selected by Reginald Jones as a successor in the early 1980s. Even though it is folklore among managers, it is worthwhile to repeat it because it is so relevant to this chapter.

Chairman Jones took the four possible successors he had identified on a long flight, one by one. The event was perceived as a routine, business flight and, of course, the discussions were business-related and broad. During the flight, with a feigned casualness, Jones would pop a question like—if I died unexpectedly in an air crash and your view was sought on a successor, whom would you choose? You can name anybody excluding yourself. And why? A conversation would ensue, during which significant points of data would be generated. This information went into the pot for Chairman Jones to churn and analyse, thus enabling him to chart a course forward.

I recount this story only to illustrate the extent and care taken by world class managers to identify, nurture and groom talent. Jack Welch has described the choosing of his own successor. It seems that on Friday night, the board had unanimously approved Jeff Immelt to succeed Jack Welch. On Saturday morning, Jack Welch waited outside his house on the driveway when Jeff pulled into the driveway. He had a big smile on his face and was barely out of the car before Welch embraced him. Welch recalled the day when Reg had walked into his room at Fairfield, Connecticut, and embraced him in just the same way.

Leaders should plan their step-off

In spite of the rich literature, it is not uncommon to see succession planning as a weakness in many organizations. Perhaps successful top executives have failed to prioritize or perhaps they do not wish to let go, or perhaps the age of retirement is flexible in that company. Or, in extreme cases, top executives feel threatened by yelping successors at their door!

With respect to top managers, there could be yet another reason for not planning succession—that the senior executive has not developed interests that could occupy him during his well-earned retirement. This is a great pity. The reality is that despite increasingly complex work schedules, executives do live longer; many are too busy to recognise this and do something about it until it is a bit late.

During my early career, I recall a study by an economist who wrote about why, despite acquiring wealth, people in the US are joyless. In a single word, his research provided an obvious answer—boredom. People had failed to develop active interests. Every person needs to develop an interest which allows him to experience 'flow', which means losing himself in that activity. It may be tennis, singing, painting, watching cricket or writing a book. Whichever it might be, it is vital.

When I was young, perhaps thirty or so, my boss Ranjit Talwar tried to persuade me to learn golf, apart from my interest in tennis, saying, 'It will give you the option of a very satisfying interest when you are my age. Have at least three or four things that can absorb you later. I learn Sanskrit, play golf and teach kids—all of which will stand me in good stead after a few years.' How right he was.

Maybe that is one reason I have written this book!

10

RICH ECOSYSTEMS THROUGH INTERDEPENDENCE

LESS RESOURCE PROMOTES COOPERATION

The breathtaking biodiversity of Australia

During budget discussions in every company, a common plea is 'we need more'—more managers, more advertising budget, more capital expenditure. I have said that to defend a higher budget to my seniors, and have had that said to me also.

The behaviour of company managers suggests that there may be a widespread perception that a shortage of resource is the greatest barrier to achieving better or superlative results. When there are a lot of resources, is it an advantage? Do people cooperate in the use of those resources? Or do they compete more?

Nature, as always, tells an instructive story.

Where resources are plentiful and rich, the environment produces incentives to compete. However, when resources are scarce, evolution actually selects against competitive species. The case of Australia is worth narrating.

According to experts, Australia has the least fertile soil on earth among all ecosystems. The soil contains about half the level of nitrates and phosphates found in similar semi-arid regions elsewhere. The absence of glacial action or volcanic activity has meant that Australia's soils have not been replenished with nutrients for a long, long time.

Plants in Australia have to work hard to get their nutrition and, having got it, need to protect it from the grass- and plant-eating animals that live in that area. In spite of these inhospitable conditions, however, there is an incredible diversity of plant life. In the perch between the karri forest of Western Australia and the sea, in particular, there exists a breathtaking variety of flora.

The heath of western Australia essentially consists of barren sand flats, almost devoid of nutrients. Yet it is host to some 12,000 species of plants, a biodiversity that can rival a rainforest. Not only is there this fantastic diversity, the ecology changes in a dramatically colourful way. Spring flowers bloom and die in a few days, and this sequence moves across the land in synchronized, successive waves. This gives the impression that huge blushes of colour are moving across the landscape slowly like clouds on a mountain top!

There is a similar pattern for coral. For more than 2,000 km along the Queensland coastline of Australia, there stretches one of the world's largest collections of coral reef. It boasts a diversity of unique species, unequalled in other terrains. Lack of physical protection makes these vividly coloured, soft-bodied, slow-moving marine vertebrates— humpback whales, dolphins and green turtles—protect themselves and their location by producing some of the world's most potent toxins. It is staggering to learn, for example, that as many as one-fourth of the chemicals derived from natural products at the US Cancer Institute are from Australia!

Thus, in an environment that may seem like a peaceful paradise to visiting divers and people who snorkel, the sponges, soft corals and sea squirts that live on the reef use chemical means to stay together and ward off predators.

The same is the story with respect to birds and other eco-systems as evolution has supported the less competitive species and supported the more cooperative ones. The Great Barrier Reef has a number of interdependent species, each one playing its own unique, distinctive role in the ecosystem.

For example, all over the world, certain bird species are known where only one sibling mates and reproduces. The others 'forgo' the right to reproduce, so that they can forage for food and feed their nephews and nieces.

What is amazing is that 85 per cent of such bird species are to be found in Australia.

Eucalyptus trees are found in many parts of the world. But in Australia, they develop large holes in their bases. A lay person would look upon this as a negative development on the assumption that this might weaken the tree base or leave the tree vulnerable to bush fires. In reality, the holes provide shelter for possums which leave nutrient-rich droppings as a sort of rent!

So what is the explanation for this phenomenon of huge collaboration and cooperation?

In the Australian ecosystem, competition for resources is a rare phenomenon. Species tend to cooperate with each other to process, recycle and retain scarce nutrients.

Zoologists have an interpretation of what is happening. Because resources are scarce, evolution selects only those species that cooperate to survive and grow. Nature favours those species that consume less, recycle efficiently and collaborate to keep the limited nutrient resource in circulation. In fact, it encourages specialization of the species so that each one is adding value and performing a unique task within the ecosystem.

Scarce resources promote cooperation

This point about scarcity promoting cooperation may seem counter-intuitive in the context of our day-to-day experiences, but there is telling evidence.

Any visitor to Dubai (which has only a little oil resource) will notice the greater hunger, the greater openness and the consequent greater encouragement to entrepreneurship in Dubai compared to the other resource-rich Gulf states. In 2005, Dubai had $30 billion worth of construction projects; it had about a sixth of the world's population of construction cranes in its few thousand square kilometres of land area!

Clearly, in a situation of extreme scarcity, cooperative behaviour may not be visible. For example, very hungry people in a famine could riot when food parcels are dropped. However, when there is no extreme scarcity of a subsistence variety, then the argument has considerable merit. Hence, in the discussions that follow, the word 'scarce' is used to mean 'less than desired' rather than 'extreme scarcity'. But what is 'less than desired'?

To explore how humans behave, let us factor in the element of ambition. Resources are scarce or plentiful in relation to human ambition. Three points can be made:

- ❂ If ambition exceeds resource, then there is a perception of resource shortage.
- ❂ If ambition is less than resources, there is a perception of adequate resource.
- ❂ Cooperation among people is fostered when the individuals realize that one person's gain need not mean a loss for the other.

Millions of years of biological evolution have given people everywhere an innate tendency to monitor the contributions of others, whether consciously or unconsciously. This has been true for centuries—here are two examples from anthropology.

A contrast: Shoshone and Kung San

Cast your mind back to many, many years ago when the world was inhabited by primitive societies. There is a comparative study of two kinds of ancient tribal people, the Shoshone in North America and the Kung San in the African Kalahari. Both lived in the wastes of desert areas, but one had shrubs and roots and the other ate large animals. There is a contrast between their different social evolutions.

The Shoshone people used to inhabit the Great Basin of North America, corresponding roughly to present-day Nevada. Sociologists found that theirs was a very simple society, where the basic social organization was the family, and the male head represented the 'total legal and political' system. It was as though a Shoshone family could live all its life by itself with very little interaction or interdependence on other such family units.

Such Shoshone families would typically go it alone, roaming the desert with a bag and a digging stick, searching for roots and seeds. It seemed that their ambitions were small, so too the resources they deployed to realize that small ambition. They matched one with the other and lived extremely simple lives with equally simple social structures. There was no big game to hunt for, but occasionally, they would spot some delicious jackrabbits.

This reflected a higher level of ambition. To enjoy this delicacy, they would employ a net which was hundreds of feet long in which the rabbits were herded before being clubbed to death. However, a single family could not handle this net, so on an opportunistic basis, a dozen or so Shoshone families would come together and cooperate under a boss. After enjoying the spoils of their cooperation together, they would revert to the more traditional structure of the family unit.

In contrast, the Kung San, who too lived in a desert area, evolved very differently. The Kung San ate giraffe meat. A simple, small family unit could not possibly overcome a large giraffe. A complex form of social cooperation evolved: some way was found to assemble larger groups.

Indeed, there might have been a surplus beyond their immediate hunger. Having no preservation techniques, they might have invited 'non-contributing' Kung San to join the feast, thus creating an obligation to be discharged on some other occasion. This would further contribute to a more complex social structure.

When the resources fell short of what was required to realize the ambition, people cooperated to do something about it. Thus cooperation was fostered by a higher ambition.

The tyranny of too much resource

The opposite happens in a resource-rich environment, which produces among the species the incentives to compete. Thus, eventually, in a rich environment, a 'super species' will evolve which will control the strategic resources in the chain.

Nobel Prize winner Joseph Stiglitz refers to what the economists call 'resource curse'. It is so named because, on average, countries with large endowments of natural resources perform worse than countries that are less well endowed. There are, of course, exceptions.

Experience around the world suggests that special skills and attitudes are required to manage abundant resources. In poor countries, the prospect of riches orients official efforts to seizing a larger share of that pie rather than developing and expanding it. In economically developed countries, a sense of indolence can creep in.

For example, in the 1970s, Nigeria and Indonesia had similar per capita incomes, both were dependent on oil. Nigeria was soon left far behind. There was too much resource and the special skills to manage were absent. By the late 1990s, Indonesia was far more prosperous compared to Nigeria. In more recent years, unfortunately, political problems have afflicted Indonesia also.

Another example quoted is that of Sierra Leone and Botswana. Both are rich in diamonds, but Botswana does vastly better than Sierra Leone.

Another example is that two-thirds of the people in Venezuela live in poverty, despite having one of the largest deposits of oil.

Stiglitz also gives the example of what happened to a more developed country. He describes the effect on the Netherlands after its discovery of North Sea oil and gas in the 1970s when it was plagued with increasing unemployment and workforce disability. Admittedly, a variety of factors were at play, but there seemed to be a connection that is difficult to ignore.

Patrick Lambe, the founder of Straits Knowledge in Singapore, compared the approaches to risk in Singapore and America. The instinctive American approach to innovation promotes competition, generous risk-taking, and aiming for large advantages. The Singaporean approach promotes collaboration, risk averseness and achievements of small wins. He felt that the US approach is so because the country has vast natural resources and has a huge domestic market. The marginal cost and risk of innovation is small. Not so in Singapore. Therefore, he wondered, whether it was inherent in the nature of Singapore to rely on collaboration and resource efficiency— a bit like the flora and fauna of Australia.

Crowd control at Kumbh Mela

There is a practical example of the application of this principle that too much resource can be detrimental in the case of crowd control at an Indian festival. The atmosphere of this festival is important so as to appreciate the mindset of the pilgrims. The Kumbh Mela logistics far exceed the Haj logistics which I had occasion to observe during my years at Jeddah.

According to tradition, the oceans were churned for the nectar of immortality. When the urn containing the nectar was grasped, a war ensued between the gods and the demons for its possession. Lord Indra's son, Jayanta, got hold of the urn and ran all the way to heaven. At four places in the course of the journey, drops of the nectar of immortality fell on the ground. This caused those four places to become holy to millions of people, who visit with a lot of religious fervour.

The 2001 Kumbh Mela had an added significance because a confluence of stars made it an event of once-in-144 years! Imagine the frenzy of the devoted pilgrims who visit to have a bath in the holy river during the Kumbh. It is essential to instil cooperation rather than competitiveness among the crowd, but it has to be planned for.

The mela has six major bathing days spread over three months, some of which have more importance than others to the pilgrims. The *Guinness Book of World Records* acknowledges that the mela area becomes the world's largest township with an influx of 20 million pilgrims on one particular day—a bit like creating a brand new and even bigger Mumbai or London or New York for just a few weeks!

When we read about the disasters at melas, or fires a cinema halls, lay people often think that more and wider escape doors are an obvious solution.

Think about what the crowd wants to achieve at such an event. Every person wishes to ensure that the specified 'holy acts' are completed within the appropriate timeframe. In other words, there must be a *feeling* of moving in an orderly fashion without anybody else seeming to move much faster; being at a standstill is anathema.

Alok Sharma of the Indian Police Service was the mela officer in 2001. Recalling his experiences, he explained how the psyche of people was influenced to promote cooperation (*Ideas That Have Worked*: Penguin India, 2004):

> We adhered to a traffic management plan to avert stampedes, accidents, drowning and boat collisions. The key to the traffic management scheme was staggering the Mela in time and space.
>
> To manage time, we let the crowd take a longer looped route to reach the Sangam, so that we had the time to evacuate the area. The second issue was staggering space. They had ten kilometer long ghats, which were full for over eighteen hours on peak days. It was also crucial to delineate the circulation space...space was at a definite premium, everyone wanted an extra inch of land. We kept seven hundred feet free space from the water line. This circulation space could hold five million people at a time.

Thus, shortage of crucial resources like free space and time were, in fact, leveraged to seek cooperative behaviour. Admittedly, such methods do not guarantee results; unfortunately, disasters will happen, especially when the resource scarcity is perceived to be extreme.

Reflection on this experience offers a lesson on how leaders can constantly try to create cooperative behaviour.

A common family experience

I now want to relate a family experience, one which many would find familiar.

When my children were young, we visited Disneyland in Florida. For a visiting Indian tourist, it was an expensive day out. Everyone in the family wanted to 'get the best value' out of the day, but that expression meant different things to each one! Layout maps were studied by each child in advance; journey plans were prepared to sequence the optimum way to maximize the rides so that all of us could hit the ground running from the moment of entry. It was not in anybody's plan that one or more might feel tired, or that the time for a snack could be a bit longer.

Once we got into the park, we were all quite excited. We were faced with an abundance of choice, more than we had imagined. The behaviour of my children played out very differently.

The eldest was systematic and wanted to follow the prepared plan, irrespective of new data.

My son, a 'maximizer', would constantly recast the plan to include new choices as every bit of information was assimilated.

My youngest kid just decided to enjoy whatever was there, so went with the crowd doing what everybody else seemed to be doing.

As a family, we lost a lot of time debating whose view should be actioned!

Less is more

It is commonly believed that offering more choices and options to people adds to their happiness and sense of well-being. That is why we have more television channels, more multi-media experiences, more shopping experiences and the list is endless.

The reality is that, beyond a certain level of choice, the psychological impact of increasing choice is actually detrimental. Increased choice and affluence have been accompanied by decreased well-being. No single factor can explain this trend, but there is evidence that explosion of choice plays an important role in reduced happiness and well-being.

The Himalayan kingdom of Bhutan sits snugly on the north-eastern border of India. It is a poor and landlocked country with a very underdeveloped infrastructure. In the late 1990s, the king announced that his country would henceforth seek Gross National Happiness for his subjects, rather than merely chase Gross National Product. It seemed a profound and laudable statement.

In 1999, he allowed television into his country—this had been banned until then. In one fell sweep, multiple television channels beamed into the country, with Rupert Murdoch's Star being the most prolific content supplier. Suddenly, these simple Bhutanese people were exposed en masse to sex, soccer, scandal et al. Of course, they lapped it up.

Contributors to the *Journal of Bhutan Studies* have started reporting some 'unusual trends' in Bhutanese society. One-third of the parents seem to prefer watching television rather than talk to their children. There seems to be a sharp increase in family break-ups, crime and drug abuse. A school principal has for the first time introduced an additional section in his annual report entitled 'Controversies'. It deals with new issues that the staff are trying to cope with.

This may be an aberration, and perhaps ought not to be blamed on television. But then, who knows?

A life without significant choice would be unliveable. But choice is positive only up to a point. The reason is that when faced with abundant choice, people respond as 'maximizers' or 'satisfiers'. Some try to get the best, but end up always being uncertain about what the best is and thus are unhappy people. There is one more suggestion that excess of resources (choice is a resource) can be detrimental to cooperation.

Society would be well served to rethink its worship of choice. The consequences of unlimited choice may go far beyond mild disappointment to mild suffering. Barry Schwartz, an author, advocates eleven lessons on what to do about this trend of excessive choice. His eleventh lesson: learn to love constraints. Of course, one should love to overcome these constraints, and avoid becoming bonsai.

The case of the panicky mice

As I conclude this chapter, I would like to mention one more anecdote from the animal world.

An experiment with panicky mice further confirms the reality that less is more and therefore better, not the other way around.

The *New Scientist* reported the results of an experiment by a University of Philippines professor of physics, Caesar Saloma, on how panicked mice escape from an enclosed area. He developed his model based on some mice escaping from a contained water pool onto a dry platform through doors of various widths and separations. First, thirty mice were introduced into a water pool. A video camera was used to film the actual escape of the mice.

The experimenters varied the width of the exits to allow just one mouse through, and then enlarged the opening to allow two mice, then three and so on. They also varied the distance between the exits. Second, each time one mouse escaped, they introduced another mouse into the pool to ensure that the level of panic among the mice would be constant. This went on until sixty mice had been involved in the experimentation process. What did they find?

The most efficient escape was when the door size was only large enough for one mouse to squeeze through, as this promoted self-organized queuing. As the width of the door was increased, the mice stopped lining up and competed with each other. This actually slowed down the escape rate.

Further, if the escape exits were positioned too close to each other, the mice arched around the exits and this too slowed down the escape rate. While scientists are interested in such studies to verify computer models on the design of escape routes, our interest arises more from the perspective of cooperation and competition.

The Saloma experiment on mice seems to suggest a

hypothesis not dissimilar to the Australian ecology lesson, that an excess of resources increases competitiveness while a scarcity promotes cooperativeness. Somehow, the psyche of the people involved must be shaped in a way that the individual believes that it is better to cooperate and be orderly than competitive.

So what can successful leaders do with this insight? The answer may be a good way to close this chapter.

The gap between ambition and resources

A feeling of fewer resources is a positive motivation. It stimulates positive action as well as the collaborative instinct among people! The manager must try to create and maintain this gap between ambition and resource.

Two hundred and fifty years ago, Samuel Johnson had said, 'Make an impartial estimate of your revenue; whatever it is, live on less.' Those were the simple days before banks invented consumer credit cards and governments invented deficit financing.

The Swiss have a dictum that seems relevant here: earn a lot, spend little, and concentrate on your work.

A management academic in the USA, Vijay Govindarajan, argues that Indians are entrepreneurial and creative. Their biggest asset is the lack of resources relative to the population, and one just has to go out into the villages to see how they do 'more with less'.

Thoughtful and well-read managers would recognise the argument from the writings of C.K. Prahalad and Gary Hamel that it is not cash that fuels the journey to the future, but the emotional and intellectual energy of every employee. They argue that it is, in fact, absolutely essential that leaders should design a gap between resources and ambition. If there are a lot of resources, then the bar of ambition should be raised. They pooh-pooh the idea of 'realism'.

If John Kennedy had been 'realistic' in the early 1960s, he would never have committed the US to a moon programme.

If the engineers of Japanese electronic major JVC had been 'realistic', they would never have developed the home video-cassette recorder.

Indeed, when the US denied India access to supercomputing technology in the 1970s, had India been 'realistic', we would never have developed our own Param supercomputer.

India has been referred to as a rich country where poor people live. This is a powerful way to emphasize the abundance of resources the country is endowed with. It was Gandhiji who said of India that there is enough for everybody's needs but, alas, not enough for everybody's greed.

Maybe this has been at the heart of India's problem. Throughout history, India has been blessed with great natural resources. However, the ruling dispensation's ambition for progress of the population at large has been modest. The goals set have been small in relation to resources. To progress, planners needed to raise targets to a level which is higher than available resources. In this way, a 'desirable deficit' is created between high ambition and the less-than-matching resources. Some of this has started to happen in recent years, and the first signs are exhilarating.

11

MARCH OF THE PENGUINS
WHEN GROUPS ARE WISER

It is believed that the best way to secure the wisdom of groups is to bring managers together into a conference for a meeting of minds. No wonder company conferences, often in exotic locations, are big business.

The belief is true that individuals influence each other, share perspectives and knowledge, and collectively come up with the 'best' solutions through such group discussions. However, this process also has the disadvantage that the more persuasive 'alpha-arguers' in the group sway others to their viewpoint: thus there is a risk of losing out on the 'average' wisdom of the group. More importantly, the outlier views, the ones at the edge, get completely lost because group discussions tend to ridicule or ignore these.

When a qualitative solution to a company problem has to be evolved, then this method works quite well. For example, what are the ways in which we can transfer good practices across the company? Sometimes, however, a quantitative or binary view is needed. For instance: we have done the analysis and the results are close, now we have to decide whether or not we should test-market this product. Here the collective intuition of the group may be sought. How does one extract this?

Animal group behaviour: The role of natural instinct

French film-maker Luc Jacquet has made a magnificent film called *The March of the Penguins*. It is a feature-length film depicting the extraordinary struggles and triumphs of the emperor penguin. For thirteen months, a full film crew set up camp in the Antarctic with no possibility of sea or air transportation. Such a film creates awe in the viewer because Nature always tells a great story.

In the wild, Magellanic penguins spend 80 per cent of their time swimming. They are furious swimmers, and come out only to moult and to breed. Off the South American coast, they swim thousands of miles in line with their migratory habits.

A few years ago, a report had appeared in the *New York Times* about the behaviour of some captive penguins in the San Francisco zoo. Forty-six penguins had been kept in captivity in a 130 by 40 ft pool. Soon, all had learnt to lead the sedentary life that zoo enclosures enjoined. They had certainly lost their penchant for swimming furiously.

To join these sedentary penguins at the zoo, there came six new Magellanic penguins. Until then, these six had spent time at a theme park in Ohio and the Sea World at San Diego, where they were not so constrained by space. At the San

Francisco zoo, they were confined in the same 130 by 40 ft pool.

Do you think the forty-six penguins influenced the six newcomers to become placid? Or did the six newcomers make the placid forty-six become active?

Within a couple of hours, the six newcomers did what came to them naturally and began to swim around furiously. After a while, the original forty-six penguins threw off their lethargy and started to swim furiously. It was almost as though they had been reminded about their natural proclivities by the six newcomers!

The zookeeper, who must be considered some sort of expert, had assumed the opposite, that the six newcomers would become lethargic. Therefore, he was extremely surprised by the outcome.

Other penguin experts, however, were not surprised. Their view was that penguins are extremely social birds, they are extraordinarily inquisitive, and to swim is to be a penguin.

Humans too are social and inquisitive, but humans do not respond the same way if a similar situation were created. New recruits into lethargic or bureaucratic organizations become listless like the others who are already there! If it were not so, organizational change would be pretty easy to introduce, would it not?

The survival instinct

Survival is a very strong motivation for group behaviour in the animal world. The following six examples emphasize this point.

Rats learn from the experience of past victims, so they manage to avoid man-laid traps and poisons unless their position is changed. That is why a rat trap in the house cannot remain in the same place for a long time and yet be functionally effective.

When 60 per cent of a group of red deer stand up, it is a signal for the whole lot to start moving. The process is unconscious, the researchers say. If democracy means that actions are taken based on a majority view, then the red deer have democracy.

Adult African buffalo females give the lead to a whole herd which is sedentary. When the adult females collectively gaze in one direction, it is the signal for the whole herd to move in that direction: a great story about female power!

Water fleas can collectively achieve what they cannot do individually. Water fleas cannot survive in an alkaline water environment. However, when several of them are together, they are able to do so. This is because in their respiratory output, water fleas emit an acidic product. Individually, the output cannot alter the water, but when there are enough of them, the acid output is enough to neutralize the alkaline environment.

When the time comes for Mormon crickets to migrate, they walk and hop by the millions. Observers have wondered for long why they do so in such large numbers. Scientists glued tiny transmitters on the 1.5 inch insects. Then they left some in the crowd and removed some others which would undertake the journey without the crowd. Guess what they found? Crickets which stayed with the crowd survived the journey. The lone crickets died, their transmitters were found chewed and pecked.

Therefore, there is one general rule of the wild—the instinct of survival. Birds of a feather stick together—irrespective of whether they are birds, mammals or fish—in order to survive.

Human behaviour in groups

Among human beings, the perception of facts from a given situation can vary quite a lot, depending on the individual.

Indians can tell a Bengali name from a Tamil name, but a foreigner cannot. Many African names may seem broadly similar to non-Africans, but the Africans can tell even tribal nuances from the name.

This has to do with the shorthand way in which we recognize situations. See how we are able to recognize so many individual faces. Studies show that each of us has stored a statistical average, a mental average of a human face. Whenever we see a new face, we do not notice every feature in detail and try to store those details in our memory. We merely notice the differences with the average in our mind, and store that difference. In this way, we are able to recognize an infinite number of faces.

The same thing happens with respect to a given situation. We are influenced by the mental average stored in our mind of the closest equivalent we have known. This influences the way humans behave in groups.

In the years of austerity before the collapse of the Berlin wall, I travelled frequently to Moscow on business. Since goods of daily use were often in short supply, it was common to see people standing in long queues in front of shop counters. Once I inquired what the queue was for. A man candidly said he was not sure, but he felt that if so many were standing in the queue, there must be something useful available—perhaps a pair of shoes his size, perhaps some clothing that might suit his son. I was amazed that citizens would stand in a queue for hours without quite knowing what they were waiting for.

In 1968, an experiment was done by two social psychologists, Leonard Bickman and Lawrence Berkowitz. They first asked a single person to stand at a busy street corner and look skywards. A small number of passers-by stopped to see what the person might be watching. The number of people looking skywards increased progressively. Now, many more passers-by stopped, at one point almost 80 per cent of them, to satiate their curiosity about what might be in the sky. The underlying assumption in both these appears to be that when things are uncertain, one might as well go along with the crowd. This might suggest that there is no particular cleverness in group thinking or action! This is not true in reality.

Human beings aggregate and congregate through well-developed social signalling. The ultimate reason for social coherence among people is the drive to survive, more often socially rather than merely physically. In order to function effectively, a society must hang together.

That is the very basis of organizational and social development. That is why management research is so focussed on how to get the best out of human groups. The old human adage, after all, is that none of us is smarter than all of us together.

In some societies, people are encouraged to think independently, individualistically and not follow the norm. This can lead to a very creative, free thinking social structure, but may not deliver the power of teams. In others, conformity is emphasized through the do's and don'ts of social mores. There may be complete submergence of individuality where people are compelled to respond only as a group. That too can turn out to be counter-productive; in fact, the term 'herd instinct' is used for such behaviour, and it has a negative connotation.

There exists great power in collective decision-making. However, the conditions for tapping such power have to be created consciously. Otherwise, either exclusive individuality will prevail or the herd instinct will. The latter could even give the false comfort that collective wisdom is being realized. The question is how to strike a balance between individuality and commonness.

How does one get a balanced approach? How can we be better off by following trends among groups?

The power of many

Three cases suggest what may be required to extract the intuitive wisdom of groups.

The first example concerns a fair for cattle, the second is about a US submarine, and both of these appear in a book entitled *The Wisdom of Crowds*. The third is a report from *The Economist* about financial managers.

The ox and the submarine

Author James Surowiecki recounts a story about a scientist, Sir Francis Galton, a cousin of Charles Darwin, who was an African explorer, geographer, writer and polymath rolled into one. He had strong views on how genius is hereditary and is present in the 'fitter' classes!

This particular story relates to the early 1900s. At a cattle fair in Plymouth, Galton found himself at a fun stall where a huge ox had been displayed. For a small fee, a visitor could buy a token and make a guess—what would be the weight of the meat when the animal was slaughtered and dressed? Using the 787 valid guesses given to him by the organizers, Galton calculated the mean: 1,197 pounds. After the slaughter and dressing, it was just about that much! Surowiecki argues that, in fact, Francis Galton stumbled on to a powerful truth—that crowds can be incredibly wise under certain circumstances.

He also cites the disappearance of the US submarine *Scorpion* in the North Atlantic ocean in May 1968. A naval officer named John Craven assembled a large number of individuals with expertise in specialist areas like mathematics, salvaging, submarining and so on. He asked them to individually imagine what might have happened and to guess where the submarine might have sunk. Craven then put all these diverse guesses together and used certain mathematical theorems to arrive at their average. It turned out that the submarine was found 220 yards away from the position he had calculated.

Predicting the economy

The *Economist* of May 2005 reported the findings of an experiment to test whether collective wisdom is better, and, further, whether collective wisdom without consultation is better than collective wisdom with consultation.

Three economists at The Bank of England devised a sort of business decision game, but applied to monetary policy. The researchers took a gang of economically literate students from the London School of Economics and tried to replicate the deliberations of the Bank's Monetary Policy Committee. The experiment was to manage the notional economy via interest rates.

The toy economy was subjected to external shocks, and the students were supposed to respond to responses of inflation and output to interest rate changes. At the beginning and at the end of the experiment, the students worked alone. In-between, they worked in committees. The findings were stunning. The average score in the committee was far higher than the average in individual sessions. Further, the average of the committee was higher than all the individual scores, bar the highest. So far, this adduces to the adage: none of us is smarter than all of us put together. However, the surprise was in the finding that those committees that were allowed to discuss their findings and views fared worse than those that were not.

The logic seems to be that articulate speakers, called alpha-arguers, tend to sway committees, nullifying individual instinct. What works is to:

- Encourage the generation of several options; and
- Recognize the outlier points of view.

Encouraging several options

Much can be learnt from the behaviour of entrepreneurs because early entrepreneurs behave in a way that encourages a profuse number of alternatives. For example, the early entrepreneurs in any industry—be it telegraph, telephone, automotive or internet—were numerous in number and all operated on the multiple pathways available. These people were always frenetic and restless, busy trying to find new ways to tap the emerging industry. Over time, there was a shake-out, the survivors consolidated and grew with scale.

Those people behaved a bit like the way bees behave when looking for food. A typical bee colony can search up to 6 km from the hive. The bees do not have a 'seminar' on where to go for the food, they just send out scout bees to search the surrounding areas. When a scout bee finds a source of nectar, he returns and does a dance. Yes, a waggle dance, and believe it or not, the intensity of the dance is proportional to the richness of the nectar source he has found! Thereafter, the other bees join him in the journey back to that source. The colony has thus found a collectively brilliant solution to their problem of food!

Nature magazine (November 2005) reported the findings of scientists at Britain's University of Sheffield. They found that foraging ants place a tiny scent marker on branches that do not lead to a reward. This pheromone acts like a 'no entry' signal to other ants, telling them not to waste their time going down that route.

A former Ford CEO, Donald Peterson, explained how he brought the people factor into Ford management. Team participation was encouraged through facilitators whose task was to go around the table and ensure idea generation from everyone.

They had to encourage 'a wide array of alternatives when trying to solve a problem or make a decision'. With pride, he recalled that the hourly workers who built the 1984 Ford Tempo and Mercury Topaz offered more than 650 suggestions, three-quarters of which were accepted.

However, merely generating profuse alternatives does not work. Managers must train to listen to the outliers.

Listening to the outliers

The wisdom of crowds seems to be conditional to three dispositions.

First, that the opinions obtained are diverse; second, that they are obtained independent of each other; third, that there is a methodology to pull these individual and diverse opinions together into an average. If these three conditions are not met, James Surowiecki argues that the wisdom of the crowd would not have been captured. This sounds plausible.

Our social training is not strong with respect to listening. If we do listen, our training is to retain things selectively, especially those that are close to our own view. If we do not have a clear view, we tend to favour those that are clustered around a common point.

In short, the outlier views which are beyond the centre of the bell curve of opinion have a natural mortality. The wisdom of crowds, it would appear, lies in capturing these outliers (in statistics, an outlier is the data point that lies 'outside' the data spread) just as carefully as those that fall at the centre of the bell curve, because they influence the average.

There lies the importance of listening to diverse views in arriving at judgements. Listening requires training, listening carefully requires a lot of training. Nobody teaches you this, you learn it by yourself. This is done by livening up the business environment, and finding the 'space' to listen and watch as diligently as one works.

However, modern management dynamics tend not to make this probable. Even though managers constantly argue in favour of collective wisdom and team working, they do not have a way to extract the wisdom of their people at large, so they become dependent on experts. Expert opinion does have an invaluable role, but it has to be pooled with non-expert views to get the best value.

Managers who listen to the outliers will benefit rather than lose out.

A successful manager has to develop the ability to listen objectively; to listen seriously to diverse points of view expressed by people independently of one another, and integrate those diverse views into a coherent representation. This is easier said than done. I have had a brush with similar experiences, but they were not controlled experiments, nor conclusive.

Using salesmen's judgement

Many years ago, the task of turning around a loss-making dairy in Hindustan Lever fell upon my boss, Bipin Shah. I was assisting him as the marketing manager. One of the challenges was the balancing of wet milk supply from the cattle with milk powder product availability in the market. Buffaloes yield three-quarters of their annual milk between October and March, the peak being in January. The summer months are low production months for the animals. That is the time when the consumer would find milk in short supply, and would look to buy milk powder to bridge the gap.

For one in the dairy business, it was crucial to figure out how much milk to dry in the winter months and when to pack it for subsequent market sales. This required the factory to receive an accurate forecast of market sales each month, a daunting task for any sales manager.

About that time, I learnt of an idea to use the intuition and experience of frontline sales staff to forecast short-term sales. Briefly, the salesmen were asked to bet on a target sales number for their own territory. Let us assume that a realistic target for a territory was RT. If he bid realistically at RT and achieved it, then he would earn 100. If he under-balled by bidding 0.8 of RT to be sure to win the incentive, and he achieved it, he would get a disproportionately low prize of only 75. If he stretched within a plausible limit of RT say 1.1 times RT, then he would earn a disproportionately high reward of 120.

Thus a matrix was created on which each salesman bid to maximize his earnings within his own risk-taking capability. The scheme was successful in meeting its aims of using the frontline sales staff's intuition and smoothening out the factory cycle; for three running months, the actual and forecast matched within a bandwidth of 10 per cent. The negative was that it took too much ongoing effort for simple-minded grocery shop salesmen to comprehend the intricacies after the initial excitement of betting against themselves died down.

Judging company profits

A second experience is more recent.

I chair a company called Rallis, which is in the business of agricultural chemicals. The company had been through a rough time for some years. From 2003, there was quite a dramatic turnaround. The company posted excellent results for the year ending March 2005 under the able leadership of Managing Director Venkat Sohoni.

Early in the financial year, Venkat and I became keen to know what profit figure the combined wisdom of the Rallis employees pointed to for the year ending March 2006. This was curiosity, not any corporate planning, I should add! We wished to compare it with the management's business plan for the year. A profit target of Rs 51 crore had been set by the company leadership for the financial year.

A conference evening provided the opportunity to satisfy our curiosity as well as to introduce some light-heartedness.

We distributed a slip to each employee at a 120-strong conference, comprising diverse functions such as manufacturing, sales, research, accounts, purchase and administration. These were people who for the most part did not deal with corporate numbers and typically had a vision of their own function or area of responsibility. Many of them were pretty junior level staff, far removed from company financials.

The survey was based on the individual gut feeling of the people present, irrespective of their knowledge level or their management capability. The members were to write down *without any consultation or deep analysis* what they intuitively felt about how much profit the company could achieve in the year ending March 2006.

Their average came to Rs 49 crore with a distribution of 60 per cent of the people within a bandwidth Rs 45–53 crore. Another 20 per cent of the people came in as outliers at a lower band of Rs 35–45 crore and the last 20 per cent came in at a higher band of Rs 53–63 crore.

Their average at Rs 49 crore was quite startling to both of us, because the number they had intuitively mentioned was very close to the management's business plan of Rs 51 crore!

The actual results of the year ending March 2006 turned out to be Rs 45 crore! This actual was certainly not spot-on to the crowd's forecast of Rs 49 crore, but neither was it far out. Bear in mind the fact that the agrochemicals business can be notoriously volatile and uncertain, and that the participating people were the 'plain Joes' of the company.

The detergent that required knotted clothes

I learnt about the wisdom of listening carefully and patiently to the outliers when I was working in Hindustan Lever. I had joined as a management trainee in the computer systems department after turning down the blandishments of the marketing director to join his department. As an engineer by academic training, I was convinced that marketing was work of a lower order compared to computer programming, which incidentally in the late 1960s was a new and emerging profession. Its sheer novelty was, in my opinion, enough evidence of its superiority compared to visiting grocery stores to sell soaps and shampoos. My impressions were severely dented when I was packed off to work as a salesman and sales supervisor for about six months soon after joining. The logic was that I could not learn to write any credible software programmes for sales managers if I did not understand their work and role from the grassroots. At that time, it was an ordeal. In hindsight, it taught me the value of how to understand a market by meeting customers face-to-face.

Later in my career, I made a fetish of field travel. In any case, the company atmosphere for achieving success forced people to do so. This could involve conversations with twenty-five retailers each day on various subjects connected with the company's products—their perceptions of what the consumer likes or dislikes about our products, the quality of packaging, the relative promotional schemes run by the company and its competitors, the level of service at the shop and almost an endless array of subjects. In some ways it was quite tiresome and boring because there were logically just that many new things that retailers could state. The feeling would periodically grow that if you had heard the first five retailers, you had heard the lot. However, that excluded the outliers and would invariably give you a partial view, thus denying you the benefit of diversity and independence in the views to be collected. In fact, numerical market research too often masks this outlier viewpoint because the responses are encapsulated in the averages and the means.

In the mid-1970s, there was an amusing experience after the launch of a heavy duty detergent powder branded *OMO*. In Germany, the promise of this successful brand was presented on the packaging through the mnemonic of clothes knotted together. The advertising stated that this product could break through the most difficult stains in the most difficult places. You could see this for yourself by tying your dirty clothes into knots—the detergent would reach the tough spots inside the knot and do its cleaning job. The advertising tested well in the Indian research, the pack received the appropriate approvals in consumer tests and the product was test launched into the Goa market.

As I 'worked the outlets' in the weeks after launch, I felt good because retailers said nice things about the product, its sales and the customer perceptions. But a few outlier opinions from some retailers kept haunting me—the customer feedback that unless the clothes are tied into knots before immersion into the detergent solution, the product would not clean! This lack of comprehension startled me, but made me want to ignore them as unrepresentative; however, it could not be ignored. Later in the qualitative post-mortem market research, it did pop up!

The product had to be withdrawn in the months that followed but not merely because of this (brands fail for many reasons). It brought to me the value of listening carefully to diverse, independent views and to somehow aggregate these decentralized views into something meaningful.

How and when to step out of line

Habit patterns and ways of thinking become deeply established in organizations, and it becomes easier and more comforting to follow them than to cope with change, even when that change may represent freedom, achievement and success. Blind follower-ship of the crowd is not good, and creates the bonsai effect. Two animal experiments illustrate this dramatically—and it is amazing how often managers can simulate such behaviour.

An American naturalist, William Beebe of the early twentieth century, once came upon a huge circle of giant ants moving around in an apparently orderly fashion. The circle was as much as a quarter of a mile in circumference, no small circle indeed! He actually counted that it took each ant two-and-a-half hours to complete one circle. The ants went round and round 'blindly' following the one in front until they were all exhausted and died.

A French entomologist, Jean Henri Fabre, did an experiment with some caterpillars creating a similar situation. A group of them were led onto the rim of a tea cup so that the leader of the procession found himself nose to tail with the last caterpillar in the procession, forming a circle without a beginning or end. Through sheer force of habit, the ring of caterpillars instinctively circled the tea cup for seven days and seven nights until they died from exhaustion and starvation. Incidentally, there was an ample supply of food within visible distance, but not in the circle in which they were moving. The caterpillars moved around in procession until they all died!

Management books encourage managers to think out-of-the-box, step out of line, and do something different. All these are valid exhortations. Those who do not will atrophy or become ineffective. The problem that a manager faces is to decide when to follow the crowd and when to step out of line.

I have found four ideas that have provided me guidance to judge when to step out of line.

- ❖ The first is not to get into the analysis-paralysis mode or the mode of inaction, but to constantly nurture the bias for positive action
- ❖ The second is to avoid the assumption that it is only the leader who should think, and it is for the others to follow, even when their own thoughts are at variance
- ❖ The third is to trust one's own judgement and motives
- ❖ The last is to answer truthfully the question, 'Do you really care?'

Such ideas help a manager to periodically step out of line and look around. Is the line going where it is supposed to? Are there alternatives? In this way, the manager should be satisfied that he is not blindly following the crowd.

12

BIRTH OF THE BUTTERFLY
THE INEVITABLE PAIN OF CHANGE

Man's obsession with the butterfly

'What the caterpillar calls its end, the rest of the world calls the beginning of a butterfly,' said Lao Tzu. The Greeks believed that the soul left the human body in the form of a butterfly. French naturalist Marcel Roland said that butterflies give us 'solace for the pain of living'.

The Natural History Museum in London, a cathedral-like building, houses one of the world's largest collections of butterflies and moths. The collection is spread over six floors, and 30 million insects are held in 1,20,000 drawers. It was started with a bequest from William Rothschild, who is better remembered for his help in formulating the 1917 declaration by the Balfour government to work towards a Jewish homeland in Palestine. Less known is that he collected over 2.25 million butterflies and moths!

This deep obsession with butterflies is not hard to explain, given the extraordinary metamorphosis it signifies.

The 'extreme pain' when a caterpillar becomes a butterfly

The word metamorphosis in biology refers to the insect's life cycle, which sees a complete change of body form and appearance. These changes are specific and recognizable.

This process is controlled by a balance of hormones. Companies too have 'hormones' which control the change processes in the organization.

The butterfly starts life as a tiny egg; the adult female lays eggs among leaves that are rich in the nutrients required by the insect. The egg hatches and there emerges a caterpillar, which marks the second stage.

The caterpillar begins to feed and grow. The joints between its body segments distend and this activates hormones. The caterpillar huffs and puffs as its skin splits and the worm-like insect steps out of its skin. It begins eating again, non-stop, until the process is repeated, in all, five times. The animal puts on an enormous amount of weight during these 'feasting' sessions. During this time, it gains 3,000 times its original hatching weight—the equivalent of a 4-kg baby becoming 12,000 kg among humans!

In the third stage, it becomes a pupa. To a bird or a lizard, pupae are a convenience food—nicely packaged, immobile, and full of nutrients, like the original energy bar!

Inside the pupa, a remarkable transformation happens during which the caterpillar's cells and tissues rearrange themselves to form the adult butterfly.

A very lyrical description by Vladimir Nabakov, author of *Lolita*, appears in his speech at Cornell about the transition of a caterpillar.

The wing disks grow the antennae needed to suck up nectar. The simple eye dissolves and in its place a new and complex eye develops. Legs lengthen and add segments.

In stage four, it is almost ready to emerge. Soon this beauty emerges with its delicate and gorgeously covered wings.

One can easily imagine why man has been infatuated with the butterfly for centuries. It is a story of transformation, pain and beauty, all rolled into one 'case study'.

If a caterpillar had the brain of a human, would it sign up for the stress of such a painful transformation?

In organizations also, pain during change is inevitable; however, it need not be gut-wrenching, as some leaders seem to assume. In reality, more often than not, less pain means more change.

Less pain means more change

Every manager knows deep down that there can be no organizational change without pain. Through the 1980s and 1990s, the management world was inundated with exhortations about change management. Jargon like creative destruction, business process re-engineering and liberation management mesmerized managers, who lapped up with great enthusiasm the calls 'to tear down the past and build from ground zero'.

Whether those authors intended it or not, readers got the message that transformation without acute pain may not be effective. Some of the iconic leaders in those days operated in harsh, gut-wrenching ways; they were idolized for quite some time for their success.

There grew to be a strong belief that the more the pain, the more effective the transformation would be. This was akin to the assumption that the more bitter a medicine, the more effective it might be in solving the medical problem. This is, of course, not true.

However, many stories of success were reported and they

involved a lot of pain—like the one about Al 'Chainsaw' Dunlap.

He was a much acclaimed leader in the 1980s and 1990s. His success in transformation was chronicled in magazines and books. Al 'Chainsaw' Dunlap was a very visible business leader. He assumed leadership of a major American paper products company called Scott Paper in 1994; he immediately fired 11,000 employees and sold off several businesses.

He had said in a speech, 'Shareholders are *the* number one constituency. Show me a company which lists six or seven constituencies and I'll show you a mismanaged company.'

The changes at Scott Paper unfolded like a military plan. Within twenty months, Al 'Chainsaw' tripled the market value and sold Scott Paper to Kimberley Clark. He himself exited with $100 million in incentives.

Thus the shareholders of Scott Paper and Al Dunlap himself became rich. However, the employees of the company were devastated. They saw Dunlap as a ruthless and self-centred leader, who led by fear and exploitation. Dunlap's effectiveness as a leader is held out these days as an example of how not to lead!

Change is a huge mindset issue; it is human nature to want to be transformed without suffering. It is assumed that if you explain why something has to be done, people will feel convinced and accept the change.

Change is risky

The truth is that knowing what is to be done does not lead to action. Preparedness for pain, courage and motivation to undertake the journeys are all essential before there can be positive action. This requires a social process. Transformation leaders have to face up to two issues.

First, the process they embark upon will be painful to themselves and to their entire organization. Second, the journey is inherently risky for their reputation. This latter point exacerbates the personal pain for the leader.

The leader of change becomes the symbol of the change. He may be a hero or a zero, depending on the outcome and the feelings of those who 'judge' him and his actions.

There are many stories from the corporate world which demonstrate the risks that leaders have to undertake. It took some guts on Managing Director Dr Jamshed Irani's part to deliver a message to the highly respected and iconic chairman, J.R.D. Tata, 'Unless we modernize our plant, both you and I will stand at the gates of the company selling tickets for a steel museum.'

As Dr Irani often recounts, J.R.D. Tata took the message seriously and encouraged his team to develop the modernization plan that changed Tata Steel. Was he sticking his neck out? Of course he was. Jamshed Irani led Tata Steel's transformation from a sleepy, old-world steel producer into a lean and flexible organization through the 1990s.

Jamshed Irani recalled another incident. For long, Tata Steel had an agreement with trade unions that, by right, any employee could nominate one son or any dependent for employment when he retired. In 1995, when he was explaining to unions the urgency of sensibly trimming the workforce, one employee shouted that that all this is fine, but the company had taken away the jobs of their sons.

'I am not worried about your son's job, I am worried about your own job and mine,' responded Irani. It was a risky repartee in a large meeting with the union and employees, but it was essential. According to Irani, that incident was a defining moment for Tata Steel.

Another example that I have witnessed is that of Tata Chemicals, which recruited Prasad Menon as managing director in 2000. He joined the company amidst difficult circumstances. The company had earlier been exceptionally successful as India's leading manufacturer of soda ash, and had been a darling of the stock markets. As the economy opened up during the 1990s and import tariffs came down, the competitiveness of Tata Chemicals became a serious issue. It recorded a quarterly loss for the first time in 2000.

Prasad realized that he was an 'outsider' in a very traditional company that had been led by charismatic leaders for a long time. He did not have the luxury of settling in gradually and sending messages to his team in a languorous and calibrated manner. He prepared a crisp communication, held open houses and answered the barrage of questions from a shocked management team in a transparent way. He took the big risk of telling the facts as they were; he earnestly sought managers' ideas on how to stem the losses and put the company back on its feet. After being viewed initially with some considerable suspicion and curiosity, Prasad survived the risks and got managers to put their hearts into positive action. By the time he moved on to become the managing director of another Tata company in 2006, he had emerged as a respected and loved leader within Tata Chemicals. In a very intelligent way, he chose the 'reduced pain' alternative to 'gut-wrenching' change management.

The case of Subir Raha

During the first half of 2006, the Indian media carried prominent stories about the stressed relationship between Subir Raha, the chairman of a public sector company, ONGC (Oil and Natural Gas Corporation) and the ministry of petroleum and natural gas. Raha's five-year term as chairman was due for review and renewal in May 2006. The management fraternity was stunned to learn that Raha's term would not be renewed. Thereafter, this prominent business leader, who was considered successful in the popular perception, slipped away quietly from the public spotlight.

What happened is a complex story and it is not the intention to delve in these paragraphs into the rights and wrongs of any party, or the merits of the government's decision. The story is being narrated purely from the perspective of this chapter—how leadership and change are inherently risky.

Subir Raha studied electronics engineering at Jadavpur University, Kolkata. At the age of twenty-one, he joined Indian Oil Corporation (IOC) as a management trainee. In those days, the management trainee cadre of IOC was considered to be quite prestigious. In twenty-eight years, Raha rose rapidly through the ranks of IOC; he became whole-time director in 1998. Three years later, at the age of fifty-two, Raha was appointed the chairman of ONGC. By the standards of careers in public undertakings, Raha's would qualify as quite stellar.

Although IOC is the country's largest company by sales turnover, ONGC is by far the biggest in assets and profits. For fifty years, ONGC had been a 'successful' PSU, considering that it was in a complex and risky business of great long-term importance to the nation. However, it was a monopoly, so it carried the accumulated scleroses of such a status.

In the perception of those who were knowledgeable, it was bloated. Over the decades, some ministers and administrative secretaries had negatively influenced the corporate independence of ONGC. The company's directors had built strong satrapies, which operated in silos. There was not much of team spirit or corporate alignment of departmental goals. Barring one, all previous full-term chairmen of ONGC had been inducted from outside the company. Obviously things needed to be changed to the new and emerging market-oriented circumstances.

There must have been recognition of these sclerotic problems. A firm of management consultants had, in fact, been mandated to study the issues and make a set of turnaround recommendations as early as 1997. However, the implementation of the recommendations certainly involved changing the internal power equations, disturbing the established bastions of powerful satraps, and realigning the leadership to a common and market-oriented business goal. To the observer, in 2001, when Raha assumed charge, ONGC looked like a candidate for a speedy turnaround, or else it was headed for the intensive care unit.

Subir Raha had worked with several government secretaries during his career. He had built the reputation of being a tough, plain-speaking and honest leader with a zest to try new solutions, a trait that had long ago been killed amongst most PSU managers. When the petroleum secretary recommended Raha for the ONGC chairmanship, these factors must have influenced the selection panel.

Whatever the internal issues, from an outsider's perspective, for the first four years, Raha had a good run. He seemed to enjoy the full confidence of the subsequent petroleum secretaries, V.N. Kaul and B.K. Chaturvedi. He converted the consultants' report into a strategic plan and got approval from his board as well as his ministry. The company and its subsidiary, ONGC Videsh, did 'unusual' deals when viewed by PSU standards. Over thirty properties in fifteen countries were negotiated in multi-billion dollar deals involving big cash outlays and proportionate risks. A joint venture company called Mangalore Refineries and Petroleum Limited (MRPL) was acquired in 2003. At the time of the takeover by ONGC, the MRPL stock price had sunk to six rupees and the annual loss was Rs 430 crore. Within the very first year, the company was turned around to profit of Rs 450 crore and to the point of being able to declare a dividend. Of course, as always happens, several factors contributed to the rapid turnaround; Raha himself would not claim for himself all the credit for this achievement. However, as chairman, he certainly carried the risks of *not* turning it around!

Throughout this period of four years, Raha's media profile

had become larger-than-life. He was required to make public announcements about his company. He was a regular speaker at public events; he received several awards, and became an office-bearer of prestigious professional bodies. As happens always with such situations, within the company and the petroleum ministry, there were three classes of eager watchers— grateful admirers (the 20 per cent who felt that he had restored a sense of hope about an assured future for ONGC), ardent critics (the 20 per cent who felt that he was messing around with established power centres, and was not sufficiently deferential to officialdom), and the fence-sitters (who were waiting and watching which way the cookie would crumble).

By 2005, some of the key players in this organizational drama had changed; detractors started to take a negative note of this larger-than-life chairman, who was so strongly in the public glare. Of course, Subir Raha, like all leaders, must have had his rough edges and weaknesses, and these became useful levers to start the process of taming him.

By May 2006, his contract came up for renewal. The issue was: should the contract of a competent turnaround manager be renewed or should the term of an unconventional and somewhat maverick PSU chairman be elegantly closed? The risks he had taken would come home to roost. The government decided not to renew Raha's term.

In the public perception, he had 'lost'.

In his own view, he had not lost. After all, he stood for something, he wanted to do certain things, and he felt he should get support for his plans for India's largest PSU. Otherwise, he would have been yet another chairman, successfully staying the course of an uneventful tenure. That was not what Subir Raha set out to be; in fact, if he were inclined that way, he would not have accepted the chairmanship in the first place.

Looking me straight in the eye, Subir Raha said, 'I felt

satisfied that I helped to save India's largest PSU. I helped to restore pride and hope in the company. In the process, if I became a sort of victim, so be it. It would have been terrible to have "happily" retired after a second term from a definitely doomed PSU.'

If it is essential for change to be accompanied by pain for both the organization and the leader—and if gut-wrenching pain is the less preferred option, then there must be some ways to achieve the 'reduced pain' alternative. There are three ways worth remembering:

❋ Understand the code of change
❋ Rearrange the existing pieces
❋ Slow down to reach quicker.

These three principles are illustrated in the transformation experiences of HLL and Tata Sons, both of which I could observe from close quarters as their respective leaders set about their tasks. The narratives that follow show how contrasting the approaches can be, yet they convey how big change was brought about.

They exemplify how to rock the boat, but not sink it.

The transformation at Hindustan Lever

Hindustan Lever was always the premier consumer goods company in India for as long as I can remember. It was considered a training ground for business leaders long before the management institutes came up. For marketing, distribution and management techniques, HLL was iconic.

In 1967, the ten-rupee share was quoted at Rs 12.50; from a stock market perspective, it was a good consumer goods company, but by no means great. There was nothing spectacular or exemplary about its technology or growth, in spite of its very high reputation for ethics and for training high quality managers.

Some of my contemporaries left after some time because they felt that the company was headed nowhere and its business of consumer products was not relevant to the nation! That view was a reflection of the inward-looking political and social ethos in the country at that time. Thereafter, for several years from 1973 onwards, the company notched up an impressive performance.

During my thirty-one years at HLL from the late 1960s to the late 1990s, I witnessed five chairmen—leaders who seemed to prepare employees for one pain or uncertainty after another. They did not tear down the company's heritage, disown the past or do any of those things that could confuse employees.

In fact, each chairman seemed to calibrate what was required as a continuum of what his predecessor had done; they seemed to run the company almost as part of a relay race team. Each of them had his flaws and critics, but they advanced the company's change agenda. It was also not as though the company had no crises or huge problems during those thirty years.

I joined during the last stretch of the Prakash Tandon years. Those were the days when price and distribution controls dominated administrative policies.

On one occasion, Prakash Tandon was in London for long-term plan discussions in the mid-1960s. An exasperated and impatient Unilever Chairman Lord Cole asked him why he could not exert his influence on the Indian government more effectively to free the business from obstructive controls. After proffering a predictable set of arguments which did not seem to satisfy George Cole, Prakash Tandon said, 'George, my influence in Delhi is not very different from yours at Whitehall. I have the same problems in Delhi as you have in changing the views and policies of the Harold MacMillan government.' The conversation apparently quickly reverted to soaps and vanaspati markets!

His successor was Vasant Rajadhyaksha, a US-trained chemical engineer, soft-spoken and ever so gentle.

He was only forty-five when he took over from the legendary Prakash Tandon as the company chairman in 1968. He found that much of the company's sales were under price control and he could not wish away the public perception of consumer products being low technology. He must have thought of and tried a series of measures to overcome the obstacles of price control. Not being successful, he resigned himself to slow down and work at the root cause of the problem, i.e., communicating continuously with officials at Delhi and trying to persuade them to do what was good for the consumer.

Rajadhyaksha did two notable things. First, he took the tough and possibly frustrating path of building a strong view in Delhi about the counterproductive nature of price controls. Second, he built on the strong technical cadre of the company. Based on the company's chemical engineering capabilities, he advocated a very contrarian view in a most reluctant Unilever that diversifying into chemicals would be good for all stakeholders in the long run.

The technical director of his board was T. Thomas, who recounted a meeting that both of them had with the Unilever chairman at Singapore. At this meeting, they proposed that HLL enter the field of fertilizers.

'There was little enthusiasm on Unilever's part, nor was there an outright rejection. Dr Woodruffe, the chairman of Unilever, was probably sympathetic,' was what T. Thomas recalled.

Within HLL, there was a perception of stagnancy and huge constraints while Rajadhyaksha would be on a flight ever so often to Delhi to explain his viewpoint. He must have been successful in nudging the rigid views prevalent. Five years later, he himself retired early to join the Indian Planning Commission, perhaps to work at changing views from within rather than from outside.

Another chemical engineer T. Thomas, who was far more aggressive, grasped the baton. Within the Unilever world, finance and marketing men got the key senior jobs, so HLL was already looking different in so far as another technical manager was assuming the company's leadership. Thomas scored two early wins based on Thomas' own aggressive follow-up strategy.

Within a year after he became chairman, HLL's product prices were decontrolled, and some years later, Unilever approved a chemical complex to be set up at Haldia.

It was during Thomas' tenure that the company implemented a major new chemical project at Haldia. This factory would make a chemical called STPP, the raw material required to make Surf detergent. Until then, the company had been buying this chemical from vendors, now it would be manufacturing it. This was a brand new activity for the company, requiring a different order of skills. Appropriately experienced senior managers were recruited, including one at the board level. However, existing chemical engineers were not overlooked; they also got suitable opportunities. Some of them like Susim Datta, Krishnan Nayar, and Gurdeep Singh all went on to occupy high positions in later years.

Thomas drove hard for cost-cutting; a sort of early *le cost killer*, a label acquired by Carlos Ghosn at Nissan, Japan, in the early 2000s. I was a young sales manager in Mumbai and I recall that there would be a control even on the number of newspapers ordered in the office, on the overtime paid to staff and other such items. Further, the company had a very difficult union situation, and this was often opposed to new cost initiatives or changes.

I remember an unfortunate episode around this time. The sales invoicing and accounting was done in the four metro cities at branch offices by highly paid clerical staff using comptometers and other manual methods prevalent in those days. There was a fire in the LIC building where the HLL Chennai branch office was located, destroying old records and some property, mercifully not any human life. It was a huge setback for the company as well as the staff. Crisis and necessity, it is said, are the mother of invention. This was exemplified in the events that followed.

The dejected office staff now had no office. They sat on the Marina beach with Marketing Director Jagdish Chopra discussing how to restore operations. While all the records of distributors and invoices at the office had been destroyed, a large part of the same data existed at the depots spread out over the southern region. Those documents could surely be used to reconstruct past records! They hit upon the idea of outsourcing the task of invoicing and cash collection to the company's third party depots.

Jagdish Chopra accepted the idea, which had originated from the staff, who knew the operations more intimately than anyone else. The board of the company used the opportunity to give the clarion call to restore normality with speed.

There were three notable features: the idea was born out of necessity; it came from the staff themselves; it was not only innovative, but it also cut costs significantly. A triple whammy!

Outsourcing was not a word invented in those days, so it was an innovative idea in its time. Over time, nationally, the entire invoicing and cash activity was shifted to the forty-odd third-party clearing and forwarding agents' depots. This changed the efficiency and cost structure in a permanent way. Its implementation involved hardship for many and invited some internal criticism, but the pain was a contained one in an overall sense.

As part of his change agenda, Thomas initiated two communications that were both far-reaching: first, in the hostile environment of the 1970s, he kept communicating that the import substitution research and development efforts of the company were extremely relevant for the nation; the second was a response to the draconian Foreign Exchange Regulation Act of 1973 (FERA) which mandated most foreign companies to reduce the foreign shareholding to 40 per cent unless they met certain criteria.

He mounted a campaign that if Unilever's shareholding came down to 40 per cent, it would be detrimental to every stakeholder. The latter was a difficult view to propagate, given the hostility to foreign companies. Even Coca-Cola and IBM quit the country at that time. Though he did a quite a lot of groundwork before the FERA issue could be resolved fully, Thomas moved to London to join the Unilever board.

His successor was Ashok Ganguly, who had risen from the research side of the business, followed by manufacturing. He pursued the unfinished agendas left by Thomas and tasted some early successes.

The first was when he overcame the new obstacles and finally secured the 51 per cent shareholding for Unilever.

The second was when he drove HLL R&D into new vistas of relevant and value creating technology development. Ashok Ganguly was proud of applying science to common products and brooked no humour questioning the association of soaps with technological accomplishment. He was once asked by the Cabinet Secretary in a somewhat derisive way, 'How long will you keep making soap?'

'As long as the Cabinet Secretary needs a bath,' was his repartee. By now, the Rs 12.50 dull share had become an icon with over fifteen years of sustained growth and success. Ashok Ganguly became a very visible business leader with quite a few accolades and a Padma Bhushan to his credit.

However, he could not be complacent. He turned over the rocks and saw the threat of low-cost detergents. The HLL response has been narrated elsewhere in this book.

He also had to gear up the company to export in order to

fulfil an obligation imposed on it under FERA. It was in this role that I came to be closely associated with Ganguly's drive and zest, his ability to focus on issues and 'to inspire ordinary people to do extraordinary things'.

Dealing with non-traditional products was not an activity in which the company had great expertise. It was most painful for soap sellers to learn and manage carpet-making or garments marketing. He led the company to do all this and more by rearranging company resources and redirecting management talent.

The stage seemed well set for his successor Susim Datta, who rode the tide of liberalization in 1991. He recognized that production capacity would no more be a constraint and progressively, competition would intensify. Rapid quality improvement would be essential to survive. How do you dislodge a whole lot of managers from the belief that 'our quality is good enough'?

Susim Datta too had risen from the technical side of the business and had a very good sense of how to dovetail manufacturing with other functions to meet the new challenges. He used the advent of liberalization to prepare the company for pain all over again. The core of the business was strengthened through major quality initiatives.

The boundaries of the company were extended through an array of mergers. Some might have thought that mergers were overdone during his tenure. It is my view that he personally favoured fewer and better targeted acquisitions, but he did whatever had to be done.

Earlier in his career, he had consolidated the chemicals business, which had by now become large and profitable. Over the years, he had helped build a strong fertilizer brand, Paras, in a market where fertilizers were treated like a commodity. Datta felt that the marketing skills of HLL managers could be leveraged to 'market' fertilizer rather than merely distribute them as others were doing. Again, it is an example of using the existing people and cultural skill sets to effect transformation in another area.

The HLL story exemplifies the point about continuous preparation for risk, managing the pain and about leadership being institutionalized. These leaders are entirely different personalities, but they ran their laps in a way which seemed part of a larger relay race for the good of all stakeholders. The influence of each leader in the transformation of the caterpillar into a beautiful butterfly was remarkable and offered a lot to mull over and reflect upon.

Long-remembered leaders manage the pain by perceiving their role as part of a larger process; they are not the process itself. They get to run with the baton for a few laps of a relay race.

As Lord Leverhulme, founder of the soap empire of modern-day Unilever said, 'The road maker is the best anonymous servant of humanity. He drives a great broad thoroughfare from town to town, and for generations, people travel over the road, with their hopes and fears, with all their cares and joys, never once asking who it were that made their way easier for them.'

The transformation of Tata Sons

The way the Tata transformation has been implemented during the Ratan Tata years provides instructive insights.

The Tata Group is over 140 years in age. Some of its ninety-odd operating companies may qualify as the oldest in the Bombay Stock Exchange still with the original promoters.

At the height of the second world war in January 1944, *Fortune* magazine of the USA carried an eleven-page feature on the Tata Group. It began with the words, 'To the Indian, the natively created House of Tata represents a source of national pride, a signpost on the rocky road toward an

industrial future.' It concluded, 'The future of the House of
Tata depends entirely on the future of India...Indeed, there is
a growing consciousness among Tata's management that
postwar prosperity for the House will be impossible unless a
concerted effort is made to raise the standard of living in
India.' Therefore, Tata is a unique case to study when speaking
about longevity, change and transformation.

I have had the privilege of sharing a small part of the
journey in recent times. My experiences have not been mellowed
by the passage of time and reflection. Therefore, in the interest
of authenticity, I wish to rely more on published accounts and
the words of Chairman Ratan Tata to illustrate a few points
about Tata's change management.

In 1983, Ratan Tata prepared a strategic plan for the
group to take it into new areas of business, including high
technology areas. In 1985, he had said in an interview to
Update magazine, 'Where we lost out was that there was no
central focusing. Decisions on entering new areas fell into the
priorities of operating companies.'

Therefore, it was only after Ratan Tata was appointed
group chairman in 1991 that he could prepare the ground to
implement his ideas for the transformation of the group. Since
1991, the Tata Group has entered and established companies
in businesses such as telecom, automotive design services,
automotive components, passenger cars, advanced plastics,
insurance and so on.

Because the companies were a loose confederation in those
early days, it was very difficult for him to implement his ideas
without first welding them together into some form of cohesion.

This had to be done without diluting the independence of
each company and its board. In other words, the challenge was
to create a unity within the diversity. Company independence
was (and is) a very key element of the Tata DNA. Ratan Tata
understood this and to him, it was clear that you could not run

Tata Group like an IBM, Unilever or GE. He had to figure out a unique path for its transformation.

There was no rigid programme to be implemented like a military plan. Each idea was debated, modified, tested and then rolled out. If that took some time, so be it. Enough time was invested in securing the buy-in of the people, so that the change would be consistent with the organization's 'code of change'. When a leader does this, it takes more time initially, and outsiders criticize the 'slow' pace of change. However, the change turns out to be more robust and durable.

A key platform was the adoption of the Malcolm Baldrige framework, branded as the Tata Business Excellence Model (TBEM). A Tata Sons director, Jim Setna, led this movement initially and with great distinction; subsequent to his retirement, the leadership was ably provided by Dr Jamshed Irani.

By now, every group company is a signatory to a formal agreement with Tata Sons. This TBEM platform became a great unifier of the till then disparate companies—it has provided a rallying post. TBEM assembles about 600 senior directors and officers of the companies twice a year to either celebrate achievement of milestones or to debate and figure out new goals and challenges in the excellence journey.

Each company has signed a formal agreement with Tata Sons, which owns and promotes the Tata trademark and brand name. The agreement allows the company to use the Tata mark, which is a sort of badge of honour for every Tata employee. However, the company in turn has to implement mandatory processes for business excellence, and be rated by assessors who are external to the company. All companies and their employees have to sign a code of conduct, a rare practice among many companies at the time of its implementation.

Reflecting on his ten years of chairmanship and changing the group, Ratan Tata wrote in R.M. Lala's *The Creation of Wealth* (Penguin India, 2004):

Broadly the plan was to critically look at various companies through a group mechanism which in fact did not exist. And so the Group Executive Office (GEO) was born. The intention was that the GEO would consist of a group of executive directors of Tata Sons who would have the responsibility of overseeing the performance of various operating companies. The GEO would also look critically at restructuring the group by way of mergers, acquisitions of our core businesses, as also divestments in companies that were in businesses that we did not consider to be our core businesses or where our market position was not predominant...

Other important 'welding' mechanisms that were introduced after I took over were:

1. The creation of a common, unified brand with a common logo which would be used and displayed by all the companies
2. A code of conduct was written to embody the value systems within the Tata group, which had never been codified before
3. A set of operating requirements for companies that use the brand.

All these are major changes for an organization to undertake which has been traditional and in a manner has had no major internally imposed change or restructuring in its entire history. Therefore, any view that this change could be overnight, I think, would be erroneous. Quite often, when you are undertaking major changes, there is a tendency to have what appears to be a negative effect for a period of time, following which there is an upturn and the benefits of what you have done to be realized...

Therefore the task was to transform this loose confederation into a synergetic group of companies with a unified direction...it has been a hard and sometimes unrewarding experience. All I can say is that I have genuinely worked hard to create an integrated, strong, well performing Tata group driven and motivated to be predominant in the

business areas in which we operate in the Indian scene and,
it is hoped, overseas.

The lessons

I would like to recall the three ways that were mentioned
earlier in this chapter about how to reduce the pain of
change—understanding the code of change, rearranging the
existing pieces, and slowing to reach quicker. What do these
mean and how are they manifested in the two cases above?

Understanding the code of change

In 1994, I attended the advanced management programme at
Harvard Business School. Michael Beer, who taught
organizational development, was a very passionate teacher,
and his face would go all red as he emoted the roles that were
being discussed! I was very taken up with Michael's way of
teaching and his ideas, and became an avid reader of his fine
book, *The Critical Path to Corporate Renewal*.

At the same time, I also got to know a young upcoming
Indian professor, Nitin Nohria. In subsequent years, I interacted
with Nitin, especially as he came to be associated with teaching
an advanced management programme for Tatas and the All
India Management Association.

Michael Beer and Nitin Nohria jointly authored a piece in
the *Harvard Business Review* in mid-2000. They expressed a
view about leaders that in their rush to change their
organizations, managers end up with a huge number of
initiatives. They get mesmerized with an enormous menu of
tools and experiences, and these result in an overload of
initiatives. Implementing all of this, in fact, confuses managers,
and rather than lessen the pain, the change programme ends
up in a muddle.

They expressed the view that leaders need to crack the
code of change.

Every company has its own code of change, a little like the number to open the combination lock, which protects that company from change. If a leader can crack the code of change for his company, then he can minimize the pain by rearranging resources, just as the caterpillar does to become a butterfly.

The key task of a leader is to watch, listen, analyse, reflect and in doing so, try and crack the unique code of change of the organization he is trying to transform.

Both the HLL and Tata stories illustrate this in parts.

Rearrange the existing pieces

A positive way to reduce the pain of change is continual renewal rather than occasional overhauls. Let me use an example.

I live in a flat in a reasonably well-maintained building which is over 100 years old, a grade II heritage building. The façade is largely in line with the original because we are able to compare it with some old photographs. The interiors are mixed in the sense that electric and telephone wires, air conditioners, false ceilings and modern sofas coexist with original wooden flooring, Italian marble panels, and very high ceilings.

There has been transformation over the century, and it was achieved by keeping the nice parts of the past, adding new things from the contemporary and developing a character which is distinctive to this building. Most of us would refer to this as evolutionary change.

On either side of our plot are two similar plots; the original builder had constructed three identical buildings in 1904. One was razed to the ground some fifteen years ago: a twenty-storey modern highrise came up in its place. On the other side stands the original, regrettably in a state of relative dilapidation.

Like buildings, companies also change through constant upgradation and renewals. That is a less painful way to achieve transformation. The equivalent of furniture, flooring, windows and ceilings in a company situation are its people, their ways of working together, their values and how they are organized.

Just as a building can be transformed, companies can be renewed with less pain by using the existing resources in different and new ways. The leader must carefully consider how to use current parts of the organization, how to recombine them for a new use, and at what past elements he can redeploy and reuse.

This is a less disruptive way to change. This point too comes out in both the examples mentioned above.

Slowing to reach quicker

The leader does have a dilemma about how to pace the change agenda. If you move too fast, you get into trouble; if you move too slowly, you get into trouble!

In my experience, the issue is not one of judging the right speed in isolation; it is an issue of matching the speed with the code. Once that is done, it is easier to judge the level of pain that can be tolerated. It is not necessary to operate at that maximum level of pain all the time, as some might suggest.

Both the Tata and HLL example show how the speed of change should be seen in a context and not in isolation of the background of the company and its culture.

Unilever had announced its *Path to Growth* in 1999, which was to last till 2004. This strategy and its execution did not work well, as reported by the company. The targets were not met, the management was tired; finally, the top management and structure was reorganized once more in 2005. The event is too recent to view dispassionately, but it certainly bore all the signs of an initiative overload and organizational fatigue.

I came across another relevant story, this one from corporate America.

Arthur Martinez was the leader called in around 1992 to turn around Sears, the great American chain. After a glorious history during the 1970s and 1980s, Sears had lost its prime position to new and aggressive entrants like Wal-Mart. One can imagine how much pressure there might have been on Martinez to deliver quickly.

That is what he set out to do. For two years till 1994, he embarked on a blitzkrieg of actions. He announced the closing of the Sears catalogue, the launch of five strategic initiatives, the closure of 113 stores with consequent downsizing and all sorts of things that left the company's people quite breathless.

He then declared his turnaround complete, and announced the next phase of 'real' transformation. These waves carried on till 1998, by when the system was frayed and people were tired. All the initial signs of success started to vanish. Around 1998, sales actually declined. By the next year, a number of other factors also conspired. The turnaround faltered and Arthur Martinez stepped down in 1999.

The protagonists of maximum pain come from the school that time is not on your side and that the competition is moving fast. This is true but with two cautions.

Firstly, the organization (people, systems, culture) has a fairly defined capacity for change, though elastic within limits. This capacity is notionally visible, a bit like the red zone on the fuel meter of the car. You cannot operate at that level all the time, you might touch it sometimes. Secondly, if the people who have to implement the change look tired and incapable of undertaking the next wave of change, you know you have an overload.

'It is when you are in a rush that you have to slow down,' says a Korean proverb.

The leader needs a way to see beyond the obvious so that he can feel and sense what is going on in the organization. The next section deals with this aspect.

First, develop huge 'feelers' as the cave cricket does so that you can reach out and sense far beyond your immediate surroundings what exactly is going on.

Second, listen to the soft, barely audible signals just outside the 'normal' hearing range, the 'infra-sound' like the pigeon. It contains messages.

Third, beware of your own power. Beware of being so obsessed with your own intelligence like the vervet monkey that you foolishly fail to interpret what you have sensed and heard. Power breeds folly.

The key is to sense, listen and feel so that you can crack the code of change and rearrange the resources of the company to suit that code—as the Hindustan Lever and Tata examples demonstrate. It is indeed the way in which the caterpillar metamorphoses into a beautiful butterfly.

SECTION V

INTUITION THROUGH PERCEIVING
BEYOND THE OBVIOUS

Knowing your own darkness is the best method for dealing with the darknesses of other people.

—Carl Gustav Jung

13

ANTENNAE OF THE
CAVE CRICKET
SENSING AND TOUCHING

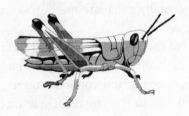

The benefits of disproportionately long antennae

For animals, uncertainty is a way of life. Animals never take survival for granted. So far as they are concerned, life is a tough grind, they are always vulnerable. Threats to survival are ever-present. For animals, there is no circumstance or time when they can be complacent.

From birth through adolescence, each species has figured out survival mechanisms to keep predators at bay. During adulthood, the challenge is to eat without being eaten.

Human beings are different; they get complacent very easily. Leaders avert this by being sensitive to the environment and adapting constantly. They sense and feel what is around them.

How do they do this?

Leaders develop enormously long sensors that read signals far beyond their immediate surroundings. This enables them to feel and touch what is going on, giving them a chance to adapt—like the cave cricket.

Crickets are jumping insects with wings that overlap each other on top of the back resembling a man with his arms slung over his back rather than hanging loose by his side. There are many types of crickets, but all of them produce those well-known chirps and songs akin to the sound produced by running a thumbnail through a comb or rubbing a file against the edge of a piece of metal—they do it by rubbing their forewings together. The rate of chirping increases when it gets warmer and decreases when it gets cooler. In one variety of crickets, you can actually calculate the outside temperature by counting its chirping rate.

Only males have the ability to produce this chirping sound. Again, the males emit different types of chirping for different signals; for instance, one sound connotes aggressiveness, while another is a sexual call to the female. These facts suggest that the cricket is quite sensitive to its environment.

While most crickets are outdoor insects, an incredible 200 species of a type called cave cricket live deep in caves where light never reaches. In this dark and inhospitable environment, cave crickets encounter extreme conditions.

They have minute eyes or are even eyeless. Unlike the land crickets, they cannot fly. They spend their entire lives underground, though their distant ancestors must have lived on the surface. They may well feel very vulnerable in such hostile surroundings.

Think about how an eyeless, cave-bound cricket finds food. Do you know they have 'feelers' or antennae up to four times the length of their body? Using these long feelers, cave crickets navigate their environment and find food such as bat droppings, hibernating butterflies and fungi. It is by the dexterous use of these extra long antennae that they survive the extreme conditions they encounter.

For many species, adapting to a hostile environment like extreme heat or cold, brightness or darkness, dryness or moistness, also poses a challenge. For another species, a metamorphosis from one form to another can cause stress and, therefore, vulnerability. The hormones and the resources of the animal adjust to such extremes and species evolve in an adaptive way.

What 'long feelers' mean

When an animal is faced with difficult circumstances, it rearranges its internal resources while watching and adapting to the external environment.

Organizational change too means that there will be a rearrangement of the resources and 'hormones' of the company; and that the organization is hugely vulnerable to predators and other threats during the transition. Under such situations, change managers and transformational leaders need to develop the equivalent of 'feelers' which are four times the length of their normal attention span.

It is but natural that the chief executive is faced with doing many things simultaneously, and sometimes even in contradictory ways.

For instance, he and the leadership team have to reach outwards, while simultaneously getting the employees to focus on the internal tasks. How does the organization survive during these vulnerable periods? The organization needs three things such as turnaround situations, mergers and industry downturns.

❁ First, it is essential for the leadership to reach out and respond to the prevailing environment. The leadership has to be aware and sensitive constantly

❋ Second, it is the time for the top team to unite internally and set aside differences, which are inevitable in any organization

❋ Third, most of the people in the company must concentrate and focus on the tasks at hand while only a few are outwardly focussed.

Reaching out

I witnessed how T. Thomas, the former chairman of Hindustan Lever reached out and established a network to deal with the issues he faced. One such issue concerned the Unilever-HLL relationship soon after he was appointed chairman of Hindustan Lever in the early 1970s.

When Hindustan Lever's profitability was seen to be steadily sliding down and heading for an all-time low in the late 1960s, people in Unilever started to take a diminishing interest in HLL's affairs. By 1973, all this had created an attitude of benign neglect towards the Indian operation.

Neither Prakash Tandon nor Vasant Rajadhyaksha faced total ruin of the company through price control, which reached disastrous proportions following the oil shock of 1972 and the subsequent inflation. There was nothing anyone in Unilever could do for HLL. Over the next ten years, the Indian company did establish relative independence while still retaining its links with Unilever.

Thomas had to develop special ways to sense the needs of the government, Unilever, and markets and meld these sometimes disparate needs together into a coherent strategy.

Thomas once told me that Unilever's offices in London were also a bit like the corridors of government offices in Delhi. He networked persistently and tenaciously with key people at Unilever there. He understood that those sitting in London would not be able to appreciate the needs of the

Indian company, and that it was part of his job to explain as many times as necessary what was good for it.

The Indian chairman could not interact as though he was the person who was to execute London's instructions. On the other hand, he needed to lobby actively in London and persuade the senior officers to approve what was right at that time for the shareholders of the Indian business. He recalled his experience with persuading Unilever to invest in the manufacture of a chemical called STPP.

If the phosphate project had a four-year waiting period with the Government of India, it had a parallel waiting period for approval by the bureaucracy of Unilever. Although HLL was responsible to the regional management, which at least began to understand the strategic importance of moving into the core sector and specifically into STPP to protect the company's supplies, the chemicals coordinator in London was totally opposed to it.

At one stage, Vice-chairman David Webb and Chairman Thomas visited London to lobby for the project. The chemicals coordinator said to David Webb, 'You remind me of the story of an old woman. An old woman had a dog with her for many years. As she became older she began to act and behave like her dog. David, your support for this project reminds me of that old woman.' Although both Thomas and David Webb were furious, they kept their cool and persisted with the rationality of their proposal. Finally, they got Unilever's approval in 1976.

When I graduated to a senior position in Hindustan Lever in later years, the deputy chairman of the Planning Commission inquired of me whether the chairman of Hindustan Lever would be obliged to follow the instructions of 'the masters' in London. I replied in the negative, and quoted the example of Thomas (and some of his successors) to exemplify that the chairman did what his role and responsibility required, i.e., what was right for all the shareholders of Hindustan Lever.

Thomas also realized that the country was going through a certain ideological medley, so he had to connect with different opinions, irrespective of whether he subscribed to those views or not. He strengthened the formal organization for government liaison at Delhi.

My long-standing colleague and friend, Suman Sinha (later Pepsi India chairman) played a stellar role in explaining the company viewpoint to policy makers. It was also at that time that Thomas recruited me briefly to be the corporate communications manager to establish and nurture links both internally with employees and externally with the media.

Apart from this, Thomas travelled incessantly and energetically to meet sales force and retailers so that he had a sense of customer issues directly from the grassroots level.

These were the ways in which Thomas developed the extra-long antennae to feel and sense what was actually going on around the company.

Uniting internally

A corporate top team by definition is likely to have a high proportion of very competent people. Those people get to where they are because they are people with ideas; they are independent and passionate. When you put such a bunch together, it is unreasonable to expect docile and aligned behaviour. They will have differences of views and style. It is the leader's role to encourage those differences, yet insist on the discipline to resolve them, and craft a common way forward. Conflict is not by nature good or bad, what is bad is leaving conflict unresolved.

In chapter 6, I narrated the story of how Ashok Ganguly and Susim Datta united the leadership of HLL to focus on the issue of lost detergent marketshare.

A couple of years ago, the *Financial Times* published an interview with a career professional, Christopher Bland, chairman of BT, the British telecommunications company. Bland had experience of being a chairman in the private sector, public sector as well as broadcasting. He had chaired organizations as diverse as a printing company, a freight company, BBC, BT and even a health service trust. He was asked what he thought of boardroom clashes.

He replied, 'In the main, they work themselves out. Usually, they are over issues of substance. If they are about territory and prestige, they are harder to deal with. From time to time, you have to have a word with whoever you think is the problem.'

He went on to enunciate what he called Bland's Law: the amount of backbiting, infighting and skullduggery in an organization is in direct proportion to the nobility of its goals. 'The worst behaviour I found was in a home for handicapped children in north London, closely followed by a teaching hospital. Compared with that Shell, ICI and British American Tobacco were relatively well-behaved.' This would ring a bell for those associated with charitable or religious trusts, sports associations and clubs or even social service organizations.

I have sympathy for this view; I find that running my building's cooperative society is in some respects more challenging than working in HLL or Tata. It has been a fine form of leadership training!

Focusing on people

When an organization is passing through a vulnerable period, it is the task of the leadership to take some critical steps. Only then can the company have the confidence to go on.

The agenda for change must be based on the wisdom of the people in the organization. As they are the ones who for some reason chose to be silent and watch the company get into trouble, they are uniquely placed to diagnose the issues on hand and find solutions. Therefore, those very people must be assigned the responsibility of implementing the agreed actions.

All this is self-evident, but with the accompanying tensions of a vulnerable organization, it is easy to overlook these aspects.

Rallis, a Tata Group company producing crop protection chemicals, reported a huge loss in March 2003, and the future of the company was threatened; the company represented more than just a livelihood for several hundreds of people, it was 'home' for them. This was a disorienting experience for everybody concerned.

At my first annual general meeting in August 2003 as the non-executive chairman of the company, I was heckled by some ex-employees and shareholders. They felt that the management had run down an erstwhile corporate success. I pleaded with the shareholders to give the management under its new leadership an opportunity to restructure and reorient the company with a new strategy, which I outlined. Fortunately, some shareholders argued in favour of patience, and that gave the management a lease of life. Every employee who attended that meeting could sense the organization's vulnerability.

Over the next several months, the new managing director, Venkat Sohoni, led the very same team through the turbulence of a successful turnaround. He talked to the 'troops', sat shoulder-to-shoulder with them to involve them in solving their own problems, developed a consensus for prioritized goals to be achieved, and built up their morale and courage.

One of the issues facing the company was a huge amount of money receivable from the trade. During the previous three years, the agricultural situation had been indifferent; most of the manufacturers of crop protection chemicals had overproduced and oversold stocks to the trade. Many peer companies had the same problem as Rallis; arguably, Rallis was worse off than its peers.

The company atmosphere at the senior levels was understandably surcharged. There could potentially have developed a blame game and scalp hunting. The people who felt most threatened were the field executives because the buck could stop with them. Ironically, it was they who held the key to solving the problem.

It was the sales executive at the field level in the company who knew precisely what risks had been taken with overloading of stocks, which dealer had been promised what, and how to resolve the problem. The best solution relied principally on his relations with the dealers and his ability to invoke implicit commitments.

Threatened people do not reveal the 'truth' lest they themselves be nailed. So Venkat Sohoni converted them into a focussed team to do the collections with rewards for success rather than merely penalties for failure. His plan was to win the trust of the people down the line, which he did. It took all of a year to get the crisis under control.

The successful outcome was because the chief executive created an atmosphere for people to solve the problems which those same people had earlier allowed to develop.

The 'inattentional blindness' syndrome

When there is a lot of concentration amidst a tense atmosphere, it is a very vulnerable time for the company. That is when you can miss huge external signals and end up inadvertently doing rather stupid things. The leadership, in particular, has to develop the antennae, or a way to watch for and listen to the subtle messages in the company and the marketplace.

It should not be surprising that when people get too focussed on solving problems, they can completely miss the implications of dramatic external signals. Two experiments help to reinforce how clever people can miss elementary signals.

The first one concerns two Harvard University psychologists Daniel Simons and Christopher Chabris who conducted an experiment which they reported in 1999. People were asked to watch a basketball game on video, but rather than just watch the game, they were given a task requiring some concentration; for example, one group was asked to count the number of times the ball was passed by the players to each other. As they watched, a gorilla walked across the screen, thumping its chest. It was there on the screen for quite some time, some nine seconds. At the end, the subjects were asked whether they had noticed the gorilla. It was incredible that half the respondents had not noticed the gorilla.

When it was pointed out that they had missed something quite so dramatic and unusual, they wanted to see the video again. Still, many did not recognise the video, believing that there must have been two different videos. The Harvard researchers called this 'inattention blindness'.

The more absorbed people are by a task, the less probable it is that they will notice something outside that task. We experience this all the time. You go to school to pick up your kid and your mind and eyes are both focussed on spotting your kid. Your best friend waves or honks at you to attract your attention. You miss him completely. Next time he meets you, he asks how come you missed seeing him. Another experience is that you are sitting in an airport lounge to catch a flight. You start to read a book which is so interesting that you completely miss hearing the announcement of your flight!

The second experiment is related by Malcolm Gladwell in *The Tipping Point*. Two Princeton psychologists met with a group of seminarians individually, and asked each one to prepare a short talk on a given biblical theme. They were then to walk across a courtyard to another building and present it to a group of their seniors. On the way, somewhere in the courtyard, each student ran into a slumped man, with his eyes closed, coughing and groaning in obvious pain or difficulty. The psychologists wanted to find out what percentage of these 'do good' seminarians would stop to help the afflicted man.

To create the right atmosphere, the seminarians were even asked to reflect on why they had joined the clergy, what their mission in life was about and so on. Naturally, all of them would have had thoughts of piety and humanitarianism oozing out. Just as they would be left alone to prepare, the experimenters told one half of them, 'It is better you head for the place soon; they are expecting you any time.' Thus a sense of urgency was introduced. The other half was told that they could go after a while, as the seniors may not be ready to hear the seminarians for some time. A sense of leisure was thus introduced.

The finding was that of the group in a hurry, only 10 per cent stopped to help the man, while of the group that had more time, 63 per cent stopped to help. The instruction was the same; the people were all similar insofar as they were all 'do-good' seminarians, only their context was changed. The effect of the context on their behaviour was quite startling. To mix the language of the gorilla experiment with the seminarian experiment, inattention blindness was induced into the seminarians who were asked to go across the courtyard in a hurry.

Company histories are full of managers with inattention blindness when they are too focussed on the tasks at hand. That is why it is important to have some way to develop feelers which are 'four times larger than the body' antennae and stick out into the marketplace.

A case of minimizing inattention blindness

I found it an instructive experience when there was a merger between Brooke Bond India and Lipton India in the 1990s.

In those days, and indeed even today, mergers and acquisitions are viewed as a high profile activity. People get awestruck with the technical aspects of mergers and acquisitions—the logic, the valuations and swap ratios, the legalities of the merger, for example. Bold headlines grab media attention and in some cases, become the talk of the town.

The post-merger scenario, which is largely about people, seldom receives the same commentary or public attention. In those days, there was not much literature about the human aspects of a merger, although that ended up being a prime focus for the top management.

Both the companies had been strong in terms of marketshare, competing in the same space of branded tea. The managers faced extreme conditions and it was a stressful period for both the companies. People who had competed fiercely for decades suddenly became colleagues to whom cooperation had to be extended. It was very confusing.

On the ground, we faced the real challenge of the post-merger situation. Susim Datta was the company chairman, I was the managing director, and we had a very talented HR chief, R.R. Nair. Under the stewardship of Nair, the company attempted to devise and implement a programme that would address the human side of this merger.

Nair helped line managers do this complex task by arranging a large number of confluence meetings at which managers of the merging companies were thrown together. It was impossible for people not to vent their feelings of insecurity, confusion and resentment about whatever was going on. This provided a release mechanism but also brought to the fore several minor and entirely addressable irritants, the existence of which the top leadership had no idea about. It took more than a year to unravel evident and not-so-evident concerns, to figure out ways to address many of them and then to concentrate on the market issues rather than on internal issues.

As a study in contrast, here is a story in which the transformation developed many complications.

A case of falling prey to inattention blindness

I serve as an independent director of ICI India Limited. This association, which began some six years ago, helped me to reconnect with a company then called Imperial Chemical Industries, which was considered iconic in the 1950s and 1960s when I was growing up. Further interest in ICI's history was aroused when Tata Chemicals bought Brunner Mond in 2005, this company having been a part of ICI until 1990.

To my mind, ICI is a story of how strong technological professionals missed the signals of a very different environment when danger was emanating from takeover tycoons.

In my younger days, the mere mention of someone working in ICI would elevate that manager to a high status. Harry McGowan, an irascible Glaswegian, put together ICI in 1926. His objective was to establish a British chemical company that could penetrate a world market with two established giants: America's Du Pont and Germany's IG Farben. ICI was the product of a great merger of four different companies and started as a company of 33,000 employees in five main industrial areas.

McGowan succeeded and, in many ways, ICI was indeed the most successful, more than Du Pont and IG Farben were. Today, eighty years after its formation, ICI is no longer an important force in British life or world business. The contemporary ICI is a shadow of that image. How come a positive transformation did not happen as must have been planned? A little peek into the context is helpful to appreciate the ICI situation.

At the turn of the twentieth century, the chemical industry was what the semiconductor or software industry is today. It attracted the largest research expenditure, it was the fastest growing industry, and it fascinated young people because of its technological prowess.

During the twentieth century, bulk commodities dominated

this industry. By the mid-1930s, the whole chemical industry was undergoing a profound change, a move away from commodity chemicals to the 'fine' organic chemistry of pesticides, pharmaceuticals, fibres and plastics. Being a research-driven company, ICI successfully reallocated its research budgets and made that transition successfully.

Not surprisingly, ICI was a company of technical people. Over seventy years, ICI developed and owned more than 33,000 patents. One of its research leaders had said, 'How can the world be changed? It is changed in the laboratory, not in the marketplace.'

The flip side was that it probably had managers who may have treated the securities markets with disdain.

On 14 May 1991, the Hanson Group, through its merchant bank Smith New Court bought a £240-million, 2.8 per cent stake in ICI. Hanson acquired a stake in the company because he felt that the whole of ICI was less valuable than the sum of individual parts. This was enough to trigger alarm about the intentions of Britain's most famous takeover barons, Lord Hanson and White. The threat of Hanson was warded off through some hectic lobbying, but the memory of that raid could not be erased. The board decided to split the company into two; one would be the more glamorous drugs and agrochemicals business (to be called Zeneca) and the other would be the more 'boring' paints, plastics and fibres business. Unfortunately, the 'boring' businesses actually became so and some new excitement had to be generated.

By 1997, a former Unilever director, Charles Miller Smith, had become chief executive of ICI. Among the roles that Miller Smith played during his distinguished career in Unilever was that of the financial chief of the Specialty Chemicals business of Unilever. It was a business that he knew well.

Soon after he joined ICI, he learned that Unilever would put this highly profitable chemicals business on the block to be able to concentrate on consumer goods. He saw a great opportunity to change ICI completely in a rapid timeframe from a boring commodity chemicals company into a successful, applications-oriented speciality chemicals company. This could be done by borrowing immediately to acquire the Unilever businesses, then quickly disposing off the old ICI commodity businesses, and then driving the 'new ICI'. Thus, ICI, a collection of cyclical, slow-growing businesses, acquired three fast growing, speciality chemicals businesses from Unilever.

ICI had to borrow heavily to do so, but had a plan to dispose off its traditional businesses to pay the debt. It turned out that it was easier to borrow and buy sexy new businesses than to raise cash by disposing of old businesses. ICI was now neither fish nor fowl; it retained the commodity chemicals and also had, alongside, the speciality chemicals business. The managers of the old businesses felt lost, while the managers of the acquired businesses did not feel rooted. Since then, it has been a long struggle for the company to get its borrowing to a manageable level and to charge up the company management to a semblance of old spirit.

One of the most charismatic chairmen of ICI was John Harvey-Jones from 1982 to 1987. The company had logged a traumatic loss in 1981, and under his leadership, by 1985, the company raced to a profit of £1 billion. He was credited with having salvaged and transformed ICI into one of Britain's best-run companies. Ironically, he himself had commented on the perils of changing companies dramatically. His comment was that many companies have changed their image dramatically, but the process of change in leaving one's own skill base is an extremely risky one—much, much riskier than trying to develop and adapt your existing business, which you know and understand, to the changing conditions of tomorrow's world.

There are many views about what happened to ICI; for me, the lesson is that you cannot accelerate too much the change of business profile and image in a company; even more so when it is a long-standing company with its own culture and traditions.

If the management had stuck out long feelers four times longer than itself like the cave cricket's, it could perhaps have picked up the signal that it takes time to rearrange the hormones and resources of a company. Quick-fixes do not work. John Harvey-Jones was right, maybe his advice was not available or relevant to subsequent managements.

An example from the Indian industrial scenario is that of the south Indian tea plantation industry. India had for long been the world's largest tea producer and exporter. Sri Lanka was a much smaller producer, but gradually became a major exporter since the domestic market was small, unlike the case with India. South Indian teas and Sri Lankan teas had some broad similarity in terms of tea types and quality.

From the 1970s, Russia became a major buyer of south Indian teas under the rupee-rouble trade agreement. When the Russians came to buy, they bought huge quantities, often at unrealistic prices because it was a managed trade, not a free trade. The south Indian industry lost its focus on quality and chased production volume almost blindly. The labour unions and the state governments of Kerala and Tamil Nadu also insisted that the wages and amenities for plantation workers be increased rapidly. This continued until the early 1990s when, with economic liberalization, it started to become obvious that south Indian teas would soon be outclassed in quality as well as in price.

However, the industry suffered from inattention blindness. Instead of focusing on the task it had to do, it continued to seek government sops and subsidies. It took another decade of decline before plantation companies started to address the core issues at hand, i.e., of developing newer models of business whereby labour would produce more for less money.

So how does a leader know whether he has developed the extra-long feelers that he needs? He knows instinctively:

❀ Am I feeling and sensing things that are remote from me?
❀ Have I made special efforts to connect with the far parts of my company?
❀ When I do connect, do I go out and connect with people or does my visit turn out stage-managed with an overdose of PowerPoint presentations?

These and many others give the telltale signals.

Apart from developing these long antennae, the top-class manager must learn to listen to the faintly audible and normally inaudible signals in the company and its environment—like the story of the homing pigeons in the next chapter. Or end up stunted, the kind of bonsai manager who is condemned to wondering just when or how things went wrong.

14

HOMING PIGEONS
LISTENING TO THE INAUDIBLE

Every organization has a unique geology

A wall in my office is adorned with a frame of phosphate-rich fossils from the bed of some mines in Morocco. It is formed of the teeth, bones and nails of animals that died 40–60 million years ago. It is very inspiring to see this every morning as it gives me a completely different perspective of time. Any temporary delusion that I am about to change the world by my decisions that day is immediately dispelled!

I got this piece during a visit to Morocco from the chairman of a company in the business of mining phosphate, beneficiating it into phosphoric acid and exporting it around the world. It aroused my interest in the Mediterranean area. How did it get the dominant proportion of phosphate deposits in the world? What caused this unique geology to occur?

The First Eden by naturalist David Attenborough provided some facts. Any geography in the world would be unique but the Mediterranean is special because it is where mankind's exploitation of the land began, and it has run its full cycle. For tens of millions of years, that arm of ocean had separated Europe from Africa.

Suddenly, some 6 million years ago, due to some geological actions, the narrow gap between Africa and Spain closed up. Thus, that arm of ocean dried out. It became roasting hot and almost lifeless. Likewise, on the eastern side, the connection from Africa to Arabia opened and then closed due to a different set of geological actions. The result was that animals in one part could cross over at certain times and were isolated at other times. Fish that could survive in a sea whose waters were constantly renewed died in a concentrated salt-water sea. The type of species that lived and died changed, leaving a lot of bone in that area, leading to the rich deposits.

In 1970, an American research ship, the *Glomar Challenger*, drilled that area and brought out samples which gave scientists some amazing insights. What interested me with regard to the current subject was the unique geology of the Mediterranean, which I might otherwise never have learned about. In fact, every land area has its own geological story, but we do not go around inquiring about this aspect when we travel.

It is not difficult to imagine why each organization and its people are unique, conditioned by its history, practices and culture. The leader has to genuinely appreciate the organization's uniqueness, invest the time required to understand it and acquire the sensitivity to let it influence decisions and executive actions. This is difficult, as is evident from the number of cases of reputed leaders getting it all wrong.

The great pigeon race

On 29 June 1997, a great race was held to celebrate the centenary of the Royal Pigeon Racing Association. More than

60,000 homing pigeons were released at 6.30 a.m. from a field in Nantes, southern France, flying to lofts all over southern England 650–800 km away. By 11 a.m., the majority of the racing birds had made it out of France and were over the English Channel. They should have arrived at their lofts by early afternoon. They did not.

A few thousand of the birds straggled in over the next few days. Most were never seen again. In pigeon racing terms, the loss of so many birds was practically unheard of, a disaster. Any one bird could get lost, but tens of thousands?

A researcher at the US Geological Survey, Jonathan Hagstrum, came up with a novel suggestion. Studying this event, he noticed a key fact. At 11 a.m., when the racing pigeons were crossing the Channel, a Concorde supersonic transport (SST) airliner was flying along the Channel on its morning flight from Paris to New York. During flight, the SST generates a shock wave that pounds down towards the earth, a carpet of sound almost 160 km wide. The racing pigeons flying below the Concorde could not have escaped the intense wave of sound. The birds that did eventually arrive at their lofts were lucky enough to be very slow racers—they were still south of the Channel when the SST passed over, ahead of them.

This story is interesting. The lost pigeons seem to bear resemblance to the very well-known, successful transformational leaders who get it all wrong in a new company, context or environment.

Organizational leaders can learn what has enabled pigeons for several centuries to navigate long and uncertain distances reliably; there are lessons for them because managers have to lead their people through long stretches of change and uncertainty. I set out to find out a bit about the history and hearing capabilities of the pigeon.

Pigeons have always reached their destination

Pigeons were first domesticated as early as 3000 BC and were used as messengers. During the thirteenth century, the Sultan of Baghdad had operated a pigeon-post system.

Even the history of Reuters has pigeons in it! This giant of the media and financial world was founded by Paul Julius Reuter, who was born into a prominent Jewish family in central Germany in 1816. Think of those days when communications were slow, though they were no less vital.

By the middle of the nineteenth century, the telegraph had spread rapidly throughout Europe as well as the United States. However, Reuter found that there was a significant gap in the telegraph network between Brussels and the western border town of Aachen in Germany. This meant that news dispatches and commercial information, for example on stock prices, had to be carried by train between these two cities for onward dispatch by telegraph. In 1850, Paul Reuter pressed pigeons into service to carry news dispatches between Brussels and Aachen.

The pigeons took only two hours, half the time, compared to the train, thus providing Reuter with significant competitive advantage. It is the premium this speed offered that launched Reuters as the world's biggest news and information empire. A postscript to this charming story is that the advantage was short-lived—one year, to be precise. In 1851, the telegraph network was laid between Brussels and Aachen.

During the first world war, the French army employed thousands of pigeons to carry vital messages. When Germans occupied much of Europe during the second world war, it was quite a problem to communicate with the resistance fighters in those territories. British planes would drop boxes of homing pigeons by parachute into German-occupied Europe and they would bring back messages to London.

Pigeons are unique in their hearing

Pigeons were chosen for such purposes because they could fly quite fast (almost 90–100 km per hour), they could fly for long distances (over 10,000 km) and they had a unique sense of precision in navigation. One needs to understand how pigeons get a sense of direction before we appreciate what happened when the birds were caught in the Paris–New York Concorde's 160-km carpet of sound.

Pigeon's ears are particularly good at detecting very low frequency sounds, called infra-sound, including the very low frequency acoustic shock waves generated by ocean waves crashing against one another. This acoustic beam always tells the pigeons where the ocean is.

Even more valuable to pigeons is infra-sound reflected from cliffs, mountains, and other steep-sided features of the earth's surface. Ocean wave infra-sound reflecting off local terrain could provide a pigeon with a detailed sound picture of its surroundings.

It is likely that this ability to hear infra-sound gives pigeons their map sense, a sense of location. This map sense is complemented by a compass sense, a sense of direction, because they can sense the magnetic north.

Infra-sound travels very far from its source, which is why you can hear distant thunder. Jonathan Hagstrum suggested that the Concorde's carpet of sound in which the pigeons were caught obliterated the infra-sound which gives the birds their sense of location. The enormous wave of infra-sound generated by the plane's sonic boom would have blotted out all the normal oceanic infra-sound information. Any bird flying in its path would lose orientation.

In every organization, there are sounds to be heard as well as echoes and sound reflections to be sensed. Those echoes and reflections are faint, and the astute manager has to strain hard to identify them and catch the message. In short, organizations too have their own unique infra-sound, and leaders must listen to this infra-sound in their organization to avoid losing their orientation—like the pigeons in the race.

The sounds change with the 'cliffs'

Metaphorically, when company leaders take initiatives and communicate with their staff, the sound frequency is in the audible range. When these sounds bounce off the departments, factories and clusters of interest groups, they produce an echo. The echo is not in the audible range, it is in the infra-range, called infra-sound. For a leader to be able to listen to this infra-sound, he has to extend his hearing range and ability. That is why it is important to understand the company geology, because it is that geology that creates unique sounds in response to its leaders' initiatives.

Each change case is unique because the sounds reflected from the 'cliffs' of each organization are different. Echoes reflected from the cliffs are unlikely to be clear or focussed.

There are broadly two types of organizations.

In a centralized authority, the jurisdiction and the lines of authority are fairly clear. In fact, such clarity is used to resolve conflicts among interest groups affected by the transformation; for instance, the erstwhile Soviet Union, Singapore and China among nations and P&G, GE among companies. The methods and rewards of transformation here are definitely different from the second type.

The second type is the confederated entity where there is an overlap in the jurisdiction and lines of authority; the result is that the number of interest groups is higher, and the means to resolve differences are more ambiguous; for example, the European Union or the World Trade Organization cannot take and implement decisions like, say, the US can. In India, Centre–state jurisdictions and roles necessarily mean that reform in sectors like agriculture and electricity will be more complex.

As the increasing number of cases appearing in the public domain suggest, among companies, family businesses do face some special challenges. In such confederated entities, the market or media perception of the speed of change does not recognize the effects of the internal dynamics which affect ways of working.

Whether it is a centralized or confederated entity, the interest groups generate the infra-sound. They represent the cliffs and valleys making up the unique 'geology' of the company.

Transformational experiences in one type of organization are not readily transplanted into others because of the unique way each organization thinks and behaves.

Infra-sound listening

The evolution of liberalization in India is instructive. The thinking and planning really started during Indira Gandhi's tenure in 1980, but was rudely interrupted by her death. Her son, the late Rajiv Gandhi, who stepped into her shoes, gave it a fresh face but got enmeshed in controversy.

When the late P.V. Narasimha Rao became prime minister in June 1991, reform enthusiasts wanted him to go for the Big Bang approach, such approaches usually being very visible. He chose the middle path, which he in fact articulated at the Tirupati Congress. He reaffirmed his commitment to Nehru's ideas, even though he would approve a completely different course of action a short while later.

He kept telling the Indian people that he would not follow the western path but draw lessons from south-east Asia and projected his policies as continuity with the past. In fact, his first foreign visit was to the Far East, not to the west.

When Dr Manmohan Singh became prime minister in May 2004, he had to define and strengthen the platforms for dialogue with the communists. If he did not listen, the government would be destabilized. If he listened too much, he would be paralysed. So he would have to send out signals on privatization, foreign direct investment and listen to the 'echoes from the cliffs' and contemplate what to do next. It is an example of listening to the inaudible as well as the clearly audible, in this case.

Another striking example is the issue of Hindi as a national language. Soon after India's independence, one group of people, mostly Hindi-speaking people, felt that an independent nation should have one single language to unite everybody. Examples were quoted of French in France, Italian in Italy and so on.

Another group of people, mostly from the south, felt no affinity whatsoever to Hindi—they regarded it as more foreign than English! The Tamil speakers pointed out that their language was older than Sanskrit, the mother of Hindi and several other northern Indian languages. So, if at all a national language was to be adopted, Tamil had a better claim.

The truth was that the concept of the nation-state itself was young, and many a nation did not have a common, unifying language until several years of nationhood. When Italy was unified by Garibaldi in the 1860s, less than 2 per cent of the population of the unified country spoke the same language! A somewhat similar situation prevailed when Bismarck unified Germany two decades later.

In India, the zealots of the 1950s agitated in a visible way, and tried to impose their language; there was a great deal of resistance. Parliamentarians from the Hindi heartland would not listen to the sounds from the South, let alone the infra-sound! There was turmoil. The southern state of Tamil Nadu even threatened to secede from the Indian Union. As a young kid back in the 1950s, I thought I might just end up not being an Indian!

This infra-sound was heard by a completely different 'bird', not the pigeons who were supposed to hear it. Although not mandated to address this task, acting in its own self-interest, the Hindi film industry listened to a faint signal: the acute need of the Indian population for entertainment was identified. Now this industry is the world's largest producer of films! Hindi films, through the provision of escapist cinema, reached every corner of the country over the next forty years, uniting Indians through the politically unacceptable Hindi language. Actors like Raj Kapoor and Amitabh Bachchan, singers like Lata Mangeshkar and Mohammed Rafi, lyricists like Shakeel Badayuni and Javed Akhtar have done more for the acceptance of Hindi than politicians like Purshottam Das Tandon.

The infra-sound in this case was that people wanted fantasies that would temporarily make them forget the stark realities of the tough life they had to lead. It did not matter to them what language that entertainment was in, as long as it entertained. The Hindi film industry in the early years attracted actors from the northern state of Punjab, actresses from Tamil Nadu and Bengal, lyricists and singers from Bengal and Maharashtra, the sort of medley of cross-cultures that would achieve integration and not merely discuss it.

There was the resultant consequence that early in the twenty-first century, even in my remote village of Vilakudi in Tamil Nadu, the streets would empty from Monday to Thursday, 9–10 p.m., as people watched the TV programme *Kaun Banega Crorepati*. So what if it was in Hindi? It offered a chance to see someone become a millionaire!

How an Indian prime minister listened

Russian leader Alexei Kosygin visited the milk cooperative in Anand, Gujarat, in March 1979. While he was impressed with the work done, he was appalled that it had taken thirty years to accomplish.

He told Dr V. Kurien, 'You have taken thirty years to do

this for the milk sector. Presumably you will take another thirty years to do the same thing with the oilseeds sector...and then another thirty years to do it for cotton and jute. If it were Russia, they would shoot you down before you got the job done.'

I reckon this comment highlights the essential difference between an evolutionary approach and a revolutionary one. The Indian politician and administrator cannot ignore society's infra-sound—which, at that time, the Russian system did.

Operation Flood, which ushered in a milk revolution in India, owes its fame to a visit by Prime Minister Lal Bahadur Shastri to Anand in the 1960s. Instead of staying at the house of Dr Kurien—there being no hotels or guest houses in Anand— he expressed the desire to spend the night at the house of a farmer in Kaira district. This caused consternation among security personnel, and logistical complications for the organizers.

To keep it a secret, one village farmer was initially told that two foreigners would stay with him; only at the last minute was he told that the guests would be the prime minister and the Gujarat chief minister. Shastriji had an early dinner with the nervous farmer and then went around the village talking to the people. Most of the villagers kept awake as Shastriji visited the colonies of Harijans, Muslims and all the others. At each place, he inquired about the milk cooperative of which they were members. This went on from 8 p.m. till 2 a.m.

Next morning, he asked Kurien to explain the secret of Amul's success; nowhere else in the country had cooperatives worked. Kurien explained the ground realities succinctly. Shastriji heard what he could not have gathered in many papers and seminars sitting in Delhi.

It was a unique way for a modern leader to listen to the infra-sound of what mattered to dairy farmers.

Leaders who fail to listen, fail

There is a story in the book *Leadership on the Line* by Heifetz and Linsky about economist Miles Mahoney of the US. This story will strike an emotional chord in almost any manager in the corporate sector or IAS officer.

Miles Mahoney was recruited for a Massachusetts state agency by the Governor himself. His mandate was to make the agency more effective. The Governor liked Mahoney's passion and commitment to strengthening the state's role in large housing projects, although these were not of the highest priority. Mahoney's office would have to approve development plans for funding. His first project was to evaluate one for downtown Boston, which elicited the enthusiastic support of every interested party—the mayor, the media, the unions and the business community. The city even chose a developer for the project, two young and somewhat inexperienced entrepreneurs who happened to be friendly with the mayor. Miles Mahoney decided to reject the project proposal since it failed to meet several requirements, strategic as well as statutory.

To carry the Governor's office with him, he explained his rationale to various officers. They were perhaps a little apprehensive when they realized how heavyweight some of the people involved were. Nonetheless, to appear impartial and professional, they encouraged Miles to kill it, and to do so quickly. The burden of their song was that the Governor would support Mahoney only if he personally and efficiently quashed the project in such a way that the issue would not linger. If it did linger, it would interfere with the Governor's other priorities.

Mahoney heard the words but not the song behind it: he heard the sounds, but not the infra-sound. It was a classic case of a bonsai manager. Interpreting that he had the Governor's full support, he turned down the project, sending its supporters into full battle mode. Six months later, Mahoney lost his job and his successor approved the project.

Another corporate example of 'a pigeon getting lost in the subsonic waves' is the case of Digital Equipment Corporation (DEC). In the late 1970s, this company led the way with its small and mid-range computers. Its smartest managers and customers, it has been reported, fed back information to the company that huge changes were occurring through the emergence of new markets like personal computing, software and systems integration. These would make the current business model of the company obsolete.

However, according to the top team and CEO Ken Olson, the company had reached the top because of the focussed development of its own technology and, no doubt, the hard work of its employees. But good ideas could not come out in the open and get discussed more broadly. Several top managers quit because DEC did not find it necessary or worthwhile to adapt to the emerging signals.

Within two decades, DEC was on its knees and Compaq bought it—a mighty fall for a market leader during whose peak Microsoft was an unknown entity!

Why leaders find it difficult to listen

The sceptre of authority and the trappings of power conspire to plug the leader's ears. Listening carefully is such an elementary lesson, why does one have to explain its importance?

Precisely because it is elementary, and life's mistakes are made by ignoring elementary things!

I served on the board of a company where the leader failed to listen despite repeated signals. Ultimately, he had to leave the company.

He was a perfectly bright and talented individual. He had enjoyed a good track record as a middle-level manager. Somehow, after becoming a CEO, he seemed to go deaf. One does not counsel a CEO as though he is a youngster. Criticism is not direct; it may be a bit circumlocutory. Some directors had conversations with him to alert him about his 'deafness', but to no avail. The CEO kept doing what he wanted to, irrespective of the views expressed by the directors. The end game took a couple of years to play out. At the unfortunate end, the CEO kept saying, 'I wish somebody had been more direct', while others kept wondering why the CEO could not see coming what many others could!

Leo Tolstoy wrote in *Anna Karenina* that 'Happy families are all alike; each unhappy family is unhappy in its own way.' Likewise, all change management cases resemble each other, but in reality, each one is unique to the prevalent culture, beliefs and mindsets. There is no 'one hat fits all' solution. Listening carefully to the unique infra-sound of the organization, however, is the most valuable tool.

Each morning as you get to work, you start to prove yourself all over again, it seems. Since dissatisfaction with the pace of change is common—it seems too fast or too slow—how does one get it right? This can be done by spending a disproportionate amount of time understanding the people within, the company's history and culture, and the unique events that shaped managerial instincts in that company.

All these exemplify the importance of leaders listening ever so carefully and responding to the infra-sound, lest they get lost like the homing pigeons.

In the next chapter, there is a story about how even after sensing, feeling and listening, the top manager, intelligent though he is, misunderstands or misinterprets the signals he has picked up—like the vervet monkey.

15

THE INTELLIGENTLY
STUPID VERVET
FOLLY OF MISSING THE CONTEXT

How clever vervets are

The vervet monkey is native to Africa and Asia. One characteristic of this monkey is that it is highly intelligent. It has been speculated that Hanuman, the monkey-god of the Indian epic Ramayana might have been a vervet monkey.

Anthropologists gain special insights from vervets because as a long-standing species, they lend themselves to studies of evolutionary influences on the brain. Vervets are considered so clever that they might even have language capabilities of some basic nature! Experts feel that there is evidence and some data to suggest that there may be man–animal parallels in the language learning process.

Robert Seyfarth and Dorothy Cheney are two scientists who have specialized in the study of the natural vocalizations of the vervet monkeys of east Africa. They have compiled and documented a range of vervet alarm calls. They transcribed them into sound spectrographs and prepared a pictorial dictionary of the vervet's calls.

They then related these sounds to specific behavioural contexts, trying to answer an intriguing question—is there any evidence of linguistic development? Apart from the genetic endowments that the young are born with, is there any positive influence from a nurturing environment that can enhance verbalization capability? If that were possible, then vervets could pass on learning from their experiences through language.

An intriguing case is that of Imo, a female monkey that lived on the Japanese island of Koshima, around 1953. She must be regarded as a sort of genius among monkeys. A team of scientists would drop sweet potatoes on the sand on the beach. Imo devised a way to dip the sweet potatoes in water, brush off the gritty sand particles and then savour the delights of the potato. That by itself would have been interesting, but there was more: within two years, 90 per cent of the grown-up monkeys on Koshima island had learnt to do the same. That was some learning.

Further, only the grown-ups learnt this; for some reason, the very young and the very old failed to learn the technique. Did the grown-ups talk to each other in some form of monkey language?

As their research continued, Robert Seyfarth and Dorothy Cheney found that a vervet was so clever that it could give three distinct alarm calls for three different predators. If it was a leopard alarm call, then it would climb onto a tree. If it was an eagle alarm call, it would dive into thick undergrowth. If it was a python alarm call, the vervet would stand upright and scan the forest for the snake.

This meant that the vervet was categorizing its predators

and selecting appropriate meaningful calls. This is solid evidence that the vervet is indeed a very intelligent animal.

Further data came from other experiments: a number of species of monkey effectively have a system of social class—rather like some human societies. Aristocrats are distinguished by their status of dominance. The offspring of aristocrats became aristocrats and the young aristocrats apparently learned to dominate with their mother's help. To curry favour with high-ranking females, male monkeys will groom themselves, pick at their fur as a sign of deference and, in general, behave not very differently from eager-to-please people in human society.

In other words, in those monkey societies, it is not what you know that matters, it does not matter how big you are. What matters is whom you know, how many high-ranking relatives you have.

Even among humans, these things happen. Career advancement comes not merely from competence, but how well you are networked. Open cultures are developed not by a rapid-fire verbal machine gun, but by exercising frankness with a wise diplomacy.

In short, intelligent behaviour comes out of viewing the issue within its context.

How stupid vervets can be

These vervets, exceptionally intelligent under a set of circumstances, act utterly stupidly in a different situation.

For example, if there are python tracks, the vervet does not sense the possibility that there may be a slithering python nearby.

If a vervet is shown the carcass of an antelope or deer hanging from a tree, it is quite likely to approach the object without assessing for a moment whether such a carcass could imply the presence of a leopard somewhere nearby.

The lay conclusion is that vervets are very good at processing certain types of 'vervetish' information, but are quite incapable of assimilating and interpreting other types of information. Their intelligence is contextual.

Managers—and indeed leaders more generally—are also like vervets, they can process some types of information and fail to process others. That is perhaps why sometimes very competent leaders do stupid things.

Why clever managers do stupid things

This is a problem for managers at all levels, though it shows up more sharply at higher levels.

I was once involved in the recruitment of an experienced middle-level manager returning to India from the US. He had a very interesting set of skills, which the interview panel thought would be useful to a deregulating Indian corporate environment. Perhaps because I was involved with his recruitment, I followed his career closely.

In all, he did three jobs during the seven years he spent in the company. All his superiors had the same thing to say of him: he is so bright, so talented, so astute—why can he not get along with anybody, just anybody? Why is he so suspicious of everyone around him?

An outstanding Unilever marketer, an Englishman, was appointed as marketing director of HLL some twenty-five years ago. His CV must have read like a dream and he arrived in Mumbai with a huge reputation. Indeed, he was a very astute and talented marketer, and I personally learnt a lot from him.

Unfortunately, he turned out to be very poor in adaptability. He could not understand or tolerate different points of view. Any difference was promptly attributed by him to either a 'hidden agenda' of someone or plain, simple 'office politicking.' Let alone revel in diversity as an expatriate manager should, he must have prayed each morning to his God that all HLL managers should behave like the ones he knew in his earlier company! It was a cross-border expatriation that just did not work out. He returned to Europe, most likely with a poor record of his India posting. He did not flourish thereafter either, and moved on from Unilever.

Business magazines and books are full of stories about highly intelligent and extremely successful CEOs, who suddenly seem to act in a silly way in spite of warning signals and danger signs.

How and why does this happen? How come perfectly intelligent managers do ridiculous, inane things? It is a significant area of management research, resulting in a large number of books. There may be a few reasons for this.

First, managers' intelligence is contextual, that is why even successful managers miss danger signals that appear obvious to others. Intelligence is a poor measure of the human ability to interpret signals.

Second, power reduces a person's ability to reflect; in this way, power depreciates intelligence and breeds folly. In fact, the greater the success of the manager, the greater is the chance of his/her missing or misinterpreting signals.

Third, he overestimates the value of his own solutions compared to those of others. This could be due to arrogance or insularity.

The dilemma of foresight versus foolhardiness

Obvious cases of stupidity are easy to observe.

There is no leader who genuinely believes that he does not listen to others. It is only later that realization dawns that listening was an issue, or that danger signals were ignored, or that those who knew that something was amiss did not speak up. At that stage, it may be accurate to term the act as folly, but it is a bit late in the day to do so!

The line between an ambitious project for the organization and a foolhardy project is a thin one. So how does one tell whether disaster is looming or an act of great vision is unfolding? I have found it very difficult to predict whether a leader is pursuing a 'sure-to-fail' mission or a 'worth-persisting' mission.

Leaders are ambitious; they tend to be hungry for power and recognition. They like to leave their stamp on the organization by expressing ambitions for the growth and prosperity of the organization. If the project is successful, history records it as an act of great vision. If not, it gets classified as foolishness.

The answers to some questions could indicate whether a project is driven by foolhardiness or vision.

- Is there greater emphasis on securing financial resources or human resources?
- Have the required expertise and leadership been made available to the project?
- Are the top leaders involved and driving the project personally?
- Has accountability to deliver been clearly allocated or is there vagueness?
- Are the initial difficulties faced due to execution or due to the concept itself?
- Do people around the project feel that they are free to express their views?
- Have plans been changed sometimes in response to suggestions from others?
- Is there a transparent financial limit beyond which a rethink is known to be due?
- Is the project motivated more by personal glory or by hard economics?

Why Jamsetji Tata was unarguably bold

It is difficult to apply these questions rigorously to the facts of individual projects in any brief reference. However, the unfolding of events when Jamsetji Tata went about setting up a steel plant offers valuable lessons by providing insights into many of the above questions. Fortunately, the story has been well told by his biographers Frank Harris and Russi Lala. Further, enough time has passed to avoid the prejudices that are inevitable in more recent events; so it may be instructive.

Jamsetji first heard about the potential of steel when he was in Britain in the 1860s. He heard a speech by Thomas Carlyle in which he said that the nation which will have steel will have gold. That speech aroused in him a grand desire that India should have steel. What might have been his driving motivation? As an American technologist, C.M. Weld, who was associated with the Tata steel project wrote many years later, 'I soon learned that Mr Tata's plan to manufacture steel was inspired by something far broader and deeper than the mere hope of adding to his fortune by a successful iron works at Chanda.'

By the turn of the nineteenth century, Jamsetji was determined to construct an Indian steel plant. Unfortunately, he did not find much encouragement from the Viceroy, Lord Curzon. In the summer of 1900, Jamsetji went straight to Lord George Hamilton in London—he was the secretary of state for India. Having received a favourable response, Jamsetji applied for prospecting licences. His personal involvement in the steel project was remarkable because initially, he ran it himself. As Lala points out in his book, *For the Love of India*, 'At sixty-three, he was still carrying samples of coal and iron ore.'

On 24 September 1902, Jamsetji set sail for Europe and America. His stated objective was to have experiments done on the coking of coal in Germany. In America, he wanted to find experts for his pet project. He had already lost two valuable years in appointing Indian agents to prospect for iron, coal and coke. So he spent the last four days of his trip in New York looking for talent. Finally, he located Charles Page Perin, a graduate in metallurgy from Harvard. 'Will you come to India with me?' he asked Perin. As Perin later commented, 'I was dumbfounded, naturally. But you don't know what character and force radiated from Tata's face. And kindliness too.' It is now recorded history that this encounter between Jamsetji Tata and Charles Page Perin was to change the life of Perin and transform the industrial destiny of India.

Jamsetji died before the project could see the light of day; it was his son, Dorabji, who saw it through. Was Jamsetji driven by a quest for personal glory by passionately pursuing what must have been an 'impossible project' in those days? Writing about the prospectus to raise funds for Tata Steel a few years later, Lala records:

> The name 'Tata' came into use for the first time for the steel company. Jamsetji never used the name 'Tata' for any company save his shipping line: it was Empress 1874, Svadeshi 1882, and Indian Hotels 1903. The prestige of his name was utilized for the first time by his sons and colleagues.
>
> —*For the Love of India*
> (Penguin India, 2004)

To my mind, the answers to all those questions lie buried in this short story; those questions are probably a decent guide to answer the dilemma referred to.

Muthuraman's reflection on Tata Steel's Gopalpur project

When a leader is going through a major and risky challenge, he may give his people an impression of self-confidence and sure-footedness. That does not mean that he is necessarily so. Contrary thoughts pass through his mind.

In a conversation I had with B. Muthuraman, managing director of Tata Steel Ltd., he said:

In 1995, Tata Steel decided to set up a green-field steel plant at Gopalpur in Orissa. It was an ambitious 10 million tonne project, to be executed in stages. There were many challenges—acquisition of some 5,000 acres of land in a populous area, displacing about 1,000 families (5,000 people), rehabilitating and resettling these families and ensuring a higher quality of life for them, organizing for basic infrastructural facilities like water (Gopalpur had long suffered from water shortage), railway lines, port and power.

I was put in charge of the project as vice-president (Gopalpur project). The project failed. We spent some Rs 160 crore in acquiring the land and resettling people. We could not proceed further due to lack of infrastructure—water and port being the main issue. We abandoned the project. We got a bad name, which is sticking to us even today. People in Orissa, aided by some of our detractors, hold a view that Tata Steel will not execute projects in Orissa and that we are only interested in taking away their iron ore to our Jamshedpur plant.

The negative impact of this project was enormous. Our relations with the Orissa government deteriorated. It was difficult to carry on even substantive conversations with people in the government and senior citizens of Orissa. It took us ten long years to get back on track, and with great difficulty. I have been, personally, in the midst of all these.

What went wrong? I have reflected on this several times. My personal diary contains many, many narrations of the events in Gopalpur as they unfolded. I have tried to introspect and tried my best to put down, as honestly as I could, the reasons why this project ultimately looked like a 'foolhardy' project instead of it being a 'visionary' project. As I planned to speak with you, I looked up my old diaries and read, for the nth time in the last ten years, what I actually wrote in those days.

The learning from the Gopalpur Project could be summed up as follows:

◈ As the project in-charge, I was driven by the sole thought that the project must succeed and that I must succeed. I had a mindset that 'I could solve everything'.

◈ The project was at a point in time in the history of Tata Steel and in the history of my own personal career where I felt a strong urge (strong urge is a mild word to what was actually going through me) to demonstrate that I could do something significant and substantial. There was a very strong 'I' element.

◈ Many in the senior leadership of the organization were not fully committed to this project. Some people were not in favour of the project, some were silent, some spoke up in 'muted' voices and generally the project was seen as being an attempt by one person or at best by one or two people—nothing to do with the rest of the organization.

◈ There were some people, especially one, who raised concerns about infrastructure and that we need to make sure of the infrastructure before we proceed. I was 'deaf' to these concerns.

◈ There was not enough 'questioning' about the project. There was no 'murder board' to ask the inconvenient and difficult questions. The contrarian's point of view was not voiced and on the rare occasions it was voiced, it was not heard.

There were many other shortfalls in this project that I won't deal with in this conversation. It is sometimes uncomfortable. There are some very searching questions for which we must pen down honest answers. I have often felt that there is, perhaps, a corporate mindset that shuns contrary viewpoints and leaders have this tendency of disregarding or not being able to cope with contrarian viewpoints and still retain the ability to function well and make progress.

I have often shared my Gopalpur experience with my colleagues in Tata Steel, in small groups as well in dialogues as well as to individuals in charge of large projects. But I am not entirely sure if the learning has got into their minds and into their systems. I sometimes get very worried because Tata Steel has, currently, very many projects, which are even more complex than the Gopalpur project.

A good project leader, any good leader for that matter, must combine in him two important but competing and contrary qualities. One is to help create a vision, and energize, enthuse and empower his people to great heights of achievements and performance. This is what the sage Patanjali said in 300 BC and I quote:

When you are inspired by some great purpose, some extraordinary project, all your thoughts break their bonds— your mind transcends limitations, your consciousness expands in every direction and you find yourself in a new, great and wonderful world. Dormant forces, faculties and talents become alive and you discover yourself to be a greater person by far than you ever dreamed.

Incidentally, each of the senior leaders of Tata Steel has this quote from Patanjali on his table.

The other quality a leader must possess—and this is a competing dimension—is architectural dimensions: the dimension of creating systems, structure and processes in the organization to ensure that the dreams and the views are properly canalized and implemented. This is where the 'questioning' comes and contrarian viewpoints surface.

It is often difficult to have, in the same person, these two contradictory and competing dimensions. Such people are rare. This is the reason why the senior leadership of an organization must have a collection of people having these two competencies and the leader must possess both these dimensions.

Jamsetji Tata seems to have had these two dimensions— without going to Harvard or Centre Europeen d'Education

Permanente (Cedep), Paris! Otherwise, it is impossible to implement what he sought to do.

Smart people have done foolish things throughout history

Ramayana

In the epic, Ravana is a flawed character. He was the demon who carried away the righteous Sita and caused the Ramayana war to occur. Every year, his effigy is burnt to signal the victory of good over evil.

In reality and point of fact, Ravana was born into a very talented lineage. Like his father and his grandfather, Ravana was an extremely learned person with an enormous capacity to concentrate. Ravana had undertaken such severe austerities that the gods themselves appeared before him and granted him a boon of his choice.

Being desirous of immortality and knowing that his death could come at the hands of a god, a *rakshasa* (demon) or an animal, he obtained the boon that he would not die at the hands of any of these three. Assuming humans to be weak, so weak that he could easily defend himself from them, he did not include a human in his wishlist.

Having done so, Ravana used the powers of his austerities and knowledge to harass people rather than serve them. All his prowess and valour came to naught with his lustful abduction of Sita, and the subsequent war with her husband, King Rama. During this war, Ravana met his death at the hands of a human, King Rama.

Coriolanus

Here is a story from ancient Rome. A flaw is revealed in the character of Coriolanus, Shakespeare's tragic Roman general.

He was a great warrior, he had a very strong moral compass, and was considered honest to the core. Notwithstanding his many talents, he had a tremendous derailer.

He just did not connect with the Roman people; he did not mingle with them or become one with them. He believed in a deeply flawed way that to do so would compromise him; it would be a form of pandering to them and, above all, a sacrifice of his integrity.

His mother, Volumnia, begged him to do so, almost like a modern-day coach might a protégé, but to no avail. Coriolanus failed to notice that Rome was changing from a patrician state to a state where common folks, the plebeians, mattered. This leader of great virtue was derailed by his peculiar flaw.

Shakespeare opens his tragedy with the Romans on the street being addressed by a mutinous citizen. He says that Coriolanus is the chief enemy of the people. If they could kill him, they would have corn at a reasonable price. Finally in their fury, the people of Rome did kill Coriolanus.

Montezuma

The Aztec state, approximating to what is today known as Mexico City, was rich, so it was attractive to predators. Montezuma was the king when the Aztec state was lost to the Spanish invaders. Although the Aztecs were advanced in arts and sciences, they were 'blind' when it came to their religion.

The folklore and religious belief among these Aztecs was that their founding god would return one day, but before that there would be omens and apparitions. This strong belief caused their downfall and ultimate surrender to the invaders.

In 1519, under the command of Hernan Cortes, a party of 600 men landed on the Mexican coast. The first act by Cortes was to burn his ships so that there could be no retreat.

A bold Hernan Cortes made alliances with the local people who were unhappy under the Aztec overlords, and pressed ahead to conquer. He sent word ahead posing as the ambassador of a foreign prince; he made no attempt to pose as the reincarnated founding god whom the Aztec folklore expected back some day.

On learning of this strange party, Montezuma summoned his council. Some of them advised stopping the strangers by force; others advised that the ambassadors of a foreign prince should be welcomed. Montezuma himself conjured up a vision that these people may be the reincarnation of the founding god whom the Aztecs had expected over the centuries. It is not at all clear how he got this fixation in his mind.

When they reached the capital city, Montezuma arranged to welcome them ceremonially. The 'guests' were escorted to their quarters and lodged in the palaces. There were only 600 raiders, and the Aztecs outnumbered them by a huge margin. Yet, they behaved in this inexplicable manner due to an excess of mysticism and superstition.

The raiders behaved as raiders would. They extracted gold and provisions ceaselessly. Montezuma's nephew denounced Cortes as a murderer and raised a revolt. Even at this stage, Montezuma remained silent and passive. At this point, Montezuma lost his authority and the people became angry. The people stoned him as a coward and traitor, and he died three days later. On 13 August 1521, the Aztecs surrendered and for the next 300 years the Spanish ruled Mexico.

When beliefs become a delusion against natural evidence, it qualifies as folly in the extreme.

Folly is the child of power

The lesson from all these stories is that folly arises from missing the context or it is the child of power.

Much of human endeavour is aimed at achieving power. The mere act of achieving the power to command itself denudes the power to think. Paradoxically, power breeds folly.

That is why enduring leaders learn to manage the consequences of power ahead of acquiring it.

Enduring leaders have four positive traits but they also have a great awareness of their negative traits. The positive traits possessed by them are pretty well-known. They have integrity, they are decisive, they are competent, and they are visionary. But they also actively manage their dark side.

They are conscious about themselves as human beings, about their weaknesses, what can derail them. Thus they not only work at enhancing the required positive traits, they also have an active plan for mitigating their negative and dark sides, their failure-producing characteristics. These are their derailers.

CEOs are particularly vulnerable to derailers because of the inherent nature of their job. They head their organization, they feel responsible for the lives and future of several thousands, and they acquire a feeling of self-importance. Further, the higher they go in the organization, the less likely it is that people will tell them about their failure-producing traits.

All these activate the derailers, which incidentally are unique to each individual. The task is not to eliminate the personal derailers; that, alas, is not possible. All that can be done is to become aware of the derailers in one's own context and to learn to manage their deleterious effects.

16

EYE OF THE FLY
EFFECTIVE, RATHER THAN EFFICIENT, LEADERSHIP

Efficiency and effectiveness

It has taken me twenty months to put this book together. It has been a journey of self-awareness, a journey of reflection and contemplation. Above all, it has been a journey of enjoyment.

At high school, I had to study Hindi as my first language. It was a nightmare; the standard of the syllabus was very high, and Hindi was not the language spoken at home. My teacher suggested that it might help if I watch Hindi movies, a pleasurable activity for a teenager. The alibi that watching movies might advance my academic record and education helped my father also to rationalize the required expenditure of time and money, which he would otherwise have disapproved of. As a result, I recall some of the Hindi movies of those days quite well.

A film called *Jaagte Raho* comes to mind, a story about a naïve man in a big, bad world. The movie was directed by Shombu Mitra, the theatre doyen of Kolkata and won the Grand Prix at the Karlovy Vary Film Festival. Of relevance here is the memorable song by Mukesh which went something like this:

Zindagi khwaab hai,
Khwaab me jhoot kya aur bhala such hai kya,
Sab such hai, zindagi khwaab hai.
Dil ne hum se jo kahaa, humne waise hi kiyaa,
Phir kabhi fursat se sochenge bura thha yaa bhala,
Zindagi khwaab hai.

Life is but a dream,
In a dream who knows what is real and what is false,
Everything is real, life is but a dream.
Throughout, I did whatever my heart told me to do,
Later at leisure, I will consider what was right and what was
    wrong,
Life is but a dream.

My professional experiences have been a bit like the dream described in the song. This book has allowed me to share anecdotes and my experiences. I hope they turn out to be of some value to the reader.

One question continued to return to me as I drew to the close.

The problems that leaders are required to solve are, by nature, foggy and unclear quite often—though not always.

Managers are trained to be efficient. In their pursuit of efficiency, they seem to sometimes lose their effectiveness.

Are efficiency and effectiveness different?

The code of an efficient organization would have characteristics such as:

- ❖ You work on things you understand quite well
- ❖ You plan in detail and review actions against that plan
- ❖ You impose a process and responsibility
- ❖ You expect completion as per an agreed time-table
- ❖ You commit resources to accomplish the tasks

The code of an effective organization would have other characteristics:

- ❖ You work on things you don't quite understand
- ❖ You find it difficult to plan in any detail as the way forward is unclear
- ❖ You try out approaches and adjust your plans flexibly
- ❖ You expect progress, but are not sure of completion
- ❖ You have to generate new options continuously, not just place more resources

It is not that an organization has a choice to be efficient or effective. It needs always to be effective. Depending on the situation and the timing, the path adopted consciously may be efficient or inefficient.

The fly goes around in circles because of its compound eye

The most efficient path between two points is the shortest, the straight line. Have you ever wondered why the common housefly is unable to approach its goal in a straight path? Why does it go round and round in a sort of spiralling circle as it approaches its destination?

Given its eye and body structure, the fly has to adapt itself to reach its goal; it gets to its goal in a way that is effective for the circumstance, even if it is not an efficient way.

The fly has two large eyes, so large that they cover most

of its head. The fly can simultaneously see up, down, forward, and backward. The fly's eye is made up of about 4,000 tiny, hexagonally packed lenses. No two lenses point in the same direction. Not only that, each lens operates quite independently of the others.

The flipside to this 360-degree vision is that a fly-eye view of the world is highly fractured; the fly cannot easily adjust for distance or see detailed patterns and shapes. Hence the fly does not have any sharp vision. It has what the biologist calls a compound eye; humans have a simple eye.

The human eye sees one large image; the fly sees the same tiny image in each of its several thousand lenses. As the fly approaches an object, the image shifts slightly in each facet. To hold in a constant position its vision of the object, the fly has to adjust its whole body. At each turn of its body, the fly is closer to the object, so the radius of the circle of approach progressively becomes smaller and smaller. If one plots the approach path of the fly, it would resemble a coil or a spiral with a decreasing radius.

Now we understand why the fly moves around in circles. Maybe this applies to organizations as well.

Organizations also have compound eyes

Where people are encouraged to think for themselves, there is bound to be a diversity of views. An organization is the sum total of these diverse viewpoints. Differing viewpoints lead to differing agendas and these naturally serve as a source of great conflict among people. These differing views halt relationships and sour human relationships along the way.

A further complexity comes from the fact that people in the organization may or may not express their genuine view in the formal forum or meeting. If the view expressed at the table is different from the real view that the person holds, there is a further increase in the complexity. That is why any organization which has a truly 'compound' eye has a very complex agenda of actions required.

Like the fly, the anatomy of the organization's 'eye' prevents a sharp vision from guiding the movement of the organization. The lack of sharp vision prevents it from moving in a straight line, the efficient path. The organization assesses its distance from a goal, makes a move, reassesses its distance from the goal, adjusts its body again and keeps repeating this till it reaches the goal: just like the fly.

Of course, it is the most important role of leadership to sharpen the organization's vision. However, sharpening the vision and causing the organization to move towards that vision does not necessarily happen with efficiency. The leader may not be able to move in a straight line from the problem to its logical solution. Examples are unnecessary, there are so many!

In fact, it would be probably correct to state that while solving complex issues, going around in circles is the more common mode of functioning; in some situations, it is the effective way for the organization to function, though not necessarily efficient.

The more complex the problem, the more likely it is that the effective solution will require the leadership to move a bit tangentially rather than straight.

The English moralist Samuel Johnson perceived the world as a 'tangled, teeming jungle of plots, follies, vanities, and egoistic passions in which anyone—the innocent and virtuous no less than the vicious—is likely to be ambushed'.

That is why we need to accept the reality that the human mind is 'a noisy parliament of competing factions'.

Yet, all our training tells us to plan for efficient outcomes and expect the organization to move along a straight line.

The greatest source of employees' exasperation about their company is that its 'leaders do not seem to do what is obvious'.

Society values efficiency more than effectiveness

Our desire for a secure future makes us want to get control of the uncertainty around us. We crave for predictability, to avoid surprises and to be in command of events rather than let events be in command of our lives.

Think of the educational and social training we impart to our children; we constantly motivate them to be efficient. If they achieve efficiency, they are assumed to be effective.

We expect our children to study diligently and complete their education in a certain number of years. We do not approve of our children 'wasting' time, we like them to use their time efficiently and well. We expect them to solve problems by developing options, and choosing the most efficient way. When they are grown up, we expect them to be successful and earn well; that makes us feel there is a 'good return' on the upbringing and education we have invested on them.

When employees join our company, we appreciate those who complete tasks on time or spend money within a budget. Managers who keep a tight diary and produce their output through excellent time management are noticed and rewarded. Those who state a problem and solve it with speed and efficiency are judged to be good; such accomplishment is rewarded with a promotion or an increase in salary.

None of the above actions are wrong. But they do have the effect of conditioning the mind to value efficiency a great deal; and it is assumed that efficiency equals effectiveness.

The problem is, of course, that this is wholly untrue if the complexity level of the problem is high. Unfortunately, leadership poses us very few simple problems to solve, especially so when one is at a level of leadership.

More often than not, managers are faced with a swirl of turbulence; complex and interrelated forces drive the turbulence. In business, as indeed in life, the course has to be charted under conditions of extreme uncertainty and accelerating change. Everyone has read and experienced turbulence in the environment. Turbulence has for long been bewildering, it continues to be so.

- ❀ Do we need to rethink our attitudes about uncertainty and the future?
- ❀ Do we need to change them, and how do we factor in that change when we plan for the future?
- ❀ Is it efficiency or effectiveness that one must seek while solving complex problems and when faced with turbulence?

Suppress or leverage turbulence: the spiral

Our erroneous attitude towards the future is rooted in culturally ingrained notions of predictability and control, a world in which change appears to be linear, continuous, and to some extent predictable. Linearity and stability are artificial ways of viewing the world. This point may seem pedantic, but it is not really so.

Peter Drucker had said that trying to predict the future is like trying to drive down a country road at night with no lights while looking out of the back window. For long, we have known deep down that the future will be different from the past.

Every science fiction writer from Jules Verne to William Gibson has reminded us of that. Our ideas about the future are shaped by our desire to eliminate or suppress turbulence. This reflects in the way we relate to, for example, the use of energy.

When we design engines or earthquake-proof housing, we seek to improve performance and ensure robustness by suppressing turbulence. On the other hand, when we are exposed to the natural forces of energy, we instinctively leverage the turbulence for enhanced performance.

- ❀ Think of how a skier comes down the slopes
- ❀ Think of how a glider pilot glides.

The skier and the glider pilot seem to realize that they cannot take a straight path because their task has to deal with the inevitable turbulence of wind-speeds or the winding nature of the slopes. In fact, they use that turbulence to their advantage.

They try to move more effectively rather than more efficiently. They never ski in a straight line, nor glide in a straight line.

In Nature, the straight line is not the most effective way to move between two points. Nature rarely, maybe never, uses such linearity in traversing from A to B—more often than not, it seems to use a spiral. A spiral moves faster towards its eye than further out.

- ❀ Water gathers speed as it whirls down a drain
- ❀ Planets close to the sun orbit faster than those at the periphery
- ❀ Witness how a wisp of smoke rises, not in a straight line but in a spiral
- ❀ Picture a galaxy, the shape of a cabbage, seashells, and the shape of our ears. All of them seem to grow from within themselves in a sort of spiral
- ❀ Water flows downhill as a stream in the same wavy way in which blood flows in our veins and the sap flows in a tree.

Clearly, the efficient way and the effective way in Nature are different. So, the issue arises: is there a choice between a straight line and spiral path, i.e., between efficient ways and effective ways? The environment is an external force that deflects our lives constantly.

Being on the straight and predictable line is the exception, not the rule. It would be nice if the two ways were identical, but are they?

Real life is not a series of interconnected events occurring one after the other like beads strung on a necklace. Rather, it is a series of encounters in which one event may change those that follow in a wholly unpredictable way. So the picture about the future must be considered chaotic.

To a student of chaos theory, however, chaos is not chaotic. There are underlying patterns in things, and there are reasons why particular things happen. There are spaces in the reasons, so you can make a difference to the outcomes. To understand the nature of the future, one needs to understand the patterns.

I was intrigued that the spiral has fascinated even mathematicians. Leonardo Fibonacci was a thirteenth century mathematician who helped to introduce the Hindu-Arabic numerals (1, 2, 3,) into western Europe. He was also the originator of a special series of numbers, now called the Fibonacci sequence, which consists of a series in which each number is the sum of the two before it, e.g., 1, 2, 3, 5, 8, etc. The Fibonacci sequence is the basis on which spirals are constructed.

The spiral may lie at the core of life's first principles, that of growth. The spiral is fundamental to the structure of plants, shells, the human body, the periodicity of atomic elements, the double helix DNA.

In short, the spiral of turbulence is the natural companion of complex problems; those who have to lead through such turbulence are mentally conditioned to suppress the turbulence and reach their goal efficiently.

A good alternative is to leverage the turbulence. You leverage turbulence by choosing the most effective path. Let me apply this principle to my experience of building a new corporate leadership in Unilever Arabia.

Leveraging diversity in a new company

When Unilever Arabia was formed, the company's top leadership had to be assembled from the management resources of Unilever globally. It was a truly multinational team.

There were sixteen nationalities working in the company. There were seven board directors—two from HLL in India, one a UK citizen of Indian origin, two other UK citizens, one French and one Dutch.

I even attended a programme at INSEAD, Fontainbleau, about how to get the best out of such a diverse team. Big diversity could either be a disaster or a huge strength, but homogenous teams would provide middle-of-the-road, predictable results. I learned some very fine lessons about managing diversity during my four-year stint.

Unilever had developed three independent legs of business in Arabia over half a century. One was a trading and distribution business. Another was a brands marketing business in homecare products. The third was a powerful branded tea business. Each of these had been nurtured by a UK-based export company. Within all these three companies, the Arabian business had acquired pride of place. None of those managements would voluntarily 'part' with those pieces of their business to a new management. The combined sales in 1990 were about $250 million with a very handsome level of profits. The plan was to get to sales of $400 million within four years.

The task was to set up a company onshore in Jeddah and Dubai with a new management. This management would have to work with the existing UK-based managers to surgically carve out pieces from the respective UK companies. It would then have to reconnect them into a single operational team with a base in Arabia. In other words, it was the management equivalent of an intricate surgery, quite a complex task.

People become the most effective glue; they can also become the most difficult obstacles.

Almost all of the team had to work with new colleagues, subordinates and bosses. New working and social relationships had to be established by everyone. Each person had come from a different part of Unilever, and each had his own perception of how Unilever operates!

There were eleven local joint venture partners spread over Jeddah, Bahrain, Abu Dhabi, Dubai and Muscat. They had their own ambitions and expectations from Unilever's new structure.

While some of these might appear like small city-states, each was a sovereign country with its own laws, currencies and ambitions; so too were the joint venture business partners of the firm. On top of all this, the managers in the UK were most reluctant to let go of this part of their company; they regarded the Arabian business as the 'jewel in their crown'.

The eye of the fly syndrome was staring us in the face every morning. Uncertainties at the individual level and company level inevitably appeared as turbulent to each person. Several managers with their families had to relocate from their home country to Jeddah or Dubai. New offices had to be found, furnished and made operational. Logistics and warehousing arrangements had to be realigned without a break in the supplies to the market. Accounting systems and controls had to transfer without a slippage. And many more such tasks.

It became important to appreciate that the mere act of presenting a logical plan would not achieve the desired results. People do not act in harmony because there are logical plans. Some other methods had to be contemplated which would win the hearts of individuals and meld them into a group. The surgery could not be done speedily, and time had to be allowed to sort out the pulls and contra-pulls that would be inevitable.

Four approaches helped the top team to leverage the inevitable turbulence—socialization, communication, understanding and patience.

Socialization

Starting with the new board directors, the new team was deliberately socialized, far more than one might have done in another situation. A calendar of board meetings, business review meetings, operational planning meetings were implemented for the whole year with a wider participation than one might have otherwise planned. Differences of views and approaches kept surfacing; managers were thankful that a forum had been planned to air these differences and authorities had been delegated to resolve these after a full discussion.

A few well-planned dinners also helped to bring people together socially—this brought some humorous and intriguing lessons on social habits. For example, our Swedish marketing manager, Laars Emnell, would turn up at his colleague's house for an 8 p.m. dinner at 8 p.m.—very Swedish, as he would reconnoitre the area on the previous evening so as to be absolutely punctual. To his horror, the host would not be ready, and the other guests would arrive from 8.45 p.m., in the case of the French, to 10.30 p.m. for the Indians!

Communication

A monthly management communication meeting was scheduled alternately in Jeddah and Dubai. All managers attended this one-hour meeting. The top team briefed the managers about developments in the business and in Unilever in twenty minutes. The rest of the time was spent answering managers' questions and inviting their suggestions. Then there were the usual annual marketing conferences and company magazines. These are, of course, routine in long-standing companies. But these kinds of actions tend to receive a lower priority in newly-formed companies, the thinking being that 'there are too many other things' to do.

The communications were quite open and facilitated by a strong sense of the daredevil in the team members. Why would anyone leave the comfort of his home country and come to 'get sand in his boots' if he did not have some such adventurous spirit? Two new factories were set up within those years; an audacious and frontal attack on a dominant detergent competitor was mounted. At these communication meetings, managers felt free to ask about a wide range of subjects. The most important outcome was the opportunity to discuss and agree why things in Arabia could not be done just as in other countries.

Our lady brand manager could not travel to Saudi Arabia from Dubai; our Unilever tea head in London, a Jewish person, could not visit Saudi Arabia. The Arabia offices were closed from Thursday afternoon till Friday evening while our London office was closed on Saturday and Sunday. So there was no communication (email had not arrived) for half the week with headquarters. On a lighter note, this was something that many of us considered a blessing!

Understanding

Socialization and communication forced a level of understanding; otherwise one could not survive in the company community. The complexities of so many nationalities working together should not be underestimated. The finance director was French. Every month he would discuss the monthly profit results with me before dispatch to London. He would take a long time to come to the point that I was interested in: have we met the profit budget? He felt I was too impatient to know the detail without appreciating the context. He even gave me a short lecture on how the Anglo-Saxon educational system focussed on the subject in isolation of the context, whereas the French educational system focussed on the context in which the subject was then placed!

On one occasion, I was meeting customers in the downtown Ballad area of Jeddah. A Tunisian sales manager accompanied me. During a short break, he asked if I, as a newcomer to Jeddah, would accept advice from a long-time Jeddah resident. His advice was a curious one: do not walk on the streets with another man's wife. I assured him that this was no known weakness of mine; however, how would the muttawah (religious police) know whether the woman accompanying me was my wife or not, I asked. With great seriousness in his eye, he said, 'If you seem to enjoy her company, they would know it is not your wife!'

Patience

Most of the managers had been trained to cut through the adipose tissues in the organization and get straight to the point. I found that, particularly for discussions with the Arab partners, this was not a good approach. One virtually had to dance around the subject for quite a while before referring to the real issue. This called for a great deal of patience and a much calibrated approach.

The partners' meeting would typically be held around 10 p.m., by which time the Arab would be preparing for dinner. I am an early morning person, and at 10 p.m., I am not at my best. Notwithstanding these differences, I learnt how to get engagement in such meetings. In fact, Unilever Arabia and the partners did achieve some important distribution and financing agreements for the business through these processes. After a year of being on the peninsula, our Arab partner said to me, 'You know, we think you are a good person for Unilever to have sent here. You are like us. You go around in circles and test the atmosphere for the discussion, just as we like to do. These English people come in a plane for a two-day trip and want to go back with an agreement. They are negotiators, you are a collaborative negotiator.'

The four approaches mentioned—socialization, communication, understanding and patience—are at the 'heart' of managing. Many mistakes are embedded in this 'heart' not functioning well. This happens when leaders lose connection with people.

Really speaking, one has to be a natural at connecting with people—or at the least, work very hard at doing so. Though there are many examples in the corporate sector, one from politics and one from history appears below.

Not connecting with people

This is an example from modern politics.

Jamil Mahuad had been the successful mayor of Quito province in Ecuador. He was extremely popular, he walked around the city to meet his voters and solve their problems spontaneously. Quite often, as the mayor, he would motivate citizens to find solutions to their own local problems. The people felt listened to and involved.

The solutions were perceived as effective; it could, however, have been argued that they were not necessarily efficient insofar as those solutions were often known in advance.

He then became the President of the country. Aides and assistants brought issues and recommended alternative 'technical' solutions as the immediate and efficient remedy. Inadvertently, Jamil Mahuad stopped doing what gave him his initial success, i.e., being visible to his people, providing hope in the face of the numerous problems and communicating about why his government needed to modernize the economy.

Initially, things went well. Unluckily, the country was then visited by an El Nino storm which wiped out a large chunk of GDP. This was followed by inflation, huge foreign debt, bankrupt banks and a whole host of problems. It is not that these were sudden developments; rather they were issues waiting to be solved and the government just had to deal with them.

There was great pressure on this 'proven leader' to deliver: not an uncommon feature in corporations. He felt he had to make some bold moves in the interests of speed.

He cut government salaries, cancelled orders for the purchase of defence equipment, reduced recruitment into the army and so on. These were probably correct solutions in the 'technical' sense, but their implementation lacked the buy-in of people.

On 21 January 2000, a coalition of military officers and demonstrators forced Mahuad out of office after just one year in office as President.

He paid the price of choosing efficient solutions over effective solutions. He had lost contact with his people. He was blissfully unaware at that time, of course, that he had lost touch. He admitted it in an interview later.

Here is an example from Indian history.

Emperor Aurangzeb died in 1707. His reign was the apogee of the Mughal empire. Thereafter, as written by Macaulay, 'a succession of nominal sovereigns, sunk in indolence and debauchery, sauntered away life in secluded places...listening to buffoons'. The longest serving emperor (1719–48) was 'Rangeela' Muhammad Shah, so called because of his quixotic ways, totally disconnected with his people. Never before did a more carefree sovereign sit on the throne of Delhi.

Within a decade of Rangeela Muhammad Shah's death, the Mughal empire collapsed, giving way to the British empire.

Perception is reality

French novelist Marcel Proust wrote, 'The real voyage of discovery consists not in seeking new lands but in seeing with new eyes.'

We spend a lifetime seeking a reality. Is there any reality other than the way we look at an issue? The fact is that we become unwitting slaves of our assumptions. Our perception of reality is shaped by our assumptions.

An example: when a train approaches a bystander at high speed, a higher pitched noise is heard by the listener as compared to when the train is pulling away. In 1842, an Austrian physicist, Christian Doppler, professor in Prague, stated this principle, that when a vibrating source of waves and an observer are approaching each other, the frequency observed is higher than the emitted frequency. If the source and observer are receding from each other, the observed frequency is lower than emitted. It is important to note that the emitted frequency is the same; it is the perception of that frequency that is different.

So, the perception is reality! It is the viewer's eye that matters, not so much the object or the event.

Think about corporate leadership.

Society celebrates the decisive, heroic leader, who makes the big and bold moves. This leader is visible and constantly in the news. He seems to achieve magical results through great clarity, sure-footedness and an unambiguous view of the world. He never compromises on his stated approach to issues nor compromises on what he states to be his principles.

On the other hand, society ignores or pooh-poohs the hesitant, unsure, groping leader, who takes tentative steps, assesses the effect and moves forward step by step.

Such a leader may have clarity on certain matters, may be ambiguous on others, and may even try to reframe the issue on yet other matters. He may achieve results in the long term, but that is only if he lasts till then—an impatient press or shareholder group may cut short his tenure.

I am neither eulogizing hesitant behaviour nor condemning decisive behaviour per se. I am advocating that while commentators and outsiders make such judgements, the context should be considered.

A man with just a stick to guide him, trying to navigate past obstacles on a mountain slope on a foggy night, is likely to progress step by step, a bit hesitantly and cautiously. We would actually expect him to do so.

However, if the prime minister of a complex nation like India or the CEO of a company trying to achieve a turn-around does so, we are critical of that leadership. I wonder whether the metaphor of the man on the slope with a stick would not apply to the prime minister or the CEO. It well could, it depends on how you look at it.

I should close with a brief reference to two other episodes.

The Tata Finance episode

The following extract from the *Tata Review*, a publication of Tatas, tells the story of the Tata Finance episode of 2001 best.

> What does a corporate house do when the managing director of one of its companies commits a fraud? Does it try to put a lid on the affair or does it make an all-out effort to ensure that the stakeholders suffer no losses? When Tata Finance was engulfed in a financial mess, the Tata Group took the latter approach...Interestingly, before the fraud could be detected by the regulators, it was the Tata Group's self-disclosure that opened the matter up...
>
> Rather than sweep the issue under the carpet, Tatas decided on a two-pronged course of action. First, the interests of the small depositors who had placed their trust in the Tata name had to be protected. Second, an open and objective enquiry would be conducted to bring the culprits to book...
>
> Tata Sons and Tata Industries made available to Tata Finance cash and corporate guarantees amounting to Rs 615 crores...Not many industrialists would have put hundreds of crores into a company that was sinking and that too without being sure that any of it could be recovered...
>
> Despite the alacrity with which the Tatas moved, the public perception of the Group and the Tata brand was affected initially...But it was the right thing to do, and Tatas did what was required to be done...

The Bhopal episode

The vagaries of a successful business career are as mysterious as life itself. To cope with success, you have to relax and not take yourself too seriously. Apart from great qualities of head and heart, it takes good fortune to get success. With that fortune and success, you have to do something for others. Obligation is born in success.

Vijay Gokhale graduated from Kolkata and studied engineering in the UK. He joined Union Carbide as a trainee engineer, and rose rapidly. He was a copybook case of success.

With twenty-five years of service and at the age of forty-eight, he was appointed managing director in January 1984. It was his best New Year. Union Carbide was a blue chip company, with fourteen plant locations and employing 10,000 people. Vijay had a lovely family, was a member of the club and was a highly respected corporate manager.

The year 1984 turned out to be a tumultuous year for the country. In a dark act, a bodyguard assassinated Prime Minister Indira Gandhi. A few weeks later, a disaster struck. In Bhopal, a deadly chemical leaked from Union Carbide's factory. The matter is sub judice and is not the subject of this article.

What happened to Gokhale, the person and manager, is the subject of this chapter.

Bhopal was the only non-US plant to manufacture this complex chemical. The plant operation was considered a tribute to Indian engineers' ability to absorb technology. For several years, the plant operation had been superb, boasting a record 2 million accident-free man-hours. Yet, the 'impossible' had happened.

Gokhale's world came crashing around him, mercilessly and relentlessly. Within forty-eight hours, Gokhale and the top company leadership were under house arrest at Bhopal.

Law and politics took their own courses. At the centre of this maelstrom was Gokhale, who, until the other day, was envied by his peers as 'a very competent and lucky manager'. How fate had changed the lives of Gokhale and, even more unfortunately, the lives of several thousands of poor and affected families.

The slings of outrageous fortune were arrayed against Gokhale. He felt like resigning: first, it seemed an honourable thing to do; later, it was an escape from depressing jibes.

An American colleague (not representing the leadership's view) said hurtfully that the Indian company had to be severed like 'an infected appendix'. Business friends indulged in insensitive humour, e.g., 'Are you Nathuram Godse?' When Gokhale offered to help with relief work, a senior bureaucrat politely said to him, 'Your visits here are an embarrassment, please do not come here.'

Then something strange happened. Gokhale realized that his success had created in him an obligation. What about those families, who were ruined by this disaster? What about those employees, whose jobs were at stake? What about small shareholders, who had invested in the company shares? How could he even think of quitting? It was just not an option.

Suddenly, Gokhale became a tornado of positive work. He was consumed with the issue of compensation to the victims. He travelled relentlessly to all his units to explain the company's response. He sold company assets to partly pay for the compensation. He got his leadership team to think of how to rescue the investment of small shareholders. He faced daunting obstacles, but Gokhale reminded himself that so had the efforts of many characters in history and mythology. There was only one way to go, which was forward.

No member of the top table left for over a year. They collectively felt fully accountable for the legal proceedings. They saved the company as best as was humanly possible. When Gokhale had become CEO, the company had a history of steady profits. Within four years of the sad incident, the profit had plummeted to 40 per cent. When Vijay Gokhale retired after another four years, the profit had reached a new peak, 110 per cent higher than when he took over. This was after paying the company's share of compensation and disposing of half of the company!

With a moist eye, he recalls, 'My most touching moment was in Cossipore factory, where I began my career. The workers had tears in their eyes. They felt I was a son of that factory, that they would do whatever was needed, but please would I lead them through this most unfortunate crisis?'

What did all this do to him as a human being?

Vijay gazed wistfully at the bay beyond the Mumbai gateway and said, 'It taught me humility. It demonstrated that obligation is born in success. It brought out the humanity in me.'

The importance of values

Doing things effectively is the natural way of doing things. When you do things naturally, you expend the least effort. Doing things efficiently requires an effort—a skill or an approach which has to be developed.

If you see Nature at work, you will see that least effort is expended. Contrast this with the effort needed to create a bonsai

Grass doesn't *try* to grow, it just grows. Fish don't *try* to swim, they just swim. Flowers don't *try* to bloom, they bloom. This is their intrinsic nature. In ancient Indian science, this was called the Law of Least Effort. Nature's intelligence functions effortlessly, frictionlessly, spontaneously. It is non-linear, intuitive and nourishing.

In a similar way, in the conduct of your business, you are in harmony with Nature when your actions are motivated by values. When you seek power and control over other people, you waste energy. When your actions are motivated by values, your energy multiplies and accumulates.

So what does it mean in practical terms to leverage the Law of Least Effort through actions that are motivated by values? There are three components to this Law of Least Effort: first, accepting that things are the way they are at this point of time; second, without blaming others, taking responsibility to change things for the better; and third, avoiding defensiveness of your view, your past actions.

Make the trend your friend! Count on your natural instinct for values.

Values are at the vortex of the spiral. We need to live with chaos and uncertainty, to try to be comfortable with it and not look for certainty where we won't get it. However, we should remember that our journey is towards the vortex, the calm eye of the centre, which represents the values we stand for.

This causes us to inquire, what is the purpose of our managerial actions? What is the purpose of our business?

If the purpose is only for oneself, it dissipates rapidly. Today, if economic progress has delivered less than society's expectations, then we know who the enemy is. The enemy is us and our own societies, because what we are fighting against is our own sense of values, our own principles.

We should remind ourselves of what Gandhiji said: 'Beware of politics without principles and commerce without morality.'

Values, and only values, can help us to withstand the political, social and economic turbulence that are inevitable.

The greatest mistake leaders can make is to assume that results alone matter, and that morality and goodness have gone out of style.

The great and more satisfying thing in life is a sense of purpose beyond oneself. This provides the values aspect of coping with turbulence.

REFERENCES

Abrahamson, Eric, 2004, *Change without Pain*, Harvard Business School Press, Boston.

Ali, Salim, 2002, *The Book of Indian Birds*, Oxford University Press, New Delhi.

Attenborough, David, 1987, *The First Eden*, Little, Brown, London.

Badaracco Jr., Joseph, 2002, *Leading Quietly*, Harvard Business School Press, Boston.

Bennis, Warren G. and Robert J. Thomas, 2002, *Geeks & Geezers*, Harvard Business School Press, Boston.

Chandiramani, G.L., (trans.), 1991, *Panchatantra*, Rupa & Co., New Delhi.

Cook, Theodore Andrea, 1979, *The Curves of Life*, Dover Publications, New York.

Daniel, J.C., 2002, *The Book of Indian Reptiles*, Oxford University Press, New Delhi.

Diamond, Jared, 2005, *Collapse*, Viking, London.

Dotlich, David and Peter Cairo, 2003, *Why CEOs Fail*, Jossey-Bass, Wiley, Hoboken, New Jersey, USA.

Dozier, Rush W, Jr., 2002, *Why We Hate*, Tata McGraw-Hill, New Delhi.

Durrell, Gerald and Lee, 1987, *Ourselves and Other Animals*, Pantheon Books, Random House, New York.

Eliot, John, 2004, *Overachievement*, Penguin Portfolio, New York.

Evans, Dylan, *Emotion: The Science of Sentiment*, Oxford University Press, London.

Gladwell, Malcolm, 2000, *The Tipping Point*, Abacus, London.

——2005, *Blink*, Little, Brown, London.

Geus, Arie de, 1997, *The Living Company*, Nicholas Brealey, London.

Howard, Michael, 1993, *The Lessons of History*, OUP, London.

Grandin, Temple and Catherine Johnson, 2005, *Animals in Translation*, Bloomsbury Publishing, London.

Hall, Judy, 2003, *The Intuition Handbook*, Vega, London.

Harvey-Jones, John, 1988, *Making It Happen*, Fontana/Collins, London.

Heifetz, Ronald and Marty Linsky, 2002, *Leadership on the Line*, Harvard Business School Press, Boston.

Ideas That Have Worked, 2004, Viking, Penguin, New Delhi.

Kennedy, Carol, 1993, *The Company That Changed Our Lives*, Paul Chapman Publishing Ltd., Sage Publications, London.

Lala, R.M., 1993, *Beyond the Last Blue Mountain*, Penguin, New Delhi.

——2004, *For the Love of India: The Life and Times of Jamsetji Tata*, Penguin, New Delhi.

——2004, *The Creation of Wealth*, Penguin, New Delhi.

Mintzberg, Henry, 2004, *Managers Not MBAs*, Tata McGraw-Hill, New Delhi.

Nehru, B.K., 1997, *Nice Guys Finish Second*, Viking, Penguin, New Delhi.

Nonaka, Ikujiro and Hirotaka Takeuchi, 1995, *The Knowledge Creating Company*, Oxford University Press, London.

Parikh, Jagdish, 1994, *Intuition: The New Frontier of Management*, Blackwell Publishers, Edinburg.

Perlow, Leslie, 2003, *When You Say Yes But Mean No*, Crown Business Publishing, New York.

Peterson, Donald and John Hillkirk, 1991, *Teamwork*, Victor Gollancz, London.

Russell, Sharman Apt, 2003, *An Obsession with Butterflies*, Arrows Books, Random House, London.

Sapolsky, Robert M., 2004, *Why Zebras Don't Get Ulcers*, Henry Holt and Co., New York.

Schwartz, Barry, 2004, *The Paradox of Choice*, HarperCollins, New York.

Surowiecki, James, 2004, *The Wisdom of Crowds*, Doubleday, New York.

Thomas, T., 1992, *To Challenge and to Change*, Viking, Penguin, India.

Tichy, Noel with Eli Cohen, 1997, *The Leadership Engine*, Harper Business, New York.

Tuchman, Barbara, 1984, *The March of Folly*, Ballantine Books, New York.

Vlasic, Bill and Bradley Stertz, 2000, *Taken for a Ride*, Wiley, Hoboken, New Jersey, USA.

Wademan, Daisy, 2004, *Remember Who You Are*, Harvard Business School Press, Boston.

Welch, Jack, 2001, *Straight from the Gut*, Warner Books, Clayton, South Vic, USA.

Winston, Robert, 2002, *Human Instinct*, Bantam Press, London.

Wright, Robert, 2001, *Non Zero*, Vantage Books, New York.

INDEX